10668765

WITHDRAWN

# A NOTE ON THE AUTHOR

CHRISTOPHER LLOYD read history at Cambridge, where he was a scholar, before becoming technology correspondent for the *Sunday Times*. Since leaving journalism, he has run a number of internet and educational publishing businesses. He was inspired to write *What on Earth Happened?* whilst doing the washing up at a campsite near Rome, during a four-month tour of Europe with his wife and two daughters.

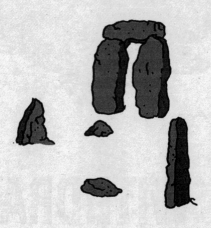

# What on Earth Happened?
# ... In Brief

### The Planet, Life and People
### from the Big Bang to the Present Day

## Christopher Lloyd

## Illustrations by Andy Forshaw

B L O O M S B U R Y
LONDON · BERLIN · NEW YORK

Comments and suggestions about this book can be posted on the discussion forum at www.whatonearthhappened.com. All notes and references to this edition can also be found here.

This abridged version also appeared in a fourteen-part serialization in the *Independent*, between 7–20 February 2009 under the title *The World: A Pocket History*

First published in Great Britain 2008
This paperback edition published 2009

Bloomsbury Publishing Plc, 36 Soho Square, London W1D 3QY

A CIP catalogue record for this book is available from the British Library

ISBN 978 1 4088 0216 8

10 9 8 7 6 5 4

Typeset by Hewer Text UK Ltd, Edinburgh

Printed in Great Britain by Clays Ltd, St Ives plc

The paper this book is printed on is certified independently in accordance with the rules of the FSC. It is ancient-forest friendly. The printer holds chain of custody.

**Mixed Sources**
Product group from well-managed
forests and other controlled sources
www.fsc.org Cert no. SGS-COC-2061
© 1996 Forest Stewardship Council

www.bloomsbury.com/christopherlloyd

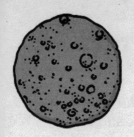

# **Contents**

Foreword to the Paperback Edition     vii

## **PART 1: LIFE BEFORE MAN**
*(13.7 billion–7 million BC)*

*How the universe was formed, and the unfolding
of life on earth before mankind*

1. The Beginning     3
2. The Age of Plants and Trees     23
3. The Rise of Animals     38

## **PART 2: HUMAN EVOLUTION**
*(7 million–5000 BC)*

*How humans evolved as hunter-gatherers
whilst living in a state of nature*

4. Early Humans     61
5. Homo Sapiens     78

# PART 3: ANCIENT HISTORY
### (5000 BC–1521 AD)

*How farm animals and crops led to the growth of a
range of different human civilizations*

6.   The First Civilizations                    101
7.   Oriental War and Peace                      121
8.   The Classical World                         142
9.   Natives and the Americas                    164

# PART 4: MODERN HISTORY
### (570 AD–present day)

*How the fate of human civilizations and the
natural world fused into a global whole.
Is our current way of life sustainable?*

10.  Islamic Globalization                       187
11.  Medieval Misery                             210
12.  European Conquest and Revolt                230
13.  The Industrialized World                    255
14.  What Now?                                   281

     Index                                       318

*For full notes and references please
visit www.whatonearthhappened.com*

# Foreword to the Paperback Edition

**HISTORY IS IN TROUBLE.** It has been splintered by experts into discrete topics and chopped up by governments to suit their educational fancies. Worst of all, it is almost never presented chronologically. How old is the universe? When did life on earth begin? Who was mankind's oldest ancestor? How did ancient Chinese science shape the modern world? Why did democracy start in Greece? Are humans really superior to other living things? Many people today are understandably confused about the answers to such a broad but fundamental range of questions when all they learned at school was a few facts about kings and queens, a world war or two and maybe a little something about creatures called dinosaurs.

This is an abridged version of *What on Earth Happened?* – a journey into the past that begins at the beginning, 13.7 billion years ago. It tells the story of everything in four simple parts: Life Before Man, Human Evolution, Ancient History and Modern History. Along the way I have tried to draw upon the widest possible range of sources and have used the most up-to-date knowledge about life, the universe and everything.

# What on Earth Happened?

This paperback edition is roughly half the length of the original hardback. It is designed specifically for anyone who wants a quick way of immersing themself in the fascinating themes of big history. Despite its condensed nature, my hope is that what emerges is a uniquely interconnected narrative that dovetails the growth of human civilizations with evolutionary biology, modern science with prehistoric art, and the rise of world religions with the irrepressible forces of mother nature.

This exhilarating project has convinced me more than ever that history cannot just be considered as simply the story of human achievement. People deserve a proper context, alongside and within the story of the planet and other life on earth. Without a more holistic perspective on their past, how can humans hope to prosper in the future?

The study of history is a powerful tool for helping our rational minds grapple with the challenges of tomorrow. I believe that it will only work if we keep on asking the one and only question that binds us all – planet, life and people: *What on Earth Happened?*

**Christopher Lloyd**
**April 2009**

# Part 1
# Life Before Man

## (13.7 billion–7 million BC)

*How the universe was formed, and the unfolding of life on earth before mankind*

# 1

# The Beginning

## (13.7 billion–420 million years ago)

*How a speck of infinite energy exploded
our universe into existence, creating
the conditions for the birth of life*

**TAKE A GOOD** look around. Put everything you can see inside an imaginary but enormously powerful crushing machine. Plants, animals, trees, buildings, your entire house (including contents), your home town as well as the country where you live. See it all get pulverized into a tiny ball.

Now put the rest of the world in there too. Add the other planets in our solar system and the sun, which is about 1,000 times bigger than all the planets put together. Then put in our galaxy, the Milky Way, which includes about 200 billion other suns, and finally all the other galaxies in the universe. See all this stuff squeezed together, reduced to the size of a brick, then a tennis ball, now a pea – finally, see it crushed even smaller than the dot on top of this letter i.

Then it disappears. All those stars, moons and planets vanish into a single, invisible speck of nothing. That was it – the universe began as an invisible dot, a singularity, as scientists like to call it.

This invisible, heavy and very dense dot was so hot and under such enormous pressure from all the energy trapped inside it that about 13.7 billion years ago something monumental happened.

It burst.

This was no ordinary explosion. It was an almighty explosion, the biggest of all time – it was what we now call the Big Bang. What happened next is even more dazzling. It didn't just make a bit of a mess; it made a huge mess, billions of miles wide. In a fraction of a second the universe expanded from being an invisible speck of nothing to something so enormous that it includes everything we can see, including all the matter needed to make the earth, the sun, the moon and the stars. And there's also a whole lot more that we can't see yet, because our telescopes can't peer that far. In fact, the universe is so big that no one really knows how wide or deep it actually is.

Just after the Big Bang, more mysterious things started to happen. An enormous blast of energy was released. First it was transformed into the force of gravity, a kind of invisible glue that makes everything in the universe want to stick together. Then the massive surge of energy created countless billions of tiny building bricks – like microscopic pieces of Lego. Everything that exists today is made of billions of particles that originated a fraction of a second after the Big Bang.

About 300,000 years later things had cooled down enough so that these particles – the most common of which are electrons, protons and neutrons – could start to stick together into tiny blobs which we call atoms. With the help of that glue – gravity – and the passing of a little time, these atoms gathered together to make enormous clouds of very hot dust. Out of these clouds came the first stars, massive balls of fire supercharged with energy left over from the Big Bang. Gravity made the fiery stars gather into galaxies of many different shapes and sizes – some in spirals, some in the shape of spinning plates. Our galaxy, the Milky Way, was formed about 100 million years after the Big Bang – that's 13.6 billion years ago. It's the shape of a large disc – like two back-to-back fried eggs – and spins round at a dizzying speed of about 500,000 miles per hour.

About 4.6 billion years ago, the left-over gas and dust cloud from previous burned-out stars collapsed and ignited to form our sun. That means our sun is only about a third as old as the universe itself.

For a long time people believed that the earth was at the centre of the universe. But we now know that our solar system is located in one of the Milky Way's outer spiral arms, called the Orion arm, and is currently travelling through a sparse and lonely part of the galaxy called the Local Bubble.

The early solar system was an extremely nasty place – and *very* unsuitable for life. An invisible rain of tiny highly charged particles streamed out of the hot, fiery furnace of the sun like a storm of razor-sharp daggers. These could cut through almost anything. They are still being fired out by the sun, about twenty billion tonnes every day. This is known as the solar wind and it can penetrate even the toughest space suits and helmets worn by astronauts.

It was hell on earth. A semi-molten crust of sticky volcanic lava burbled across the planet's surface like burning-hot treacle. There was no solid ground and definitely no life. The unstable earth spun so fast on its axis that each day was only about four hours long.

What happened next was a freak. Experts believe two young planets happened to be on the same orbit around the sun, but moving at different speeds. One was the earth, the other another early planet called Theia. About fifty million years after the sun began to glow these two newborn planets ploughed into each other. With a massive jolt, the ailing earth fell on to its side, out of control, a crippled, hysterical, shaking wreck.

Thousands of volcanoes erupted following the impact. Huge volumes of gas, previously trapped inside the earth's core, now spurted through the surface, giving birth to the earth's early atmosphere.

Theia's outer layers vaporized into billions of tiny particles. Debris flew everywhere, surrounding the earth with an enormously thick blanket of hot dust, rock and granite. Trapped by the earth's gravity, this fog of rubble swirled around in the sky making everything go dark. For months not even the brightest sunlight could penetrate the thick layers of dust which were once planet Theia. Her heavy, molten-iron core converged into the centre of the earth. It caused an almighty shock wave that fused the two planets' cores into a single, tight, metallic ball, thousands of degrees hot, which plunged deep into the middle of the stricken globe, crushed by the force of the impact.

It's just as well for life on earth that this almighty collision happened. The earth's metallic core gave birth to a magnetic shield that deflects the most lethal effects of the solar wind away from the planet's surface. The shield also prevents the solar wind from splitting water ($H_2O$) into separate hydrogen and oxygen atoms, preserving the earth's vital supplies which would otherwise diffuse into space. Without this shield life on earth might never have evolved. Other planets that do not have an iron core, such as Mars and Venus, appear never to have developed life.

Today there is no physical evidence on earth of the impact of the collision with Theia – no crater – because such was its force that all the outer material vaporized and exploded into space. But visible evidence isn't far away. The dust and granite that wrapped itself around the earth soon stuck together again, thanks to the glue of gravity, and turned into an enormous ball of dust. Only about a year after the giant impact the earth had a new companion – our huge, bright, crystal-like moon.

## The first living things

One hot sunny afternoon in the autumn of 1951, Professor Harold Urey strolled into his lecture hall at the University of Chicago. The room was filled with students eager to hear this great scientist talk about his pet subject – the theory of the origins of life on earth.

# The Beginning

For more than 150 years scientists had been struggling to come up with credible theories of how life began. The problem, as Urey knew, was that so far it had proved impossible to actually *demonstrate* how life could have started from a ragbag of primitive or 'primeval' substances such as those found on the early, hostile earth. As a result, no one could agree on the origins of life.

Urey dreamed of concocting a laboratory experiment that would simulate conditions on the early earth, and show how life had been created out of a lifeless jumble of nothing. One of the students in the audience that day was utterly gripped by what Urey was saying. Stanley Miller had stopped off in Chicago on his way across America. He was in the process of trying to decide on a research project that would complete his training as a scientist.

The more Urey spoke, the more excited the twenty-one-year-old Miller became. At the end of the lecture he went up to the professor and – after a great deal of talking – persuaded Urey to work with him on a project to try to create life in a laboratory out of nothing more than a cocktail of chemical junk.

The two men set to work by designing an elaborate glass apparatus, in the middle of which was a large jar that would contain all the substances which they believed existed at the time of the early earth, such as hydrogen, methane and ammonia. Steam was fed into the glass jar through a tube connected to a flask of boiling water. Inside the jar were two metal rods, or electrodes. A powerful electric current would surge through these to make sparks – re-creating smaller versions of the violent lightning strikes that were common on early earth. The whole apparatus was designed to reproduce the earth's early atmosphere, complete with thunder and lightning.

Miller started off the experiment by boiling the water in the flask. Steam climbed up through a tube connected to the large glass chamber, where it mixed with the primeval gases. Next, he flicked the electric switch. Some 60,000 volts of electric current surged into the electrodes, beginning a constant stream of mini lightning strikes.

To his bitter disappointment nothing happened. A despondent Miller left the lab that night with nothing to show for his efforts.

But when Miller arrived the next morning he found that the water in the flask had turned pink, indicating that some kind of chemical reaction had taken place. After running the experiment for a week the results he had hoped for were unmistakable: the clear water had turned a definite shade of red. The water now contained amino acids – the vital ingredients for life, used by all plants and animals (including you and me) to construct their living cells. Surely this was the demonstrable proof that Urey had so strongly believed in! Life, Urey and Miller concluded, began by chance on the hell that was the earth some 3.7 billion years ago because the Goldilocks-like conditions for it to do so happened to be just right.

Yet for all the science and technology, and the brilliant academic minds that have tried to come up with an explanation, no one has actually solved the riddle of how those chemical building blocks re-created in the laboratory by Miller and Urey turned into living cells, the stuff of you and me.

## What is life?

The magic of a living cell is that it can reproduce. It can have buds, offspring, make replicas of itself. Usually single cells make exact copies of themselves – as viruses and bacteria do today, although sometimes a copying error creeps into the system to form a mutant cell. The ability to multiply is what makes life so completely different from anything else in the known universe. Nothing dead can do it.

Some experts believe the magical leap from life-giving amino acids to single-celled living organisms may have taken place deep down in the early oceans. Methanogens – one of two basic types of single-celled bacteria – evolved deep within the oceans so they could hide away from the lethal effects of the sun's solar wind. They thrived next to volcanic vents called black smokers, which belched out thick, black, acrid fumes from the ocean floor, providing chemicals for food and warmth.

The other type of single-celled life form probably evolved from a copying error when food was scarce. It adapted to live off a completely new energy source – sunlight – which it used to split carbon dioxide ($CO_2$) and water ($H_2O$) into food. This simple but ingenious feeding process is what we now call photosynthesis.

Unlike the methanogens, these cyanobacteria needed to live close enough to the surface of the seas to feed off the light of the sun shining through the water. Their photosynthesis transformed the planet's atmosphere, because its waste product is oxygen. Over billions of years cyanobacteria caused surplus supplies of oxygen to build up in the air.

## How oxygen changed life on earth

To begin with, the oxygen bonded with iron on the sea floor left over from the giant impact with Theia. The iron became iron oxide, a rusty-red mineral ore. When all the available substances that oxygen could bond with ran out, it was simply left to hang around in the air – which is where it has remained ever since. Oxygen now accounts for about 21 per cent of all the air we breathe. The rest consists mostly of nitrogen (78 per cent), with a little water vapour and a number of other trace gases in small measures under 1 per cent, including carbon dioxide.

Without oxygen, life on earth would have carried on, but it might never have developed beyond columns of sticky, microscopic bacteria. Humans could never have evolved, because oxygen is an energy-rich gas that sustains all forms of advanced animal life. Also, high up in the atmosphere, oxygen provides an essential protective blanket in the form of the ozone layer, which protects land life from the sun's powerful ultraviolet rays.

About two billion years ago, thanks to another mutation, a

single-celled bacteria began to feed off the oxygen-rich atmosphere. Oxygen's enormous energy-giving properties meant that this process – called respiration – could produce up to *ten times* more energy than other ways of life. Soon the oceans were filled with highly energetic microscopic cells that fed off oxygen dissolved in the oceans.

So energetic were these microscopic cells that some found they could drill their way *inside* other, larger cells and strike a mutually beneficial bargain. While the smaller cells fed off the larger cells' waste products, the larger cells used up surplus energy created by the smaller cells' respiration. Through such a collaboration, called endosymbiosis, these new combined cells were now better equipped for survival in the increasingly oxygenated world.

Some found that the best survival strategy was to link up. Gangs of cells joined together to form the world's first multicellular creatures. Some of them became the forefathers of all animal life while others turned into the ancestors of today's plants and trees.

Already we have travelled more than *three billion* years since the earth was first formed. If we think of the earth's history as a twenty-four-hour clock, the first signs of life emerged at about 05.19. So far, we have already travelled to about 16.00, leaving just eight hours to go for all the rest of life to evolve. Although miraculous signs of life have already appeared in the form of complex microscopic bacteria, hundreds of millions of years have yet to pass before fish, animals, plants and trees make their first appearance.

They only ever made it thanks to another piece of extraordinary teamwork – one that prepared the planet for yet more dramatic changes to life on earth.

## *Life's increasing complexity*

Doctors in a medical emergency always have the same top priority: to protect the body's vital life-support systems. If a patient's internal transport system – the blood – cannot carry oxygen from the lungs and nutrients from the stomach to the cells in the body, then the victim quickly starves. And if waste products such as carbon dioxide and toxic acids are left to fester because they cannot be removed, the body is almost as quickly poisoned.

During this period of earth's history a global life-support mechanism emerged that works in a strikingly similar way to the human respiratory system. Without this mechanism microscopic bacteria from two billion years ago could never have evolved into plants, animals and people.

The first and most simple part of the earth's life-support mechanism is very well known. It is rain. As the sun beats down on the planet's surface, the seas get warmer, and some of the water evaporates into vapour. Once in the air, this vapour cools to form clouds, which get blown about by the wind across the planet, eventually to fall elsewhere as rain. Without this automatic fresh-water supply, most living things on land and sea would almost certainly perish. No pipes, no pumps, no need for power stations, no people to watch over the machinery – it just happens, every day, the most precious of all free gifts.

Beneath the surface of what seems a very simple process, an important partnership between the earth and its living things developed some time between 3.7 and two billion years ago.

For rain to fall, clouds need to form. Steam molecules can condense back into water only if there is some kind of surface or 'seed' around which they can cluster. Luckily, waste gas produced by early bacteria provided a perfect surface around which water vapour could turn back into water to form rain. In this way bacteria help nature operate one of her most important life-support systems by seeding clouds. Cloud cover also creates a reflective blanket that sends many of the sun's scorching-hot rays shooting back into space. And so clouds help to cool the planet, greatly improving conditions for life on earth.

This is just one of a number of partnerships between the earth and living things that help control the climate and prevent excessively hot temperatures from harming life. Another of the earth's life-support processes helped reduce the levels of salt in the sea, preventing the poisoning of early life. It is called plate tectonics.

As you read this page, you are sitting on a crust which is floating like a giant raft on an underground sea of boiling-hot lava. The earth's crust is split into a number of floating plates that are in constant motion, like enormous, slow-moving bumper-cars (see plate 4). Each plate is either drifting apart from, or bashing into, another one. When they collide they form massive mountain ranges that soar high into the sky. When they drift apart, huge ocean ridges form in their wake. So much pressure builds up in the rocks of the earth that the movement of the earth's plates causes massive earthquakes and volcanoes, hot geysers and tsunamis. This process has helped secure life on earth by removing excessive amounts of poisonous salt from the seas. Because the earth's crust has split into separate plates that move around, like giant pieces of a puzzle, evaporated sea salt is safely stored deep beneath mountain ranges – millions of tonnes of salt are today buried beneath the European Alps and the Himalayas. As long as the plates continue to move, mountains of salt will always be safely buried under the rocks, leaving the levels of salt in the sea low enough for life to continue to thrive.

For billions of years this tectonic cycle has been churning up the surface of the earth in ultra-slow motion, drastically changing weather patterns, burying dangerous salts and minerals, making and destroying super-continents and crumpling crusts as if they were pieces of tin foil. Such are the earth's life-support processes that seem to have kept everything – from the composition of atmosphere, global temperatures and the saltiness of the sea – sufficient for life to thrive. Without these systems, the evolution of complex life as we know it would have been impossible.

## The coming of sex

Life on earth consisted of only two kinds of living things until about a billion years ago: the original, simple single-celled bacteria that produced methane and oxygen as waste products, and the newer, more complex multicellular organisms that fed off the increasingly abundant supplies of oxygen in the air.

For billions of years these tiny organisms were all the life there was. Then something triggered a spectacular and dramatic increase in the pace of the evolution. About one billion years ago living things developed a radical new form of duplication called sexual reproduction. It revolutionized the way life evolved.

Sexual reproduction helped life shoot forward in complexity, equipping it to survive the challenging conditions on the planet in far fewer generations than it would have taken without it. While it took 2.5 billion years for life to evolve into types of microscopic organism, it took less than half that time for life to transform completely into everything we know today – from fish, amphibians and reptiles to plants, trees, birds, mammals and man.

One of the first men who worked all this out was Gregor Mendel, a monk, born in 1822 in what is now the Czech Republic. He spent most of his life absorbed in the natural world, especially in his favourite place for study, the monastic vegetable garden. Brother Mendel became so interested in cultivation that between 1856 and 1863 he studied more than 28,000 different pea plants. What intrigued him was that when these slightly different plants had seedlings, their differences (or characteristics) would often be carried forward to the next generation. The seedlings had *inherited* features from their parent plants.

# What on Earth Happened?

The concept of inheritance was first described by Mendel in 1865. He went on to devise a number of laws that could predict how living characteristics are passed from one generation to another through sexual reproduction, massively increasing the variety of living things.

## Finding fossils

We are now on the edge of an enormous transformation. The time is just past 9 p.m. on our twenty-four-hour trek across earth time. The rest of history will be played out in the final three hours. There's still no life on land, no plants, no trees, no flowers, no insects, no birds or animals, let alone humans. The earth is very old, but human history is not. Compared to the age of the earth, everything else we will discover is either young, very young or just hatching out. Mankind is among the youngest of all.

About 550 million years ago the first full and clear pictures of what life on earth was actually like begin to emerge. When the fossil record begins it is rather like a theatre curtain being pulled back to reveal a stage bursting with actors in the middle of a play.

Fossils are the impressions of long-lost creatures that had hard surfaces such as bones, shells or teeth, which sometimes leave impressions in rocks. They are wonderful for helping investigators identify what kinds of creatures have lived on the earth.

Charles Doolittle Walcott was born near New York in 1850. As a young boy he found school rather boring. It wasn't that he had no interest in things, rather the opposite. He was so curious that he wanted to get outside and explore the world for himself – in particular he liked to look for minerals, rocks, birds' eggs and fossils.

By 1909 Walcott had become a well-established fossil collector. One day a freak accident changed the rest of his life. While he was walking high up in the Canadian Rockies his mule slipped and lost a shoe. In the process it turned over a glistening rock of black shale, a type of rock made out of compacted mud and clay. When Walcott stooped to pick up the rock he saw a row of remarkable flattened silvery fossils. These were perfectly preserved creatures from the Cambrian Period.

It turned out that the mountainside had collapsed about 505 million years ago, smothering these creatures, killing them instantly and burying them like a time capsule for posterity. Walcott's discovery became one of the richest hoards of fossils ever. It is known as the Burgess Shale, named after Mount Burgess, near the site where Walcott found the fossils. Walcott returned to the site many times and eventually wrote a library shelf of books about his finds. And what a bizarre range of creatures they were.

First, there is the strange-looking *Anomalocaris*. This was one of the biggest sea hunters of its day and could grow up to a metre long. It used a pair of grasping arms to capture and hold its prey. For a long time the fossils that make up this extraordinary creature were thought to be three separate living things. The body was identified as a sponge, the grasping arms as shrimps, and the circular mouth as a primitive jellyfish.

Another was the remarkable *Hallucigenia*. This curious worm-like beast also kept fossil hunters and scientists scratching their heads. It was thought to have walked on stilt-like legs and to have had a row of soft tentacles on its back which it used for trapping passing food. Thanks to the discovery of similar fossils in other parts of the world, particularly in China, fossil investigators now think they've been looking at it upside down. Instead, it walked on paired tentacle-like legs and used the spines on its back as a form of body armour to protect itself from being eaten.

But nothing in the wildest imagination of science-fiction writers could conceive of such a beast as *Opabinia*. This swimming gem had five stalky eyes, a fantail for swimming, and a long grasping arm for feeding. It was smaller than other predators, being only about four centimetres long, and there's nothing remotely like it alive today.

One of the most common forms of animal life at that time, and the most common of all the fossils unearthed in the Burgess Shale, were trilobites. Their fossilized remains look like giant woodlice and have been found all over the world. Trilobites were probably the first creatures ever to be able to see. They had eyes, like those of today's flies, which divide into hundreds of different cells, giving them a kind of mosaic view of the world under the seas.

To create a realistic picture of how life on earth actually evolved, it is important to know when each species lived and died so they can be pieced together in chronological sequence. The genius of one man helped work out how to do this. Charles Darwin (1809–82) worked out that all living things have evolved according to a sequence that is still unfolding today.

## Natural selection

Darwin's book *On the Origin of Species* (published 1859) explained, for the first time, the theory that all living things originally evolved from a single common ancestor. Darwin worked this out because the fossil record frequently shows new creatures emerging and others disappearing. His conclusion was that all living things are related to each other, but that only those species best suited to the environment of the day survived. His theory gave scientists the first ever way of arranging fossils in different groups and eventually into a rough chronological order. Darwin's theory came to the inevitable conclusion that even humans must be descended from simpler forms of life, like apes, and before that from mice, reptiles, fish, and ultimately from those bacteria found at the beginning of life on earth.

Fossil records of now-extinct species became the key for Darwin's understanding of the evolutionary process. By studying fossils and comparing them with living things today, he could see that each species has adapted itself according to a principle that he called natural selection. Over successive generations those creatures best equipped to live life on earth at that time survived, flourished and become dominant, while those least well equipped died off, their species eventually becoming extinct.

Many people were outraged at the implications of Darwin's

theory when it was first published. Some still are. The suggestion that humans are descended from animals – more specifically apes – threatened the widely held view that mankind was somehow different, superior, to all other living things. Equally as implausible to many was the idea that humans are just another natural species, which, like all others, is destined one day to become extinct.

Today, scientists have discovered powerful new ways of dating rocks and fossils which back up Darwin's theories of how creatures have evolved over time. They have been able to construct an accurate picture of how life on earth has changed since fossils began to appear in rocks about 550 million years ago. They have also made a map of the past called the geologic column (see plate 1), which is divided into a number of chronological eras and periods.

## A snapshot of prehistoric life

The best way to get an idea of what life was like several hundred million years ago is to use our imaginations and dive down to the ocean floor. Before we start, here's a quick time check on our twenty-four-hour clock. On our first stop we will see what life was like between about 9.05 p.m. and 10 p.m. Here are some of the key species that evolved in the prehistoric seas.

## Sponges

These were among the simplest of all animals living in the ancient Cambrian seas. There are still many types alive today. About 5,000 different species of sponge have been discovered so far. They attach themselves to rocky surfaces at the bottom of the sea. The reason we use them for washing ourselves is that their bodies are full of absorbent holes. Sponges use tiny hairs called flagella to beat sea water through these holes to extract a diet of microscopic nutrients.

For a long time people thought sponges were plants, because they are rooted to the sea floor and they don't seem to move, but actually sponges are in a distant way relatives of mankind. We are much more closely related to a sponge than to, say, a daffodil. Sponge fossils have been found dating back to the earliest part of the Cambrian Period (*c.*530 million years ago). A famous place for finding them is in the Sponge Gravels of Faringdon, Oxfordshire.

## Corals

Most people have heard of coral reefs, but what many probably don't realize is that these enormous constructions were built over hundreds of thousands of years by tiny marine organisms which secrete their homes on top of the skeletons of their ancestors.

When coral fish die their bones pile up to create vast underwater mountains that provide an ideal marine habitat for future generations of corals and other sea creatures. It is thought that up to 30 per cent of today's marine species camp out in the earth's biggest existing coral reef – the Great Barrier Reef off the coast of north-east Australia. This colossal structure, composed of more than 1,000 islands, stretches for more than 1,000 miles.

Coral fish need sunlight in order to live. As each generation of coral dies the underwater mountain gets taller and taller so the top of the reef is never far from the sunlit surface. Some reefs have broken through the surface, becoming small islands. These are now amongst the world's most popular tourist destinations such as the Seychelles and the Maldives in the Indian Ocean.

Coral reef habitats seem to create an amazing degree of trust between different species. For example, small fish are often seen cleaning larger fish – even entering their mouths to wash their teeth. Communities of these small fish run cleaning stations, where larger fish come for rest and relaxation. Corals in the Cambrian seas would have been perfect examples of natural co-operation and community.

## Jellyfish

These are part of the same family as corals, but nowhere near as friendly. The family, or phylum, is called the Cnidaria. Like sponges, they are primitive creatures, although they can swim using a pumping action of their bell-like heads. Jellyfish have a very simple nervous system, no sensory organs and only one opening – a combined mouth and anus. They were very common in the Cambrian seas and some could pack a punch worthy of a lion using a lethal arsenal of harpoons dangling from their tentacles.

Jellyfish hunt in packs. Great herds of them would have been seen in the Cambrian seas, rising to the surface at night to feed off green algae and falling to the depths by day to avoid being eaten by fish like squids.

## Ammonites

Any fossil hunter would recognize these creatures, even though they have been extinct for many millions of years. Fossils in this characteristic spiral shape crop up everywhere. Although they look like snails, their closest relatives are actually cephalopods – the family that includes today's octopus and squid.

Ammonites first appeared about 400 million years ago, in the Devonian Period. The animal's living parts were contained in the last and largest of its shell chambers. Shells were ideal protection against sharp-toothed predators. Ammonite fossils have been discovered showing teeth marks, scars from unwelcome attacks.

## Sea squirts

These look like giant sacks anchored to the sea floor. They filter massive volumes of water each day in order to extract particles of food. At first glance they seem similar to sponges, but actually they're a lot more sophisticated. Not only were squirts a common feature of the prehistoric sea bed but the way they evolved was important for all kinds of creatures fortunate enough to live on earth in the future – and that includes humans.

Sea squirts have babies that swim about like tadpoles. They propel themselves with a special tail that contains a very primitive form of backbone called a notochord. Descendants of sea squirts developed these notochords into vertebrae – the bones that form our spinal column. Animals that have nerve cords or spines belong to this group, called the chordate, which includes all the fish, amphibians, reptiles, birds and mammals. Baby sea squirts are the most basic form of chordate that has ever lived and so must go down in prehistory as the first forefathers of human beings.

## Lancelets

Our first fish-like creature may not be big, but it's very old. Something like today's lancelet emerged about 500 million years ago. It seems to have evolved from some copying mistakes in those baby squirts – perhaps one that never glued itself properly to the bottom of the sea.

Like all fish, the lancelet is a distant relative of ours because it has a spinal cord running the length of its body. But that's just about where the similarities stop. Unlike us, it cannot be called a vertebrate, because its cord is not surrounded by bones. The lancelet has no brain but it does have small gills at the side that breathe sea water in and out. It uses these for feeding by filtering small food particles. These fish protect themselves from predators by burrowing into the sand on the ocean floor.

## Placoderms

Among the most fearsome creatures of the prehistoric seas were the now extinct placoderms. These were among the first fish with jaws and teeth. Recent research has shown that some species of placoderm had one of the most powerful bites of any creature ever known. Their teeth could tear a shark in two with a single snap. A placoderm could grow up to ten metres long and weighed over four tonnes. It was built like a tank. Heavy, articulated armour plating covered its head and throat, and its body was thickly scaled. Even its fins were encased in armour-plated tubes.

Placoderms were some of the world's first true vertebrates. Their spinal cords were protected, like ours, in a series of bony segments. Ugly as they were, they are our cousins nonetheless. They died out in the late Devonian Period, during one of the earth's extinction phases.

## Sea scorpions

Here's a good reason why fish like the placoderms needed to protect themselves with such highly developed body armour. The now-extinct sea scorpion or eurypterid was formidable. It had a long spiked tail equipped with a deadly venomous sting. The creature could grow to more than two metres in length, making it one of the largest underwater creatures of its day.

Sea scorpions died out along with many other species in what's called the Permian Mass Extinction, 252 million years ago (see page 41). More than 200 fossils of these terrifying creatures have been discovered. In fact, some fossilized tracks made by a 1.6-metre-long sea scorpion were found recently off the coast of Scotland.

## Lungfish

Imagine being a medium-sized fish fighting for survival in the violent, dangerous prehistoric seas. Forefathers of today's lungfish were among the first creatures to develop the equivalent of an escape hatch from the prehistoric seas by adapting one of their gills into a primitive air-breathing apparatus. There are only six species of lungfish alive today, but something closely related to them emerged from the oceans around 417 million years ago.

Lungfish look like powerful elongated eels. They burrow into the mud and use their lungs to survive dry periods when water is scarce, a process called aestivation. They lived in the estuaries of rivers, and learned to survive in dried-up river mouths by breathing oxygen from the air. They developed other features that helped them live on land, including four highly developed fins, well adapted for 'walking' across hard, dry surfaces. Such devices provided the key to surviving in a dramatically different habitat.

Now it's time to explore the emergence of life on land.

# 2

# The Age of Plants and Trees

## (420 million–65.5 million years ago)

*How seaweed eventually evolved into tall trees and forests, and how the ground was covered in a blanket of nutrient-rich soil*

FOR MILLIONS OF years heavy rain fell on the earth's barren land masses, wearing down the ground into a lifeless muddy silt. High levels of carbon dioxide in the atmosphere at this time meant the rain was acidic, increasing rock erosion and weathering. The first plants were just squidgy things that looked like small seaweeds and green mosses. They were descendants of the ancient blue-green algae – the oxygen-producing cyanobacteria – and they clung close to beaches, rivers and streams.

The transformation of these small, soggy clumps of moss into tall, graceful trees that can live thousands of miles from the water's edge demonstrates some of nature's most spectacular feats of biological engineering.

Think how hard it would be to design a tall tree that could flourish in the wild. For a start, there is the business of staying upright. Ideally, a forty-metre-high tree should be able to withstand a force-ten hurricane without toppling over. Next, a steady supply of water and nutrients is needed to sustain the whole tree. The bits of the tree that make food – the leaves at the top – must be as near to the sun as possible, which in a thick, dark forest means being tall enough to make sure that all the other trees don't block out the sunlight. But being tall means being further away from the main source of water, which is stored somewhere in the ground. Finally, if the tree's family is to flourish in future generations, it must be able to reproduce successfully. That means just dropping seeds willy-nilly on the ground below simply won't do, because young trees can't thrive if they have to compete with their parents for sun, food and water. Seeds have to be spread further afield. How is this to be done when trees can't walk or swim?

Designing a tree is no simple thing, which is probably why the earliest plants – mosses, liverworts and hornworts (the family is called the bryophytes) – stayed exactly where they liked it best: near to the water's edge, thriving only in inlets and bays in river mouths and beside streams. They completely ducked the idea of being tall; their strategy was to hide from the wind by staying small.

These plants had no proper roots, leaves or internal plumbing system to deliver water and nutrients. But if trees and plants were to colonize the vast tracts of barren land a half-hearted attempt at escaping from the sea like this was no long-term solution. About 420 million years ago, the first signs of a new approach began to emerge in the form of vascular plants. Ultimately, all the world's trees and forests are derived from them.

### The wonders of Rhynie chert

The first vascular plants weren't anything spectacular to look at. They comprised smallish shoots, only about fifty centimetres high, with thick stems and firm spiny leaves. We know about these plants thanks to a bizarre discovery in a Scottish village called Rhynie, about forty kilometres north-east of Aberdeen. In 1912 local doctor and amateur geologist William Mackie made an extraordinary find when he was exploring a piece of ground: he discovered perfectly preserved species of plants fossilized in the rocks.

About 400 million years ago Rhynie was like a steaming cauldron with boiling-hot pools of bubbling mud. Every so often a giant geyser would spout a huge fountain of scorching water filled with silicon from deep inside the earth. Silicon is one of the elements that form sand and rock. When this silicate water landed on nearby vegetation and plants it didn't just kill them instantly; when it cooled, it petrified them into perfect fossils of stone.

The fossils of Rhynie are so well preserved that scientists can see exactly what the plants were made of and how they worked. These vascular plants had evolved a chemical called lignin, which toughens the walls of plant cells. Plants that have little or no lignin stay small and floppy – like herbs or garden flowers. Although the stems of plants like these can feel rigid, they are held up only by the force of the water within them. If the water supply dwindles, the herb or flower wilts.

Plants with lignin in them can stay upright even when a drought sets in. With great precision, lignin-toughened cells are stacked and interwoven in carefully constructed layers to make wood – the magical stuff of trees. Lignin also provides tubes through which minerals and water are transported up and around the tree.

The first evidence of lignin came from plants called rhyniophytes (named after their place of discovery in Scotland). These are now extinct, but their descendants are all round us – indeed, everything woody ultimately comes from these early pioneers of the land. Mind you, it took a while for these small plants with toughened stems to become tall, graceful trees. At least forty million years.

By the time we get to the Carboniferous Period (360 million years ago), trees were growing in huge numbers. The earliest, called lycophytes, were simple structures. They had roots and branches which divided into a 'Y' shape. But they could also be very big, with some specimens, such as the lepidodendron tree, as wide as two metres and as high as a twelve-storey building.

## Life in the world's first forests

Except for the wind, and maybe a scratching sound inside a hollow log or a faint buzzing in the branches, it was eerily quiet in this prehistoric world. There were few animals, and no birds – it was still far too soon for them. And the landscape looked pretty much the same in all directions – an endless thick, dark greenish-brown, a blur of identical-looking trees. Very few varieties existed at this time. There were also no flowers. The earth would have to wait at least another 150 million years before it could witness a first bloom. Compared to trees, flowers are a modern fad.

The lycophyte trees that dominated ancient forests lacked one ingredient that ultimately led to their graceful decline into extinction some 270 million years ago. They lacked true leaves. They mostly used scales on their trunks and thin green blades on their branches for photosynthesis instead. It was left to a relative of the vascular plants found at Rhynie to come up with the concept of creating little green solar panels attached to the tips of branches. These were the euphyllophytes – literally 'good leaf plants'. Most trees alive today descend from them. Euphyllophytes quickly grew into several varieties, including ferns and horsetails.

If it weren't for lycophytes, ferns and horsetails, our modern lives would be very different indeed. These early trees colonized the land in their millions. When they died, most of them sank into swampy marshes, where over millions of years they were compacted, hardened, chemically altered and metamorphosed by heat and pressure, ultimately becoming coal. This source of chemical energy eventually fuelled the Industrial Revolution (see page 260).

While lignin helped trees become strong and leaves trapped the energy of the sun to make food, trees still faced the difficulty of finding a steady and reliable supply of water that somehow had to be channelled all the way to the top of their canopies – water that was often dispersed many metres below the ground. Trees rose to that challenge in two ways. The first relied on cultivating a good crop of friends to help. The second was down to ingenious design.

Tree roots grow downwards to find water. But to help them, they often enlist the support of another group of highly versatile living things. Neither a plant nor an animal, although for a long time they were grouped with plants, fungi form their own separate, almost invisible underground kingdom.

### How fungi helped plant life to thrive on land

They came on to land from the sea because their tiny light spores were so easily blown by the wind. They arrived at about the same time as the earliest plants started to grow on the shores. Since then fungi have developed into a huge variety of life forms, ranging from the smallest to the largest living things on earth. Small fungi are just one cell big. Yeast is an example, used in cooking all over the world to make bread. It grows by using a process called fermentation, which converts sugar into alcohol and carbon dioxide. Most fungi live underground. They have elaborate networks of hairs, called hyphae, that gather together in clumps called mycelia. A mushroom or toadstool, which most people think of as a fungus, is simply the fruit of the mycelium, which occasionally pops up above the ground to spread spores so that it can reproduce.

Fungi can have massive mycelia. In fact, the largest living thing on earth today is a fungus. Found recently in the American state of Michigan, this hairy beast stretches underground for over five kilometres, and is estimated to weigh more than ten tonnes. It is also one of the earth's longest survivors, having lived for well over 1,500 years.

# What on Earth Happened?

Fungi are the world's ecological dustmen. They process and digest dead and decaying matter, from the leaves on the ground to the dead skin in between your toes. When human dustmen take away rubbish it is often just burned or thrown into a pit in the ground. Nature's dustmen, the fungi, not only rot away the dead rubbish of life, but turn it into materials rich in nutrients that fertilize plants and trees to help them grow. Fungi are vital links in the earth's ongoing cycle of renewal – of life and death.

As so often in nature, different groups of living things team up to mutual benefit. The fungus passes on some of the nutrients and water it gathers to the tree and in return the tree feeds the fungus with sugars produced by its leaves. In this way the tree's capacity for gathering water and nutrients is dramatically increased, and the fungus gets fed. Sometimes a single fungus lives underground and attaches itself to many trees – so in this way the trees are actually connected together, linked up in a chain as if poised for a medieval dance. This relationship is called mycorrhiza. It has been estimated that 80 per cent of all flowering plants today have some sort of mutually beneficial relationship with underground fungi.

Even with its roots in water, a tree still needs to transport it up to the all-important leaves which manufacture food – and that's a long way in the case of some trees. For a long time no one could work out how trees did this. Of course, they have no moving parts like heart pumps to do the job for them. It was once thought that external air pressure caused water to flow upwards, as it does when you suck a straw, but air pressure simply isn't strong enough to pump water up a one-hundred-foot tree.

The answer is down to the ingenious design of tree leaves, which contain millions of tiny perforations, or holes, called stomata. Trees open or close these pores depending on the weather and conditions of the day. When it is hot, water in the leaves evaporates through the stomata, making the sap in the tree trunk more concentrated. This drags underground water up through the trunk and into the leaves at the top of the tree. The name of this process is transpiration.

The trees' final challenge is to find a way of spreading their offspring, even though they cannot walk or move. The earliest species used the wind to spread spores in much the same way as fungi. The problem is that spores need exactly the right conditions to germinate – usually they must land in wet places, such as marshes or bogs. In dry climates this is a big problem. Then, about 360 million years ago, trees came up with a much better solution. Seeds.

Unlike spores, seeds contain a partly formed tree embryo as well as a substantial food store of sugar, protein and fats. The embryo, with its larder stocked with food, is then encased in a coat (testa), ready for a sometimes epic journey, using one of a number of alternative transport systems.

Seeds dramatically increase a tree's chances of successful reproduction. They are tougher than spores; they can survive droughts; they take their own food rations with them and some can even float. The first seed-bearing trees were the cycads, which have been traced back to about 270 million years ago – about 40 million years before the first dinosaurs appeared. About 130 species of cycads are still living today, although many are under threat of extinction owing to the destruction of their habitats. These trees also mastered the art of sexual reproduction, which usually requires the genes of two different trees to combine to make a seed. But that leaves a final, apparently insuperable challenge: how could two different parents mix their genes when they are both, literally, rooted to the ground?

### How rising levels of oxygen transformed life on land

The solution came from other forms of life that had emerged on to the land. A few small worm-like creatures probably emerged from the sea at about the same time as the earliest plants and mosses, about 420 million years ago. What tempted them ashore had something to do with the rising quantities of oxygen in the air. Oxygen levels had steadily increased over millions of years until they levelled off at the beginning of the Cambrian Period, about 530 million years ago. Then there was a blip between four and two hundred million years ago.

This blip was caused by the luscious green forests now covering the land. Plants and trees dramatically increased the amount of oxygen in the atmosphere. The effect was a bit like lining the shores with sweets. Life in the seas just couldn't resist the temptation to come ashore for a taste. When the first sea creatures came crawling out they found that the adjustment wasn't too hard, with all that extra oxygen in the air to give them a boost. Today about 21 per cent of the air we breathe is oxygen. But 350 million years ago, with the arrival of the carboniferous forests, oxygen levels shot up to perhaps as much as 35 per cent.

## An age of giants

Extra oxygen explains why Stan Wood, a sharp-eyed commercial fossil hunter from Scotland, did so well out of a dilapidated old limestone farm wall that he spotted next to a school football field in 1984. He thought the wall might contain some interesting fossils, so he bought it from some developers who were about to knock it down – for twenty-five pounds.

The fossils Wood found inside were so important that he ended up selling them for more than £50,000. He spent some of the money buying the disused quarry in East Kirkton where the limestone in the wall had come from. After bringing in some heavy digging machinery, he made some even more amazing discoveries. He found the fossil of a giant air-breathing scorpion at least thirty centimetres long, with a vicious-looking barbed tail and a protective outer skeleton. This huge creature, an eurypterid, probably grew more than two metres long, bigger than most humans.

The higher concentrations of oxygen in the air meant many

creatures could grow much bigger than their living descendants can today because energy-rich oxygen could diffuse further into an organism's breathing system. Stan Wood's scorpion, estimated at about 335 million years old, shows how this ancient beast had mastered two of the essential challenges for creatures that came ashore. It used primitive lungs for breathing air. These were adapted from its gills and protected by pockets of hard outer skin. The giant scorpion also had pairs of legs, so it could walk on land.

## The Beast of Bolsover

Some of the world's first insects also belong to this period. Dragonflies were the most spectacular of all. How they learned to fly is still a mystery, but it probably had something to do with the arrival of plants and trees. Wouldn't it make sense for an insect to just jump or glide from one tree to another, rather than climb all the way down and then up again? Something like this is what led the dragonfly to develop its wings. They grew out of the same kind of pockets of hard outer skin as those found in the giant scorpion.

Perhaps to begin with they used these small flaps just for jumping, maybe to add a little extra distance to a big leap. Gradually the flaps grew larger, until such acrobatics as gliding, diving and finally flapping became possible. Of course, flapping is an extremely energetic thing to do. Happily, in the oxygen-rich atmosphere of those days these first flyers were immersed in just the right stuff for trying something new and tiring. The extra oxygen also made the air thicker, so it was easier for the dragonflies to lift off.

Extra oxygen also helped them grow big. These colourful prehistoric flies were as large as today's seagulls. They leaped, jumped and flew from tree to tree totally unchallenged. They had complete command of the skies, feeding off other insects as and when they liked. They had no rivals.

Smaller insects eventually developed an ingenious design to protect themselves. They evolved sophisticated folding wings, just like those we see in houseflies today. Folding wings allowed the smaller insects to crawl into narrow spaces where the larger, fixed-winged predators, the dragonflies, could not go. Flying (neopterous) insects are by far the largest group alive today, which means that the folding wing probably counts as one of nature's most successful ever inventions.

Another important requirement for land-based creatures is the ability to see. Dragonflies developed highly sophisticated compound eyes with 30,000 facets, each one a tiny eye, neatly arranged to give nearly 360-degree, or all-round, vision.

Dragonfly fossils have been found in many parts of the world, but the most spectacular came from the small mining town of Bolsover in Derbyshire, England, where a giant 300-million-year-old dragonfly fossil was discovered by two coalminers. With a twenty-centimetre wingspan, this is the oldest known dragonfly fossil, and far bigger than any dragonfly alive today. For a few days dragonfly fever gripped Britain, the newspapers had a field day and the legend of the Beast of Bolsover was born.

## Worms emerge and insects evolve

The first ever land animal was probably a relation of the velvet worm. It wriggled out of the sea, feeding off the earliest plants and mosses that were clinging to the shore. Descendants of this creature, the common ancestor of the arthropod family, went on to develop legs, becoming the first millipedes and centipedes. Once on the land, these early arthropods gradually evolved into a wide variety of insects, combining the first few segments of their worm-like bodies to form a head, and adapting at least one pair of legs into feelers. Over time other segments merged to form the thorax (upper body) and abdomen (lower body and tail).

One of the most significant insects to emerge was the beetle. Today there are probably more species of beetle than of any other living creature. Over 350,000 different types have been discovered so far, which is about 40 per cent of all known insect species, but experts believe there may be between five and eight million types in all.

Beetles bring us back to the final engineering challenge faced by the world's first sexually active trees, the cycads. These were the insects that came to their assistance. As they rummaged in the undergrowth and up into the leaves of the trees, they transferred yellow pollen powder from the male parts of one cycad tree on to the female parts of another, so fertilizing the trees' genes to produce a new crop of seeds.

## A blanket of nutrient-rich soil

Beetles, other insects, worms and fungi are jointly responsible for attending to the land's most precious sustaining life force of all: the soil. Like constant gardeners, they recycle organic matter – fallen leaves and rotting trees – into nutrients that fertilize the soil for tomorrow's plants and trees. Without living things, there would be no soil. The earth would be nothing more than dust and rock, like the surface of the moon, Mars or Venus. Some of the rock might weather and dissolve in the rain to be washed back into the sea in the form of mud and silt, but the crumbly black-brown stuff that makes vegetable gardens grow would never have formed were it not for life on earth. Over the course of millions of years all the soil on earth is renewed and regenerated. This is called the soil cycle.

There is nothing now left of the soil from the Carboniferous Period. The oldest soil today is just a few million years old. Wind, water, ice and the movement of the tectonic plates mean that soil, like rock and salt, is always being churned up or washed away. Soil, which is made up of weathered rock, minerals and organic matter, appeared first when plants and trees started to grow on the land in large numbers during the Carboniferous Period. Plants established themselves in cracks between rocks that had been pummelled by centuries of rain and weather. Their developing roots broke down the rock further.

Since plants were a rich source of food, they attracted fungi, worms and other tiny arthropods such as mites that live off organic matter. For the last 400 million years these creatures have been digging up the earth and turning it over, exposing it to the air and rain with their burrowing, allowing the weather and the elements to break up the soil so that it's always ready for new life to take seed.

With plentiful supplies of food in the form of plants and trees, more oxygen than ever, a cooling climate and a landscape ideal for providing shelter (either in the branches of trees or in soil which could be burrowed into), the scene was now set for life's next major episode. What would the descendants of those backboned, four-finned creatures such as the lungfish make of this rich, earthy paradise?

### Flower power

Charles Darwin wrote in 1879 in a letter to a friend, the botanist Joseph Hooker, that he could not understand the sudden appearance of flowering plants in the fossil record. Where on earth did they spring from? 'The rapid development of all the higher plants in recent geological times is an abominable mystery ... I should like to see this whole problem solved.'

To this day, no one has really come up with a decent explanation. Unlike some of those wilder theories about life's ingredients arriving on earth via a meteorite from outer space, there is no question of the same being true for flowers. Yet about 130 million years ago the world's first flower fossils suddenly start to show up.

Some experts think flowers arose as long as 250 million years ago, but fossils this old have never been found. Others think that several evolutionary phases occurred in quick succession, accounting for flowers' sudden appearance in the rocks. The fact remains that flowers appeared for sure only about 130 million years ago, and as yet there is no clear evidence that they lived much before then.

Flowering plants and trees made a massive impact on life on earth. Without them, life today would be very different indeed. More than 75 per cent of all the food humans eat (directly or indirectly) comes from flowering trees and plants. No longer was the earth dominated by endless streaks of browns, greens and blues. For the first time there were blooms of red, yellow, orange, purple and pink.

The flower is a powerful technology used by many plants and trees to reproduce and spread. Evolution must have been at its magical best when the first flowers evolved, because the designs it came up with to aid fertilization and spread seeds are among the most spectacular of all.

Plants used the tried and tested strategy that the older trees knew best: they put all their effort into making friends. Flower power helped plants and trees recruit armies of other creatures to help them spread to all corners of the earth. It is maybe no accident that flying insects such as bees, moths and butterflies first appeared alongside the earth's first flowers.

Flowers and pollinating insects such as bees evolved together – a process called co-evolution. Flowers needed bees as much as bees needed flowers. Each developed ways of helping the other survive better because they both stood to make gains from mutual co-operation – one providing food, the other a means of transport. With the help of a pollinator such as a beetle or bee, genes from male and female flowers could mix to produce new seeds with their own unique genetic code. Flowers developed a huge range of incentives to get animals on land and in the air to carry their pollen and seeds to other places.

*Fruit juice*

Fruit is the female part of a flower, the ovary, which once it has been fertilized changes its shape and form to help disperse seeds. Sometimes these seeds travel on the wind, sometimes by water, or sometimes by sticking to an animal's fur. So the downy white parachute of a dandelion seed is a fruit. And so is the acorn from an oak tree, or a prickly burr. The most ingenious transportation method of all is to bury seeds in a ready-made meal. A passing animal might help itself to the fruit, digest it for a day or two, and then obligingly spread the indigestible seeds as it moves along by scattering them in its dung, giving them an additional growth shot in the shape of a godparent's gift of manure. Seeds are built to be tough. They can survive the most upset, unpleasant of stomachs.

Not all fruits rely on being eaten. Some trees, like the coconut palm, developed other strategies, such as floating their large seeds over thousands of miles of water from one coast to another. Or there's the curious sandbox tree, whose fruit explodes like a firework, scattering its seeds up to a hundred metres away. Cotton fruits produce fibres that stick to animal skins as a way of spreading their seeds. Nuts are edible seeds designed to be carried off by animals which hoard them for the winter. Almost always they leave some uneaten, allowing these seeds to grow into new plants in a new place.

Before fruit there was the wind – nature's most traditional method of spreading pollen and dispersing seeds and spores. The wind is still a favourite among many flowers, especially grasses like wheat and barley. Dandelions have tiny parachutes to catch the breeze, and the helicopter-like wings of the sycamore seed work well too. Flowers that use the wind for pollination as well as seed dispersal have no need to attract animals or insects, so they don't bother with big, showy flowers. They save energy by keeping their petals small and discreet.

An important new group of plants evolved during the Cretaceous

Period (145–65.5 million years ago) called monocots. Unlike most other plants (called dicots), they came up with the ingenious trick of growing back to front. Instead of new growth being added to the tips of the leaves – a conifer's greenest, youngest shoots are always at the ends of each branch – a monocot's leaves grow up from a central, often submerged, bud. The new design was an instant success, because it meant that if a plant's leaves got nibbled by a passing dinosaur it didn't lose its most recent growth, because this was safely tucked away at the bottom. Grasses are monocots and use this design to recover quickly after being grazed by animals. In fact, many grasses *like* to be grazed. It strengthens their stems, but doesn't damage their potential for new growth, since the growth bud (called the apical bud) is always kept beneath the ground, out of harm's way.

So successful was this design that grasslands have come to cover as much of the earth's surface as all the other plant and tree species combined. What's more, some time during the Cretaceous Period a completely new type of tree evolved. Unlike the ancient cycads and conifers, monocot palm trees grow from a bud at the top of a thick, scaled trunk. There are more than 2,600 types of palm trees alive today. The most ancient palm tree fossils – from the nipa palm – date from around 112 million years ago. Nipas are rather special, because their trunks and roots are sunk in marshy swamps or riverbanks. Their way of spreading themselves takes some beating. These are trees that swim. They tie themselves together by the roots and, using the force of the tides and water, break loose into floating islands that can carry cargo in the form of small groups of animals, which use them as rafts to float from one place to another.

Although today an enormous amount of research has gone into studying the fossil record and the genetic ancestry of modern plants and trees, many pieces are missing in a puzzle that was, and is still, Darwin's 'abominable mystery'.

# 3

# The Rise
# of Animals

**(420 million–7 million years ago)**

*How terrestrial living was transformed by
the evolution of better adapted species*

**LIFE ON LAND** is about to take a big lurch forward. First, we will complete a tour of the Carboniferous Period (360–299 million years ago) and then head into the Permian (299–251 million years ago), when reptiles ruled the earth. Then we must pick our way through a dramatic episode called the Permian Mass Extinction, when most of the life on earth was wiped out, before emerging into a bright new dawn. There we shall meet our first dinosaurs. At this time many of today's familiar insects will also arrive: bees, butterflies and moths. We will also see our first feathered bird. A quick check of our twenty-four-hour clock shows that in this part of our journey we will be travelling from about 10.24 p.m. to 11.58 p.m. – leaving just two minutes for the final evolution of all living things to unfold into human history.

Our tour begins with a rare and most important piece of evolutionary evidence provided by the fossils of a creature called *Tiktaalik* which were discovered on Ellesmere Island, in Canada, in 2004. They represent what are known as transitional fossils, and show key features from two different species: one is the lobe-finned fish, the other the next-to-evolve tetrapod (four-limbed creature). Tiktaalik lived about 375 million years ago, towards the end of the Devonian Period, just as the early plants and mosses were adapting to life near the shores. This creature developed the first genuine arms, with shoulders, elbows and wrists – brilliantly suited for heaving its body on to the land or wading through shallow bogs.

Several million years later we come across the almost impossible to pronounce *Ichthyostega*, which lived between about 357 and 362 million years ago. This land lover was about 1.5 metres long and had seven toes on each foot. It was one of the first genuine tetrapods, and certainly no longer a fish. Young ichthyostega could easily leap ashore and move around without having to drag an enormous heavy body. Land was also safer than the sea because there was plenty to eat and fewer large predators.

The transition from fish to amphibian was finally completed about 340 million years ago with the evolution of the first known family of amphibians, the temnospondyls. These could be as large as a fully grown crocodile or as small as a newt. *Eryops* is a fine example, and first appeared in the fossil record about 270 million years ago. It had a stout body and wide ribs, grew up to 1.5 metres long, and had a strong backbone that prevented its body from sagging under its own weight.

Reptiles differ from amphibians because, if necessary, they can live their lives away from the water. They have waterproof skins so that if the weather becomes very hot, the water inside their bodies doesn't evaporate, reducing the likelihood of dehydration. They were also the first creatures to be able to lay eggs on land. These were encased in tough waterproof shells that contained a portable ocean in the form of a liquid membrane to protect the embryo and give it all the nourishment it needed until it was old enough to hatch out and survive on its own in the air.

One of the most successful species was *Dimetrodon*, a reptile which first appeared in the early Permian Period, between 260 and 280 million years ago. Growing up to three metres long, this lumbering giant walked on four side-sprawling legs and had a long swaggering tail. It was the largest meat eater of its time. The success of this bizarre-looking creature was mostly due to the spectacular sail on its back, which it used as a radiator to heat itself up more quickly than other creatures at the beginning of each day.

This was the beginning of warm-bloodedness, a feature of all mammals, including humans. It allows living things to maintain the same internal body temperature regardless of the conditions outside, allowing such creatures to hunt at night or whenever it is safe to go out. Dimetrodon also evolved other mammal-like features, such as different types of teeth. Dimetrodon means 'two-measure teeth'.

### Life's biggest brush with death

Bizarre creatures like these ruled the world on land for about sixty million years. Their success came to a sudden and dramatic end 252 million years ago, when life crashed into a deep abyss from which it almost never recovered. This was the single most serious threat to prehistoric life on earth, a time known as the Permian Mass Extinction.

By now all the earth's land masses had collided, forming a massive single supercontinent, Pangaea (the name comes from two Greek words: *pan* meaning 'all', and *gea*, meaning 'the earth').

When enormous continental land masses collide, one thing is certain – there will be a huge increase in the number and violence of volcanoes. Experts think this is one reason why such a horrific mass extinction occurred 252 million years ago. An enormous super-volcano located somewhere in what is now northern Russia exploded with unprecedented fury. Initially it flooded about 200,000 square kilometres of land in Siberia with boiling-hot lava (forming the

Siberian Traps – an area larger than Florida). Then, amazingly, it kept erupting for more than a million years.

This massive eruption devastated the earth's environment, triggering a catalogue of disasters. As the Permian Mass Extinction took place over an estimated 80,000 years, only the very toughest, most well-suited creatures survived the darkness and the enormous swings of temperature. Only those which luck had blessed with specific genetic differences that improved their chances of survival in those extreme conditions lived on. Everything else perished. These were desperate times for the earth, her life-support systems ailing from a string of unmanageably chaotic events.

## The age of dinosaurs

Nine out of ten species that existed on the earth were killed off by the Permian Mass Extinction. After those catastrophic years, the most successful species were nature's loyal brigade of cleaners and recyclers – the fungi. When times get really tough, history shows it's best to be small – like insects, bacteria and fungi. For a while the earth belonged to them.

Only one species of mammal-like reptile survived at all: the *Lystrosaurus*. If this creature had perished, evolution would almost certainly have shunted yet-to-come mammals and humans into life's might-have-beens, consigning our ancestors to the waste bucket of life, an experimental cul-de-sac. No matter, then, that our reptilian saviour wasn't exactly blessed with good looks, being something like a cross between a hippopotamus and a pig.

No one knows quite why or how the *Lystrosaurus* survived the trauma of the Permian Mass Extinction, but for millions of years it thrived across all Pangaea. There is almost no record of any other vertebrate alive during this time, 230 million years ago, which is called the early Triassic Period (see plate 1).

Then, out of the barren sands of extinction, came a completely new generation of land-living reptiles – one that grew into the most fearsome and dominant prehistoric force that had ever trodden the earth. Dinosaurs were reptiles that lived on land. They had rearward-pointing elbows and forward-pointing knees, with hips that allowed many of them to walk on two legs. Most were large – their average weight is estimated at 850 kilograms, whereas the average weight of a modern mammal today is only 863 grams.

The name 'dinosaur' was coined by the first curator of the Natural History Museum in London, Richard Owen, in 1842. It comes from two Greek words: *deinos*, meaning 'terrible', and *saurus*, meaning 'lizard'. More than 500 different species of dinosaur have been identified so far, although nearly 2,000 are thought to have existed. Some walked on two feet, some on four. Some ate plants, some ate other animals, some ate both. The first known dinosaurs were the prosauropods. These were plant eaters that could grow up to ten metres long with small heads and enormously long necks. They usually walked on four legs, but sometimes climbed on to just two when reaching to nibble at the top of a tree.

Gideon Mantell was the first person ever to discover a dinosaur bone. He was a doctor and amateur fossil hunter who lived in Lewes, in East Sussex. Near his home lay the remains of an ancient forest that was a goldmine for fossil hunters of the period. In 1822 Mantell found several remarkably large teeth. Mantell calculated from the size of the teeth that the animal must have been at least eighteen metres long – that's nearly as long as two back-to-back double-decker buses. After years of dispute Mantell's teeth were eventually recognized as belonging to a new type of creature, never before known. He called it the iguanodon because it was reckoned to look like a much larger version of a modern iguana.

Mantell's discovery made people realize for the first time that the earth was once dominated by a family of huge, now-extinct monsters. The world went fossil mad.

The place that went maddest of all was America. In 1858 a fossil hunter called William Foulke discovered the first ever near-complete dinosaur skeleton in a quarry near his home of Haddonfield in New Jersey. This dinosaur was named after Foulke and the place where he found it – *Hadrosaurus foulkii*. Soon after, two of America's leading palaeontologists, Edward Cope and Othniel Marsh, began scouring the land for all the dinosaur fossils they could find.

At first Cope and Marsh worked together, hiring men to dig up the quarry where Foulke had made his discovery. They found several other almost complete dinosaur skeletons, but their friendship soon turned sour when it emerged that Marsh had secretly bribed the men digging out the quarry to tell him first whenever any new fossil discoveries came to light. A war – and not just of words – broke out between them. Both men were wealthy and they spent their riches trying to outsmart each other with dinosaur discoveries.

At one stage Cope was so angry with Marsh for stealing his fossils that he had a trainload full of Marsh's fossils diverted to his own collection in Philadelphia. By the end of his life Marsh had clocked up eighty-six new species, including the now famous triceratops, diplodocus and stegosaurus. Cope discovered fifty-six, including the first ever dimetrodon (although that is not technically a dinosaur). The result is that we now know a good deal more about these mighty beasts that once ruled the world, and why they were so successful for so long.

## How dinosaurs came to rule the world

Like the dimetrodon that thrived before the Permian Mass Extinction, dinosaurs benefited greatly from living in a era when it was literally possible to walk from pole to pole. Thanks to the arrangements of the earth's continents into one giant land mass,

Pangaea, the strongest land-based creatures of this era had a unique opportunity to evolve into a position of unassailable dominance. Natural barriers, such as oceans, never got in their way. It was almost inevitable that their success would lead to a reduction in the variety of other land-living things.

The dinosaurs were the first creatures ever to have their legs directly under their bodies at all times, whether walking, running, galloping or hopping. This is called a 'fully improved stance', and meant that many of them could walk upright. This may have been the biggest single biological factor in the dinosaurs' success. Animals with a fully improved stance could grow bigger, move further and walk faster than other living creatures, allowing many body types and lifestyles to evolve.

Some of the biggest dinosaurs were the sauropods, such as the diplodocus. These beasts, which walked on all four legs, could grow up to 27.5 metres long and weighed up to eleven tonnes. Their survival strategy was simple: they grew so large that few other creatures were big enough or strong enough to kill them. So they did very well. In 1994 a 147-metre-long fossilized sauropod trackway was found along an ancient muddy estuary in Portugal. The huge footprints showed scientists how these creatures walked, confirming that they held their bodies above their legs and lifted their long tails to stop them dragging along the ground, allowing them to walk more easily.

Others were fast. Hypsilophodons grew only to about the height of an adult human's waist, but could run as fast as a modern deer. More than twenty of their skeletons have been found fossilized on the Isle of Wight, England, where they unwittingly wandered into a pool of lethal quicksand. With long, thin feet and short thighbones for rapid forward and backward movement, these two-legged creatures had self-sharpening teeth and lived off plants. They survived purely thanks to being able to run away from danger so fast.

Other dinosaurs could walk on either two or four legs, such as the iguanodon discovered by Mantell. This beast couldn't run out of harm's way. Instead its thumb was cleverly crafted into a terrifyingly sharp dagger which it used to defend itself, usually standing upright on its hind legs to fend off attackers.

But one of the strongest beasts ever to have stalked the earth was the tyrannosaurus rex, or T. Rex for short. It belonged to the therapod family, which originated in what is now western North America.

T. Rex walked on two legs, and had a massive skull, balanced by a long, heavy tail. Its hands had just two fingers, and its forearms were quite short compared with its massive legs and tail. At twelve metres long and weighing the same as a modern elephant, this was one big dinosaur. It dined off either dead carcasses or live prey – possibly both.

Some experts think T. Rex could run fast despite its huge size – perhaps up to thirty miles per hour. Others think it lumbered around at a more modest ten miles per hour. No one knows for sure how powerful its muscles actually were, because all that remains are skeletons reconstructed from the more than thirty specimens found in rocks around the world. But with jaws more than eight times as powerful as a lion's, the T. Rex could literally pulverize bones to extract the nutritious marrow inside. Its teeth were like a shark's, continually being replaced throughout its life.

The most complete T. Rex skeleton to date was discovered on 12 August 1990 in a place called the Hell Creek Formation in South Dakota by Sue Hendrickson, an amateur fossil-hunter. This almost complete skeleton, called 'Sue' in honour of its finder, measures some four metres high and thirteen metres long. Finding fossils like this is a serious business. After a protracted legal fight over its ownership, Sue was ultimately declared the property of landowner Maurice Williams. He eventually sold her at auction for $7.6 million.

# What on Earth Happened?

## The origins of the family unit

The majority of dinosaurs were peaceful, plant-eating creatures that developed the earth's first strong social communities. Herds, packs and families of dinosaurs were commonplace. Many fossils have been found where groups of dinosaurs died together, such as the ones which sank in the quicksand off the Isle of Wight. In Alberta, Canada a mass grave has been discovered containing at least 300 grazing dinosaurs of all ages and sizes. This herd was swept to its death by a flash flood while trying to cross a deep river. In Montana, in the USA, an even bigger herd of about 10,000 dinosaurs has been discovered. These creatures were poisoned by volcanic gases and buried in ash. Their fossilized bones stretch out in a straight line for more than a mile.

Modern understanding of how dinosaurs lived together was transformed by a fossil specialist called Dr Jack Horner, who made a most extraordinary discovery in the mid-1970s. Horner and his team were fossil hunting in Montana when they came across America's first dinosaur nesting site. They found a number of dinosaur eggs as well as the fossilized remains of dinosaur embryos. They called these creatures maiasaura, which means 'good mother lizard'. Each season maiasaura returned to the same breeding grounds where they refurbished their old nests. These dinosaurs lived in colonies and looked after their young in herds until they were old enough to start families of their own. Here, beyond all reasonable doubt, lie the origins of the family unit. More than 200 dinosaur-egg sites have now been found across the world. The eggs range in size from a small pebble to some as big as footballs.

Other dinosaur-like creatures, too numerous to mention, also lived through these times. The pterosaurs were enormous flying reptiles that dominated the prehistoric skies. One of them holds the record for the biggest wingspan of any creature ever to have lived. At nearly twenty metres across, its wings were as large as those of a Second World War Spitfire.

## The mystery of feathered flight

Hermann von Meyer, a German fossil hunter, thought he'd got the answer to this puzzle in 1861 when he announced the discovery of what he claimed was the first ever bird. He called it archaeopteryx. It was about the same size as a modern magpie, and was definitely bird-like. Its feathers were arranged in just the same way as modern birds', with an aerodynamic configuration to make flight possible. It even had bird-like claws on its legs, and a wishbone.

Von Meyer's fossil dated back some 140 million years, about the same time that the first flowers were beginning to bloom (see page 34). Since then a further ten archaeopteryx specimens have been found in a region of Germany called Solnhofen. But for years a mystery remained. From what did these creatures descend, and how did they learn to fly? So perplexing was this puzzle that the birds were shunted into their own separate group, neither reptiles like the dinosaurs, nor mammals like man. They were just, well, birds.

Then, in 1995, Chinese scientists announced that they had dug out a fossil which proves conclusively that some dinosaurs did indeed have down-like feathers. Sinosauropteryx caused a sensation. It was a 1.5-metre-long two-legged dinosaur with the jaws and flattened teeth typical of meat-eating dinosaurs. It had clawed fingers, and its hind limbs show that it must have been a fast runner. At last, the puzzle of where birds descended from seemed to have been solved. They are indeed the last and only surviving branch of the dinosaurs.

## The earth's first civilizations

We are now roughly a hundred million years from the present day, that's about 11.20 p.m. on our twenty-four-hour clock, and at last we see the first signs of civilization. Not human civilizations, but belonging to insects in the form of wasps and their descendants, bees and ants. There were also termites, a different branch of life altogether, related to beetles. From these creatures new, more advanced social ways of living developed that became the prototypes for all subsequent civilizations to evolve on earth.

Bees descended from wasps and emerged alongside the first flowers. They switched from dining on other insects to a diet of pollen and nectar instead. There are about 20,000 different species of bee alive today. Some of these – especially honeybees, bumblebees and stingless bees – form highly social groups that offer a deep insight into how nature's civilizations work.

Eusocial creatures divide up jobs between themselves. They pass knowledge and learning on from one generation to another, care for their youngsters and even, in certain circumstances, sacrifice their lives for the benefit of the group. Such characteristics were for a long time thought to be unique to mankind when it first organized itself into tribes and eventually cities and states. But, as any beekeeper will tell you, that is not so.

Queen bees are in overall command of a group of male drones and a third type of bee, sterile female workers. Bees communicate with each other through the language of dance. When they return to their hives they dance to inform the others as to the whereabouts of good sources of food. The round dance means that food is within fifty metres of the hive. The waggle dance, which may be vertical or horizontal, provides more detail about both the distance and the direction of the located food source. Then there is the jerky dance, used by the bees to decide whether to increase or decrease the amount of food gathering they need to do, depending on the hive's overall requirements.

Ants belong to the same family as honeybees. The oldest ant fossil yet discovered is a specimen trapped in amber, estimated at more than eighty million years old. Their civilizations feature the earth's first schools, what look like the beginnings of slavery and even a bizarre attempt at behaving like an early type of computer. There are many similarities between ants' nests and honeybees' hives, but ants do not dance. Instead, they communicate through chemicals called pheromones that other ants can smell. When an ant finds food it will leave a trail of scent along the ground all the way home, to lead others to it. The ant then finds the way back by remembering certain landmarks often using the position of the sun as its guide. As other ants follow the first trail each one leaves more scent, until the food source is completely exhausted. Once the ants no longer leave a scent the smell evaporates, and the trail is lost for ever.

Ants' smells say other things too. For example, if an ant gets squashed, its dying gift is a smell that triggers an alarm to all the other ants nearby, sending them into a mad panic as they run around trying to avoid the same fate.

Ants are also the first creatures we know of that learned to teach each other. When a young ant makes its first journey out of the nest an older ant will tutor it in the art of finding and fetching food. These tutors slow down to allow the pupil to catch up, and speed up when it draws close (this behaviour has been observed in the species *Temnothorax albipennis*). They have even been known to link together over gaps to form chains, allowing other ants to cross streams of water like an army with its own portable pontoon bridge.

Termites evolved alongside the dinosaurs during the Jurassic Period (199–145 million years ago) – fossilized nests are thought to date from as far back as 200 million years ago – and grew more numerous from the Cretaceous Period (145–65.5 million years ago) onwards (see plate 1). These creatures can create the biggest microcities of all. Termites often live in colonies that number several million individuals. A termites' nest is a monarchy, but this time the king rules with one or more queens by his side. A pregnant queen can lay several thousand eggs a day. She gets so large (sometimes up to ten centimetres long) that she is often unable to move. If she needs more space, thousands of worker termites heave her up and push her to a newly built chamber. In return she rewards them with a special form of milk.

Termite civilizations show very high levels of collective intelligence. Compass termites build tall nests that point north–south, to help drive hot air currents through their elaborate network of tunnels. Temperature control is vital for the maintenance of their growing gardens of fruiting fungi.

The story of civilized insects is largely untold in histories of the earth, but their worlds go on around us, with important consequences. Sometimes they are under the control of mankind – bees pollinate our orchards and make us honey – and sometimes they cause humans annoyance and distress. Whatever their reputation today, these creatures' powers of organization, intelligence and self-sacrifice for the greater good of their kind are the very hallmarks of what we humans have come to call civilized.

## Extra-terrestrial impact

What on earth happened to the non-avian dinosaurs? The rocks speak clearly for themselves: after dinosaurs dominated life on land for more than 160 million years, from about 65.5 million years ago another mass extinction occurred and all traces of dinosaur fossils disappear completely. It wasn't just the dinosaurs that were wiped out. The last of the pterosaurs, the flying reptiles, also vanished, as did all the sea reptiles – except for the turtles, which somehow survived. It was also the end of the road for the ammonites, those bizarre spiral-shaped fossils, relations of today's octopus and squid (see page 19).

Life on earth survives inside a thin, delicate layer of atmospheric skin on top of a lump of hard, lifeless rock. That's exactly how it would have looked to the six-mile-wide asteroid hurtling towards earth 65.5 million years ago at a speed of some 70,000 miles per hour. Far in the distance, a bright blue-green dot would have been growing larger and larger by the day. As the dark chunk of deadly rock and ice made its final approach, planet earth would have resembled a sparkling jewel in the black sea of space.

# The Rise of Animals

Freakish misfortune powered the asteroid on its lethal journey, and when the end came it was as colossal as it was spectacular. Not that the earth isn't used to googlies bowled by chance from outer space. Asteroids, meteorites, comets – they all fall from the skies in a constant rain. Usually they vaporize as they cut through the dense atmosphere, burning up with the shock of suddenly encountering the earth's thick, heavy air. But not when they are this big. Down it came, possibly splitting up into several pieces before finally making its rendezvous with an unsuspecting world.

At the point of biggest impact, just at the edge of the Yucatán Peninsula in Mexico, the asteroid would have blasted a crater more than a hundred miles wide, destroying in seconds everything within a 600-mile radius. The force would have been equivalent to thousands of nuclear bombs exploding all at once, vaporizing anything and everything into nothing more than a cloud of deathly, blisteringly hot, toxic gas.

The noise and sight of the impact would have deafened and blinded countless living creatures. Many of those not killed by the blast would have been drowned by the waves. For perhaps as long as a year the earth, enveloped by heavy, acrid clouds, was without light from the sun.

## The mammals inherit the earth

Had that asteroid missed the earth 65.5 million years ago, would many of the animals we know and love today, including mankind, ever have evolved? No one can possibly know the answer because life on earth cannot be rerun through a computer program to see what would have happened if the dinosaurs had survived.

What *is* clear is that evolution took a dramatically different path following their extinction. The disappearance of the dinosaurs provided an opportunity for another group of animals to take centre stage and become the next masters of the earth. When the dinosaurs were in charge, mammals clung on at the edge of the world's families of living creatures.

Mammals back then were mostly small and squirrel-like. They emerged from their underground burrows only when it was safe to do so, often at night. When the coast was clear, they'd scuttle off to feed on insects – easy food for ground dwellers or for those who chose to hide out of harm's way safely tucked up in a tall tree.

Many of them developed evolutionary tricks to help survive the terrifying dinosaurs. Most gave birth to live young, so they didn't need to leave eggs lying around for someone else's breakfast. They were so scared of leaving their burrows that they developed their own personal soup kitchens, in the form of breast milk, so they could feed their young at any time, day or night, without leaving the nest. They also grew fur, which helped them keep warm. Finally, warm-bloodedness let them hunt at night when it was cold outside and safer from predatory dinosaurs. So when disaster struck 65.5 million years ago, these small, furry mammals were well placed to survive the impact and the dreadful blackout that followed.

Once the dust had settled, mammals could enjoy the sunshine without the threat of being eaten by reptilian monsters. Birds were now the only living branch of the dinosaurs left, using their survival advantage of feathered flight to avoid the worst of the meteorite storm, and going on to fill the world with song as the earth moved into a fresh new dawn.

Things got off to a quick start. Within three million years shrew-sized mammals had evolved into creatures as large as dogs. Within five million years, mammals of all shapes and sizes roamed the land. With the dinosaurs gone the land was a place of relative peace and tranquillity. This period, from 56 to 34 million years ago, is called the Eocene (see plate 1). The name comes from the ancient Greek meaning 'new dawn'. Extraordinary mammals filled every available corner. In the forests there roamed deer, boars, bears, koalas, pandas, monkeys and apes. On the grasslands grazed cattle, bison, oxen, sheep, zebra, pigs, horses, giraffes, kangaroos and donkeys. In burrows dwelt rabbits, badgers, hedgehogs, mice and foxes. In rivers and swamps splashed rhinos, elephants, beavers, otters and hippos. Across the deserts trekked camels, llamas and rats. In the oceans swam whales, dolphins, seals, walruses. And in the air flew bats.

Mammals evolved into three main groups. Two of them, including nearly all of today's mammals, originated in Laurasia, the northern fragment of Pangaea, and one in the southern part, Gondwana. It is only the monotremes that survive from Gondwana. They are a very strange lot. And the most famous of them all is very strange indeed.

## Monotremes

Is it a duck? Or perhaps a weird fish? Or maybe a bird? Or even a beaver? The question baffled experts when the duckbilled platypus was first discovered by Europeans in Australia in the late 1700s. To begin with the creature was dismissed as a hoax, a kind of half-bird, half-mammal. Surely someone was having a laugh: naturalists suspected that perhaps it was a duck's beak sewed on to the body of a beaver – they even tried to find the stitches with a pair of scissors. But by 1800 people accepted that this animal was something completely unknown but most definitely natural.

Duckbills are definitely mammals because, even though they lay eggs, their babies are fed by milk produced by their mother's mammary glands. Platypus fossils dating back 110 million years show that these early mammals originally waddled over to Australia from South America before the two land masses fully broke up into separate island continents.

## Marsupials

The name means 'pouch' in Latin. These mammals rear their young in a special pouch on their outer skin. They give birth to extremely tiny babies which crawl up the mother's belly and tuck themselves inside her pouch, latching onto her nipple for food and drink. There they stay for a number of weeks until they are big enough to leave the pouch on their own, returning for warmth and food as and when they want.

Marsupial species developed similarly to non-marsupial mammals. There is still a marsupial version of the mole and a marsupial mouse. Once there were marsupial cats, dogs and lions on the Australian continent too.

But their luck began to change with the arrival, about fifteen million years ago, of bats and rats, which came over from Asia as it drifted close enough for them to fly or raft across the sea. Then, from about 40,000 years ago, people arrived in canoes. In time they would introduce dingoes, rabbits, camels, horses and foxes (for hunting), all of which have undermined the native ecosystem for indigenous Australian and Tasmanian marsupials such as the Tasmanian Tiger, the last of which died in Hobart Zoo on 7 September 1936. Shortly before her death a black-and-white film was made of her pacing up and down in her enclosure. As a final farewell, she bit the cameraman on the backside.

## Placentals

The third, and by far the biggest, group of mammals is the placentals. These creatures (to which humans belong) keep their babies inside their bodies until they are well developed. The baby's blood and the mother's blood are brought into close contact by a food-exchange organ called the placenta, through which nutrients pass from the mother to the baby, and waste passes from the baby to the mother's blood. The first placentals to evolve, the afrotheres, were probably relatives of today's elephants – not that they looked like elephants since all mammals in the early days were small, furry and fed at night for fear of being eaten by dinosaurs.

About fifty million years ago several members of the same family as the elephants returned to the sea (see plate 2). These are the sea cows. They use their front feet for swimming underwater and their tail as a rudder for steering.

Ungulates are mammals that evolved independently about 54 million years ago in Africa. They have survived to become today's deer, sheep, antelopes, pigs, goats, cattle, giraffes and hippos. Some of them also returned to the water. Today's whales and dolphins are actually related to ancient seafaring hippos that lost contact with the land, shedding their legs in a process of evolutionary tidying.

Meanwhile, in North America (not yet connected to its southern counterpart), other types of ungulates evolved. Their descendants are today's horses, camels and rhinos. They include the hyracotherium, a tiny horse about the size of a small dog. Originally these creatures lived in forests, but as the climate dried out, from about 35 million years ago, many forests were replaced by open grasslands. Open spaces meant that small horses were more exposed. Only those with longer legs, those that could gallop out of harm's way, survived. So, over millions of years, the dog-sized hyracotherium evolved into today's much larger and faster steeds.

Bizarre as it sounds, camels also originated in North America. They eventually spread to other parts of the world, along with horses, crossing a land bridge from Alaska into Asia and then into Mongolia, finally reaching the Asian steppes and the deserts of the Middle East by about two and a half million years ago (see plate 2).

Next came paws. *Carnivora* is a mammal family which evolved about 42 million years ago and whose living descendants include cats (for example lions and cheetahs), dogs (for instance wolves and jackals), weasels, bears (including the panda), hyenas, seals, sea lions and walruses.

Shortly after paws came claws. These are the rodents – today's descendants include mice, rats, rabbits, hares, gerbils, voles, hamsters, beavers, squirrels, marmots and guinea pigs. They are notorious for spreading diseases such as plague, including the dreaded Black Death (see page 220). In South America some rodents grew to an enormous size, such as the giant capybara (also called a proto-hydrochoerus), which grew as large as a donkey.

### How primates spread across the earth

Monkeys are placentals and first evolved in Africa, but they now live in both Asia and South America. About twenty-five million years ago one or more groups of African monkeys somehow found themselves on a raft bobbing across the Atlantic Ocean, eventually to be washed ashore on the coast of modern-day Brazil (see plate 2). This is when the first South American monkey fossils appear, providing evidence that by then they were thriving up in the trees of their newly adopted home.

These New World monkeys are distinctive for their flat noses and for using their tails to help them swing and balance in the trees. They can happily hang from a branch by their tailbone alone, using it like an extra hand.

As if one perilous transatlantic crossing wasn't risky enough, other African monkeys set off in the opposite direction, trekking through Asia, across the land bridges of the Middle East and Arabia. Gibbons and orang-utans are found today in places such as India, Malaysia, China, Borneo, Indonesia and Java. Whether they lost their tails before they left, on the way or later, isn't entirely clear.

Recent genetic evidence and fossil finds suggest that African great apes evolved from species such as gibbons and orang-utans, which once lived only in Asia. This means that about ten million years ago one of these groups of apes, either the orang-utans or the gibbons, made their way back across the Asian land mass into Africa. Here they evolved into today's gorillas and chimpanzees (see plate 2).

Gorillas are mild-mannered vegetarians that live on grasslands, not up in the trees. Only two species survive today. Both are endangered. Several hundred died in 2004 of Ebola virus, for which there is currently no known vaccine or cure. Gorillas are highly intelligent. Koko, born in 1971, is a captive female gorilla living in California. She has been taught sign language from the age of one. Her trainer, Dr Penny Patterson, claims she can communicate using a vocabulary of up to a thousand words. Something of a scientific debate has been raging for years since Koko first showed off her language skills. Does she really understand what she is saying, or is she just prompted by the prospect of a reward if she says the right thing? In August 2004 Koko indicated that she had a toothache. According to her handlers she communicated that she was in pain. She could even indicate its level on a scale of one to ten.

Koko shows other human-like traits too. She is one of the few animals other than humans ever to have been known to keep and care for a pet. In 1984 Koko asked for a cat. She selected a grey male kitten from an abandoned litter. She named him All Ball. Koko cared for the kitten as if he were a baby gorilla, until All Ball escaped from Koko's cage and was hit by a car. Koko cried for the next two days. Since then she has adopted a number of other pets, including two more kittens, Lipstick and Smoky.

Humans are apes. Until the 1960s it was thought that mankind split from apes about twenty million years ago – mostly because so few fossils had been discovered to prove, one way or another, what happened and when. There was also a strong feeling that the split had to be at least that far back or there could never have been enough time for us humans to have evolved into such apparently superior beings. We talk; we build things; we invent amazing machines; we are clean (generally), ingenious, and we appear to have mastered nature, tailoring it to our own ends.

# What on Earth Happened?

But in the early 1990s molecular biologists discovered that we humans share at least 96 per cent of our genetic code (DNA) with the other great apes – chimpanzees, gorillas and orang-utans. Their analysis showed that humans are descended from an ape which probably lived some time between four and seven million years ago – just ninety seconds before midnight on our twenty-four-hour scale of all earth history.

This ape's offspring divided into chimpanzees and their cousins the bonobos on the one hand, and into early human beings on the other. Exactly who this ancestor was, and where he or she lived, is one of the greatest mysteries in all human knowledge, one that is still waiting to be solved.

# Part 2
# Human Evolution

## (7 million–5000 BC)

*How humans evolved as hunter-gatherers whilst living in a state of nature*

# 4

# Early Humans

## (7 million–195,000 BC)

*How climate changes brought apes down from the trees, and how some of them learned to walk upright and developed larger-than-average brains*

**REMEMBER THOSE** old-fashioned rides at traditional funfairs? Carousels, the helter-skelter and, best of all, the dodgems or bumper cars? Bizarre as it sounds, we are all riding on top of the earth's very own natural set of dodgems. They aren't quite like those in man-made funfairs, because the earth's bumper-car ride travels extremely slowly. Also, whenever its dodgems crash into each other they seem to have a rather dramatic impact on the world's weather.

Welcome to nature's fairground. Gradually, over the course of the last 200 million years, the earth's restless crusts of land have broken up to form today's giant continents. Actually, this was quite good for life on earth, because it made it much harder for any single type of living thing, like the dinosaurs, to dominate the land. Seas and oceans forged natural barriers as the crusts split apart. New species evolved, many learning to thrive in different habitats with less competition. Scattered continents also increased the number of beaches, sea shores, wetlands and salt pans – all serving to bolster life on earth.

# What on Earth Happened?

Since the extinction of the dinosaurs 65.5 million years ago, the amount of carbon dioxide gas in the earth's atmosphere plummeted from nearly 3,000 parts per million (ppm) to just 284 ppm by 1832. Less $CO_2$ reduced global temperatures significantly during the same period, despite the sun warming up by as much as 30 per cent since the beginning of our twenty-four-hour journey. Such changes in the earth's atmosphere and temperature have, in large part, been caused by the constant collisions of its crusts, which, although they move slowly in human timescales, have had dramatic consequences for life on earth.

## Continental chaos

About ninety million years ago the Indian subcontinent sheared away from Africa, becoming, in effect, a giant dodgem on the loose. It raced north at the unprecedented speed of fifteen centimetres a year, swivelling and crashing into Asia about forty million years ago, having travelled 3,000 kilometres. Scientists believe it moved at such a speed because its plate is so thin compared with most others'.

When it collided with the larger, slower-moving Asian continent, it created the biggest mountain range on earth. The Himalayas and the enormously high plateau of Tibet are thought to have been responsible for reducing global temperatures in a dramatic way. The annual monsoons they create have removed large amounts of $CO_2$ from the atmosphere by dissolving the greenhouse gas in rainwater.

Meanwhile other land masses were slowly but chaotically making their way across the globe, crashing together with no less spectacular results. At about the same time that India rammed into Asia, Africa pushed up against the seas that separated it from the same continent. The ocean floor buckled up, forming a series of land bridges across the ancient Tethys Sea, a stretch of water that once connected today's Middle East to the Indian Ocean. These bridges are what probably gave the African monkeys their land route into Asia, where they then evolved into the first members of our family – the apes (see plate 2). The first horses and camels came across from North America into the grasslands of Asia via another land bridge, connecting Alaska to the eastern tip of Russia, allowing them to settle finally in the deserts of the Middle East.

Africa bounced off from this collision, pushing northwards into Europe – a process that threw up the European Alps, which stretch from France through Switzerland, Italy and Austria. Then, in the middle of this multiple pile-up, which began about twenty million years ago, Africa crunched up further into the Middle East, closing up the Tethys once and for all.

The earth had already slipped into an Ice Age thanks to another land mass on the loose on the other side of the world. When Antarctica split away from South America, about forty million years ago, it slid south towards the South Pole. Cold water from the Southern Ocean was now forced to circulate around Antarctica instead of moving north to mix with the warmer waters of the Pacific and Indian Oceans. As the region cooled, a massive ice sheet developed over this once tropical land. Today's Antarctic ice sheets are more than a mile thick and stretch across a land mass fifty times larger than the United Kingdom. Such an enormous ice desert caused sea temperatures to plunge by as much as ten degrees, its bright white ice reflecting the sun's rays back into space causing temperatures to cool even more. With a gleaming ice cap on its South Pole, the earth now entered a new Ice Age – its first in at least 250 million years – all due to the chaotic journeys of its out-of-control land masses.

## How life adapted to a cooler, grassier world

Cooler temperatures tend to mean that less water evaporates from the seas, resulting in reduced rainfall in many inland areas. Such conditions gave birth to the great grasslands of today, which replaced forested areas that need larger quantities of rainwater to sustain them. The prairies of North America, the pampas of Argentina and the grassland steppes of Europe and Central Asia all emerged during this Ice Age. Animals adapted to these new conditions, evolving into larger species and more numerous herds as competition for survival increased in the wide-open spaces. The spacious grasslands offered feeding grounds for birds, which rose to the challenge of the conditions by migrating in vast flocks to find the best (and avoid the worst) places to live. Grasslands rich with seeds provided convenient stopping-off points for feeding. Blackbirds, meadowlarks, sparrows, quails and hawks all thrived thanks to these new steppes, which eventually came to cover more than 25 per cent of the world's land surface.

The last continental dodgem of significance in the earth's giant fairground ride was South America. About three million years ago it collided with its North American neighbour, joining up via a thin sliver of land – today's Panama. The collision of these two continents had its own dramatic effect on the earth's weather. Atlantic sea currents were forced northwards, and were prevented from mixing with the waters of the Pacific because their path was now blocked by land. A new weather system spluttered into life as a result. The Gulf Stream began pumping warm air north, heating up north-west Europe by at least ten degrees. It also brought more water vapour, freshly evaporated from the Atlantic. As its clouds blew northwards towards the cold Arctic, rain turned to snow, which settled over time in layers on the cold seas, where it turned into thick packs of ice. The effect was that by three million years ago the earth had donned a second ice cap, this time in the Arctic.

With ice caps now on both poles, the earth grew colder still. Much of it was plunged, literally, into a deep freeze. Colossal ice sheets groped down from the poles, sometimes as far as modern-day London, Paris, Berlin and Moscow. They stretched past the plains of Canada, over the Great Lakes and as far as New York. Most of Russia and all of Greenland were iced over. For thousands of years the seas all around were thick packs of ice, often soaring skywards more than a mile high.

Sea levels plummeted because so much water was trapped as ice. It was possible to walk from where Dover, England is today across to Calais, France. There was no English Channel, just flat, desiccated tundra. Even beyond where the enormous walls of ice ended, it was still too cold for anything much to grow.

In northern Europe temperatures often fell as low as −80ºC, while winds whipped up to speeds of 200 miles per hour. Massive frozen rivers of ice were also on the move. They advanced like gigantic bulldozers, slowly but relentlessly scratching their way down the sides of the earth and then gradually retreating as temperatures rose again, melting as they went and leaving freshwater lakes in their wake. These glaciers carved out many of the world's most spectacular lakes and valleys – from the Lake District in England to the Swiss mountain valleys, and from the Great Lakes of North America to the fjords of Norway.

Conquests of ice like these have occurred as many as thirty times in the last two million years. On each occasion huge boulders of rock have been carried miles away from their mountains of origin by the ice, rock faces have been squeezed and scratched into the most contorted shapes, and the ground has been pushed down – only slowly to bob upwards again after the massive packs of ice retreated. The United Kingdom, for example, is still rising after the retreat of the last massive ice sheet 10,000 years ago – but only by about one millimetre a year.

Life thrived despite these enormous and dramatic events, because nature's changes were slow enough for succeeding generations of species to adapt successfully. Not all life was affected. It was still warm in the tropics, and some rainforests remained, although they were far fewer than before the Ice Age began approximately forty million years ago.

It was now a cooler, grassier age. One where the seas rose and fell, opening and closing causeways to other lands, and where relentless thick packs of ice came and went like clockwork. It was into this dramatic world that mankind was born.

## The earliest human ancestor

Lucy lived in Ethiopia about 3.2 million years ago. She was discovered by an international team of scientists headed by Donald Johanson, an American fossil expert. On 30 November 1974, next to the Awash River, Johanson and one of his students, Tom Gray, were searching for human fossils when they found the fragments of an arm bone poking out from an upper slope. After scrabbling through the earth they found further relics – a jawbone, more arm fragments, a thigh bone and ribs. Gradually, piece by piece, more than 40 per cent of a complete skeleton was unearthed.

They called her Lucy because she was clearly a woman, and at the time of the find Johanson was listening to the Beatles' song 'Lucy in the Sky with Diamonds'. She was about 1.1 metres (three feet eight inches) tall and weighed about twenty-nine kilograms (sixty-five pounds). When her discovery was announced to the world, Lucy caused a sensation because scientists could tell from the shape of her pelvis that she was the earliest known ape to have definitely walked on two feet.

Four years later another team of fossil hunters made a second extraordinary discovery, in nearby Tanzania. At a place called Laetoli they found a series of footprints perfectly preserved in powdery volcanic ash that further backed up the idea that, like us, Lucy-like creatures walked upright. Were these footprints made by a family of early humans walking towards a nearby watering hole? Soon after they passed, a volcano erupted, its mountains of ash preserving their tracks as trace fossils in the rocks. These footprints have been dated to 3.7 million years. There could be no mistake: they were made by creatures that walked on two feet.

## The advantages of two feet over four

Until the discovery of Lucy, scientists had assumed that it was because of their superior intelligence that early humans had decided that walking on two feet was a good idea. Walking upright meant they could use their free hands to make technology, in the form of tools and weapons, that would help them prosper and survive. What was so surprising about Lucy was not simply that she walked on two feet, making her species a candidate for the earliest human ancestor, but that her head was not much larger than that of a chimpanzee.

Generally speaking, a smaller head means a smaller brain and less intelligence. What Lucy tells us is that walking upright came long before humans got big brains and big heads – probably long before they had the nous to work out that walking upright was a smart idea. So what was it that made her want to walk upright, when a life on all fours must have made perfectly good sense? What's the big advantage of two feet over four? Escaping from danger or chasing prey are just as fast on four feet as two (witness the fleeing of a deer or the hunting of a cheetah), and it's just as easy to climb trees with four legs as with two and a pair of hands – look at a squirrel or a monkey. There are also some serious drawbacks to life on two feet. To walk comfortably, two-footed females have to have a much narrower pelvis, making childbirth extremely painful and much more dangerous to both baby and mother.

No one is sure what it was that made Lucy-like creatures stand upright. Perhaps it was as simple as the fact of squatting on the forest floor searching for food, which over time made their feet become flatter so they could balance better. Then, generations later, they got into the habit of walking upright. If this was the case, the long-term consequences of such an apparently simple evolutionary adaptation were probably the most monumental in all history.

A recent study has compared humans walking on treadmills to chimpanzees. It showed that walking on two feet uses only 25 per cent of the energy used by walking on all fours, suggesting that two-legged creatures may have enjoyed a significant survival advantage when times got tough. Walking upright meant that these creatures could feed on the move – just as people do today with takeaway hamburgers and hot dogs. With their hands free, these creatures could now carry food more easily to makeshift stores, helping them survive harsher environments. This gave them the confidence to spread beyond the trees and hunt in the vast grasslands that were still displacing many forests as the world's weather turned worse.

Since Lucy's discovery the bones of many other similar creatures have been found. A recent discovery was of a three-year-old child called Salem, meaning 'peace', unearthed in Ethiopia in the year 2000. Salem has since been painstakingly excavated to reveal a complete skull, collarbones, ribs and kneecaps. These are the ancient remains of creatures called Australopithecus, the oldest of which, Little Foot, dates back as far as 3.9 million years, after being accidentally discovered in 1994 by Ronald Clarke, a fossil hunter who was rummaging through a bag of old cow bones. For molecular scientists Lucy and her ilk provide excellent support for their theory that chimps and humans descended from a common ancestor some four to five million years ago. Lucy and her newly found trick of walking on two feet also provide definitive evidence of the first major distinction between humans and modern chimpanzees.

But was Lucy human? If being human is just about being ape-like and walking on two feet, then Lucy's our woman. But if it's about having larger brains and much greater intelligence than other creatures, then we must wait another 800,000 years, until about 2.4 million years ago, when the bones of the first *Homo habilis* appeared. He was smaller than us (about 1.3 metres tall), but a lot taller than Lucy, and a more upright walker too. More importantly perhaps, his brain was nearly twice the size of Lucy's, although at 650 cubic centimetres still only half that of us, *Homo sapiens*. *Homo habilis* makes Lucy look and seem much more like an upright-walking chimpanzee than the first human being.

*Homo habilis* was the first species of human for which there is evidence of the intelligent use of tools – sharpened flint stones for cleaving meat from the bone. This marks the beginning of what is known as the Old Stone Age, and *Homo habilis* is the point where we can safely say humans join the earth's nature park. He was the first of our kind, the world's first *Homo*.

## Why humans have larger-than-average brains

Walking upright allowed *habilis* to start developing craftwork skills. Carpentry or stone sculpting requires very precise hand-to-eye co-ordination. Skills like these need well-developed motor-neurone skills and sophisticated hand and finger co-ordination – processes that probably provoked the evolution of bigger brains. Recent studies have shown that, relative to other mammals, *Homo habilis* had a brain at least four times larger than it should have been for his size and weight.

Bigger brains use lots of energy. To power our brains we need about twenty watts of energy, or 400 calories a day – that's about 20 per cent of our total energy consumption – just to be able to think. There's a good deal of truth in that old expression, 'food for thought'. So began a most important evolutionary spiral. Big brains need lots of energy, which is best supplied by eating meat. The most successful means of getting meat is by hunting for it, using tools and weapons. The creatures that were best adapted to making such tools were those with the biggest brains. An avalanche of evolutionary changes kicked in, all thanks to Lucy's fortuitous swivel up on to her two feet. These were adaptations that led, almost inevitably, to hunting, weapons, tools and intelligence, to the genus *Homo*, the species *habilis* and beyond.

# What on Earth Happened?

Some of Lucy's ancestors stayed in the trees, so they didn't need to bother with walking upright. They evolved into today's chimpanzees and bonobos. Without free hands, the evolutionary spiral that led to bigger brains and modern human intelligence never took off and their brains stayed small. After all, if you don't need a bigger brain to survive, don't have one. It's far more energy efficient.

Chimps and humans are genetically so close because these evolutionary changes happened so recently in history – probably no more than about four million years ago. Despite this short space of time, a big difference has emerged in terms of intelligence and brain size. An apparently simple change in circumstances, such as having freely available hands, seems to have triggered an evolutionary revolution.

But just how big is the difference between humans and their closest animal relatives? Chimps, like gorillas, have been known to communicate. Kanzi is a bonobo ape, born in 1980, who now lives in Georgia, USA. He can understand more than 3,000 spoken English words, many more than Koko the gorilla (see page 57). When Kanzi wants to 'talk' back, he points to a series of pictures so he can be understood by humans. It was reported in November 2006 that Kanzi was taken for a walk in the woods after having touched the symbols for marshmallows and fire. Once in the woods, he then proceeded to snap twigs and make them into a pile, light a fire and toast his own marshmallows on a stick.

## Africa, the cradle of humanity

Most African people today are desperately poor and suffer terribly from disease, poverty, famine and war. You'd think there was good reason to flee – and they do. Thousands of Africans try to escape the continent each year, many of them across the Straits of Gibraltar into Europe. History is repeating itself.

About two million years ago *Homo habilis* had evolved into a new species of human, *Homo erectus*, who looked much more like us. For a long time experts thought that the ancestors of modern humans originated in China, or maybe Java, because that's where the bones of *Homo erectus* were first discovered, dating back at least 500,000 years. Now, thanks to the discovery of a ten-year-old boy mysteriously swept to his death in an African swamp near the shores of Lake Turkana in Kenya some 1.8 million years ago, we know that he first appeared in Africa at just about the same time as *Homo habilis* died out.

Turkana Boy was found in 1984 by a team of fossil hunters led by Richard Leakey, a British palaeontologist who lives in Africa. The implications were far-reaching, as Leakey himself explained soon after the find: 'In 1984 his bones were painstakingly excavated to reveal a species on the brink of becoming human. All people on earth have one thing in common. We share a single African ancestor; the same as this young boy.'

When alive, Turkana Boy was black-skinned and sweaty. His kind, *Homo erectus*, had lost their body hair because of the blistering African heat, which meant there was no need for fur. Dark skin and sweat glands helped these early people survive the harsh, arid heat of the African grasslands. Like us, Turkana Boy would have had hair on his head as a natural sun hat. A decent crop on top protects upright walkers from the sun's burning ultraviolet rays.

The boy had a long, protruding nose unlike his *habiline* ancestors, again useful for helping cool the blood. His pelvis shows that he walked more upright, and his skull shows a marked increase in size: now as big as 1,100 cubic centimetres, nearly twice the size of *habilis*. Bigger brains need more food. Unlike his evolutionary ancestors, who sometimes fell victim to a hungry cheetah or a pouncing lion, *erectus* was the first human to make spears. In contests with wild beasts, he almost always won.

## Fire and language

*Homo erectus* had several key advantages over anything else alive in the wild: his hands, his brain and, perhaps most important of all, his control of fire. This would have helped scare away the large animals that so bothered his ancestors. It also meant that *Homo erectus* eventually became the world's first cook. Well before they became extinct 70,000 years ago these early people had figured out that cooked food releases energy more quickly than raw meat. It also takes less time to digest. The remains of human campfires nearly 1.5 million years old have been found in Africa and Asia (man-made fires magnetize the soil leaving telltale signs). Who taught man how to light a fire? How did he learn to control it?

The ancient Greeks had a myth that tells the story of a Titan called Prometheus, who stole the fire of the gods and smuggled it down to earth in the stalk of a fennel plant. He paid dearly for his crime. When the king of the gods, Zeus, found out, he had Prometheus tied to a rock. Each day an eagle was sent to pick out his liver. Each night his liver would grow back so that it could be picked out again when the eagle returned. Zeus also took his revenge on man for gaining the knowledge of how to use fire. He sent a box down to earth along with a pretty girl called Pandora, who was told never to open it. Of course temptation eventually got the better of her, and when she lifted the lid suffering and despair were unleashed upon mankind for ever.

Fossil evidence shows that *Homo erectus* mastered the art of making fire by using stones. Pieces of scorched flint dating back 500,000 years have been found at several of their campsites located in northern Israel.

*Homo erectus* lived in groups of about a hundred, hunting together using sharpened flints, following wherever the scent of blood led them, chasing and trapping wild animals for food. Their tools were more sophisticated than those first made by the *habilines*. The biggest difference was that axes were worked on both sides of the blade into a sharp point. These biface tools have cutting edges up to four times bigger than those of the older technology, ideal for hacking wood, digging out roots, butchering animal carcasses and skinning hides.

Could *Homo erectus* talk? Scientists think Turkana Boy's bones suggest that he could not because the nerve openings in his vertebrae were not large enough to contain the complex nerve systems needed to control the breathing required for speech. Maybe he developed a sign language of some kind, or perhaps something similar to modern-day texts? F we cn gt by ths wy, I hve no dbt thy cld 2. With their portable toolkits, the protection of their communities and the magic of fire, these were people ready to walk wherever needs must to make sure they were fed. *Homo erectus* was the first human species to explore life outside Africa – humanity's first migrants, Africa's ancient Marco Polos.

## *Early globetrotters*

With the earth's continents arranged more or less as they are today, it was possible then, as now, to travel overland from Africa across the Middle East into south Asia, India and China. Could Stone Age man really have made it all that way without roads and tracks, let alone cars, boats or planes? Unlike most of us, these people had one huge advantage: they were not in a hurry.

*Homo erectus* lived on average about thirty years. Even at a supremely leisurely pace of travel, say ten miles a year, it still would have taken them only 600 years to wander across the 6,000 miles of land from Africa to China. That's about thirty generations. The earliest *Homo erectus* fossils found in Africa date back 1.8 million years. People had more than enough time to make the journey. In fact, they could have walked there and back dozens of times (see plate 3).

Early humans walked their way around the habitable continents of Africa, Europe and Asia from the time of *Homo erectus*. The first evidence of humans in Britain dates from 700,000 years ago. Boxgrove Man, a human skull found in Sussex, is a *Homo erectus* descendant, known as *Homo heidelbergensis*, dating back about 500,000 years. Did he build a raft or wade across when the sea was shallow, or simply walk across to Britain when there was no English Channel? Either is possible.

While *Homo erectus* was populating Asia the climate turned much worse, as the beginning of a deep Ice Age chill caused glaciers to move down over the continents. For *Homo erectus*, who had wandered so far and wide, such cold conditions were a big problem. Even the miracle of fire wasn't always enough to ensure survival in the bitterly cold temperatures that sometimes descended on much of the European and Asian continents for thousands of years at a time. Nature had its own answer, of course, in the form of Neanderthals.

## The most recent human species, apart from you and me

In 1856 quarry workers near Düsseldorf, north Germany, found what looked like human bones in the Neander Valley. Their discoveries first alerted naturalists to the possibility that there may have been several species of humans that lived before our own *Homo sapiens*, and that man was almost certainly descended from apes. What they didn't know then was that, genetically, humans were actually a branch of the ape family itself.

Since then, bones from many Neanderthal sites have been found. The oldest date back about 350,000 years, which means that several species of humans must have lived simultaneously for a very long time – at least until about 70,000 years ago, when the *Homo erectus* line disappeared, probably as a result of climate changes and the arrival of a yet more powerful species. Experts believe that during this period at least five different species of humans were living on the planet: *Homo erectus*, *Homo ergaster* (the African form of *erectus*),

# Early Humans

*Homo neanderthalensis, Homo heidelbergensis* and *Homo rhodesiensis.* There may have been more, and scientists are still unsure if some of these are subspecies rather than separate species. Did they fight? Did they live together or in their own separate communities? Did they interbreed? Could they talk?

There are still a lot of unanswered questions. What does seem clear is that once *Homo erectus* migrated out of Africa (see plate 3), from about 1.7 million years ago, several different species of humans evolved in separate parts of the world, and that geographical and climatic differences caused small but significant evolutionary changes. Chances are that these species didn't mix much, because back then there were very few humans around – maybe a million or so spread widely across Europe and Asia, continents which hold more than four billion people today.

## The birth of human culture

Neanderthals first appeared in Asia and then spread northwards and westwards into Europe as the weather permitted, even crossing to Britain, where the remains of a jawbone in Kents Cavern, Torquay have been found dating back as recently as 35,000 years ago.

Neanderthals have had a bad press. To call someone a Neanderthal is usually meant as an insult, implying that they are thick, old-fashioned or brutish. Pictures of Neanderthal people were, until recently, more like apes than men. They were shown walking with a stoop and bent knees.

This is wrong. Neanderthal brains were at least the same size as those of modern humans, if not a touch bigger. They also walked as upright as we do, although they were more hairy and usually shorter. They were stronger than us, with broad noses and foreheads that jutted out above the eyebrows. Almost all these adaptations helped to reduce the surface area of these early humans, helping them conserve heat in the bitterly cold Ice Ages.

# What on Earth Happened?

Neanderthals were highly skilled at using tools. Recent archaeological evidence shows that their hands were at least as nimble as ours. The most famous site where tools have been found is at Le Moustier in the Dordogne, France. In 1909 archaeologists found an almost complete Neanderthal skull there, less than 45,000 years old. Hundreds of sharp skilfully crafted stone tools were found alongside the bones.

Neanderthals used some of these as weapons. Their spears were not designed to be thrown, but were used for stabbing and clubbing. Stone tools helped them build impressive shelters – the first human houses – and they are the first people known to have buried their dead, often leaving ornaments in the graves of those they loved to help them on to the next life. This means that these people almost certainly had beliefs, perhaps religions, and developed societies in which some individuals were thought to be more important than others.

Perhaps the most significant discovery of all was dug up in 1995 by Dr Ivan Turk, a fossil hunter from Ljubljana, Slovenia, next to a fireplace in a Neanderthal house. He found a hollowed-out bear bone with several holes bored in a straight line. This could be a fragment from the world's oldest known musical instrument – a Neanderthal flute. What tunes were played on this prehistoric pipe? It's hard to say, because no one knows for sure how long the original flute was, or how many holes it had, as only a small section remains. Some researchers believe it would have played what we would recognize as a minor or blues scale today, with a flattened third note.

In 1983 a Neanderthal bone was found in a cave in Israel that is almost identical to a bone in modern humans called the hyoid, which connects our tongues to our throats. This means that Neanderthals almost certainly had the capacity to speak. Also, the size of openings in Neanderthal vertebrae for the nerves that control the tongue for speech are about the same as in modern humans – unlike Lucy's people – meaning that they could produce a wide range of sounds.

Music, ceremonies, weapons, tools and conversation are the stuff of people possessing intelligence, brains, culture and an appreciation of beauty. The Neanderthals were certainly big and burly enough to cope with the hardship of living in caves through an Ice Age, but there's nothing to suggest that they were any more brutish than us. What happened to these strong, intelligent, well-adapted folk? To understand this, we must look at ourselves properly, face to face in the mirror.

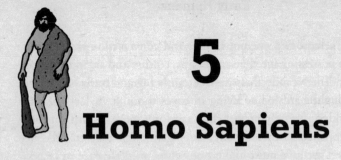

# 5

# Homo Sapiens

## (195,000–5000 BC)

*How a single species of humans, sapiens, became the last to survive on earth*

**ANY IDEA HOW** close we are to midnight on our twenty-four-hour clock of earth history? A few minutes left to go, perhaps? After all, we've still got all human 'recorded' history to tackle, starting from when the first large-scale human civilizations emerged in the Middle East through to today, with approaching seven billion of us living on the planet.

How about three seconds? That's it. Imagine how short sitting doing nothing for just three seconds would seem compared to doing nothing for the length of a full day. Anyone attempting that rather daft experiment would get a good impression of how much earth history actually took place before the first *Homo sapiens* could be heard calling across the hot, dusty African plains.

We now know it was from Africa that *Homo sapiens*, or modern humans, came. We did not descend from the Neanderthals. The two species lived at the same time for thousands of years, and while there was probably a little interbreeding, recent genetic evidence suggests that there was not much. Red hair, freckles and pale skin are features that may have been handed down from the Neanderthals.

Instead we must look back to Africa – to the descendants of *Homo erectus*, Turkana Boy's people (see page 71). Bones from twenty-one sites across Africa have been found, stretching back almost 500,000 years, and they paint a picture that shows how small evolutionary steps along the *Homo* line led to who we are today.

The oldest *Homo sapiens* fossils yet found came from southern Ethiopia. In 1967 two human skulls were discovered buried deep in mud at the bottom of the Omo River. They have recently been re-dated, and are now thought to originate from about 195,000 years ago. These skulls, called Omo I and Omo II, certainly look as if they belong to the immediate predecessors of modern humans. They are slightly larger than modern human skulls, but otherwise strikingly similar. They have been classified as a subspecies of *Homo sapiens* called *idaltu*. They have flat faces and prominent cheekbones, but not the protruding brow ridge of the earlier *Homo erectus* and the Neanderthals.

Genetic research supports the idea that all humans alive today emerged from a single evolutionary line in Africa from about this time. But one strange feature remains unsolved. There is surprisingly little genetic variation between people alive today – much less than in most species of mammals. Even our closest cousins, the chimpanzees, show genetic differences ten times greater across the spectrum of their species than we do.

Such a small variation can only mean one thing: at some point *Homo sapiens* must have shrunk to a very few individuals – perhaps between 1,000 and 10,000 people – all of whom shared a very similar genetic code. This idea has set experts off on another hunt, to find some event that fits in with the idea of *Homo sapiens* suffering an almost fatal collapse in population early on in its history.

One candidate for such an event is a massive Category 8 volcanic eruption that occurred about 75,000 years ago at Toba, on the Indonesian island of Sumatra. A giant hot spot of molten lava is thought to have burst through the earth's crust, releasing energy 3,000 times greater than that of the huge eruption of Mount St Helens in Washington State, USA in

1980. One site in India today still has ash deposits from the eruption of Toba that are six metres thick. Such an enormous explosion would have created a blanket of dust in the atmosphere, blocking out the sunlight for months or even years, triggering a sudden drop in global temperatures and possibly even starting an Ice Age all by itself.

Maybe there are other reasons. A virus, perhaps, that wiped out large parts of the human population? At the moment, no one knows. But from a very small stock of African ancestors, *Homo sapiens* walked its way around the world, copying the migrations of his ancestors, eventually to supplant all other species of humans. The last of these, the Neanderthals, survived until about 24,000 years ago, which is the date of their very last known traces, in Gorham's Cave, Gibraltar.

Did we kill them? Did we eat them? Or did they die because of climate change or through lack of food during an especially nasty Ice Age snap? It seems that changes in the climate about 30,000 years ago were especially severe in Central Asia and northern Europe, which is where the Neanderthals lived.

## The great migration

It was probably a warm interglacial interlude within the Ice Age, between about 130,000 and 90,000 years ago, that initially triggered large-scale *Homo sapiens* migrations across Africa. Then, from about 70,000 years ago, the climate cooled, causing glaciers to form on the tops of mountain ranges so that parts of north-west and north-east Africa were cut off from each other, as well as from the south. As Charles Darwin discovered, whenever a species is physically separated, small variations begin to creep into its respective gene pools, creating diversity. So it was with modern man, giving us our four main ethnic groups: Khosian (African), Caucasian (European), Mongolian (Chinese and American Indian) and Aboriginal (Australian).

# Homo Sapiens

From about 60,000 years ago, these four groups of humans emigrated from Africa separately and in their own time across the world, exporting their small genetic differences with them (see plate 3). Some *Homo sapiens* swept across Asia, displacing the last of the Neanderthals either by depriving them of food, hunting them or maybe occasionally absorbing them into their own species through limited interbreeding. Some turned south and reached India and China. They learned to build rafts. From about 40,000 years ago, Australia, for many millions of years the preserve of marsupial mammals, became another human hunting ground as the first people paddled ashore.

The first *Homo sapiens* to arrive in Europe walked eastwards out of Africa about 50,000 years ago, and then came north via the Middle East. They brought with them enormous changes in lifestyles, technology and culture, including the world's first spears specially designed for flight rather than close-range use, as with Neanderthal-style clubs.

The time from about 50,000 years ago marks the beginning of the final one second to midnight on the twenty-four-hour clock of earth history. It has been described as the 'Great Leap Forward' because the complexity of human tools increased dramatically. Bones, tusks and antlers were used for the first time to carve out ornaments as well as to craft useful household items such as needles for sewing, and spoon-like oil lamps that burned animal fats. Jewellery, in the form of necklaces and pendants, has been found buried in the graves of these people. The first ceramic pots date from this period, as do the world's first known sculptures such as the Venus of Willendorf, a female fertility figure found in Austria in 1908 which is thought to date from about 24,000 years ago. Some of the first known cave paintings date back to the same era. They can be seen to this day in the caves of Lascaux, in the Dordogne region of France.

The earth was far cooler back then. The last of the great ice sheets swept down from the North Pole about 22,000 years ago, to disappear rather quickly 12,000 years later. During this time some people adapted to the changes in climate by developing paler skin, which helped produce sufficient quantities of vitamin D for bone formation despite the weaker sunlight of the Ice Age.

*Homo sapiens* arrived in Britain about 20,000 years ago. They walked across the Channel from France, since it didn't flood until the end of the last big Ice Age melt, about 10,000 years ago. But they weren't the first to arrive. Up to seven previous attempts were made by earlier people to populate the British Isles, starting with *Homo erectus* some 700,000 years ago. Each time, the populations of humans died out, probably because of the horrendously icy conditions that periodically swept over the islands as far south as present-day London. Even in the very south the cold would sometimes have been too much for any type of human to bear.

About 15,000 years ago giant glaciers still locked up much of the earth's waters, lowering sea levels so that a massive land bridge the size of Poland, called Beringia, connected the eastern tip of Russia to Alaska across what is now a ninety-five-kilometre-wide stretch of sea called the Bering Strait. In those days people could cross by foot from Asia to North America – a land that until then had probably been free from human habitation, although some scientists think people may have rafted there a few thousand years before from south Asia via the Pacific islands. North and South America were the last of the great habitable continents to be populated by man, and are still appropriately called the New World even today. It was an opportunistic walk all the way across Asia, following big animals, hunting on the move, making the most of nature's twisting and turning climate changes.

With another land bridge via Panama linking the two great Americas, it wasn't long before the first people from North America wandered down to the southern American continent, where the climate was warmer and the land rich in vegetation and game.

# Homo Sapiens

The arrival of Stone Age humans in this part of the world – as in Australia – came with dramatic consequences for much of the earth's wildlife. Although a few of nature's ecosystems lingered on without any human representation – New Zealand and Iceland were untouched by humans until about 800 AD and 1000 AD respectively – many of the world's living creatures were by now beginning to succumb to mankind's growing influence as he spread out to envelop the whole of planet earth.

## *Life in a nomadic state of nature*

Until about 10,000 years ago there were few, if any, permanent homes or villages. People moved around all the time from place to place. Men would hunt animals, and women gathered wild fruit and nuts. Sometimes the women helped with the hunting too, especially when trying to catch an animal, like a deer, which needed to be surrounded on all sides to prevent it from escaping.

Living as a traveller, a nomad, meant people had few if any actual possessions. All they had was what they could carry. In cooler climates they wore animal skins and furs; in hotter areas many went around almost naked. Why carry what you don't need? They took essential provisions with them, such as water inside gourds, vegetables belonging to the pumpkin family which can easily be hollowed out to make bottles. They would also carry spears or bows and arrows for hunting, and flint implements for skinning dead animals and lighting fires.

These people needed little else. The whole idea of owning anything was completely alien to them. Their habit was to share things with each other, because it meant there was less to carry. There was no need for money, because they hunted and gathered whatever and whenever they needed. They had no use for storage areas or farm buildings. They had no property, and there were no signs saying PRIVATE – NO HUNTING HERE because no one owned any land. It was, like the air we breathe today, something common to us all, a resource to be shared between all living things: plants, animals and people.

People lived in this state of nature from the time of their first appearance as *Homo habilis*, or even as far back as the Australopithecus, Lucy's people, dating back at least three million years. They hunted when they were hungry, slept when they were tired, and when the land was void of fruit and meat they moved on elsewhere, giving the earth a chance to restore, recover and renew.

Were the people living this wandering, possession-free lifestyle happy with their lot? It is interesting to note that before people started living in towns and making weapons out of metals like copper, bronze and iron there is little evidence of extensive warfare or violence.

A deep regard for all things natural was the basis of the hunter-gatherers' mythology, or religion. For them the woods were full of magic and wonder. They contained the spirits of their dead ancestors, who returned in the afterlife to protect, guide and comfort the living – or so they thought. The woods were their ultimate source of food, warmth, habitation, medicine and shelter. To them, nothing was more important than looking after nature's forests. They trusted completely in her abundance and her resources.

Perhaps the biggest long-term strength of the hunter-gatherers' lifestyle was that it provided an inbuilt control on the overall level of human population. Hunter-gatherers relied on travelling by foot so it was necessary for them to have their children well spaced apart – one every four or five years at most – because it is impossible to carry too many children at once. A stable population of about five million hunter-gathering humans lived on earth for tens of thousands of years. It was a natural limit, a sustainable level, founded on a nomadic way of life.

## *Adapting to climate change*

Dramatic cliffs of ice have repeatedly bulldozed their way down from the ice caps over the last three million years. Sometimes they have covered as much as 30 per cent of the earth's entire land mass in glaciers and ice sheets more than a mile thick. But because such climate changes happened reasonably slowly, life generally adapted well.

Large animals became furrier, like the woolly mammoth, so they could live in the cold. Humans became smaller and hairier, like the Neanderthals, and some of them even turned white, preserving heat and helping to reflect away dangerous ultraviolet rays. Such natural evolutionary adaptations saw them through the worst of the cold. The last glacial period ended rather suddenly. About 14,000 years ago average temperatures on the earth rose by six degrees, easily enough to flip the climate from severe Ice Age to the much balmier conditions we have today.

Swings in temperature on earth normally happen because the planet veers slightly nearer to or further from the sun during its annual orbits, making the climate hotter or colder. Another factor is the way in which the earth spins on its axis. It actually behaves like a slightly out-of-control spinning top so that over long periods of time its tilt can vary from twenty-one to twenty-seven degrees, making big differences to the temperatures of the poles. Scientists are fairly sure that it was thanks to these orbital variations and spinning-top cycles that, between about 14,000 and 11,000 years ago, temperatures warmed up enough to give a hot spell of a few thousand years in between the bitter conditions of the Ice Age.

Warm episodes within an Ice Age are called interglacials. We are experiencing one now – it began about 14,000 years ago. Thanks to human-induced global warming, this one may last much longer than others, or it may even spin the world's climate out of its forty-million-year-old Ice Age altogether if the polar ice caps melt completely.

# What on Earth Happened?

About 18,000 years ago, when the last ice glacial was at its height, the North American landscape, south of the enormous ice sheet that covered the Great Lakes, looked like parkland – a mixture of trees and grasses, a paradise for roaming wild mammals. Large carnivorous mammals such as lions and sabre-toothed cats fed on mastodons and massive woolly mammoths.

Bison roamed across the rich pastures. But these bison were no cows – they were almost as big as elephants. Beavers, which we know as smallish river creatures, grew as large as today's biggest grizzly bear, and the bears back then were almost twice the size they are now. The earth was full of enormous mammals, known today as megafauna. Big beasts fared better in the bitter climate because their large bodies helped protect their vital organs from the extreme cold.

## *Upsetting nature's balance*

There have been at least thirty ice-overs and melts in the last two million years – some more severe than others. Each time nature and her living things bounced back as individual species adapted to different climates, hot or cold. The last big melt, which reached its height about 14,000 years ago, should have been just like any other. But for some reason this time something went catastrophically wrong. Scientists and historians are still trying to figure out exactly why. The consequences of this disaster continue to shape human and earth history to this day.

At least eighty mammal families were alive in North America when the ice sheets melted. Some of them had survived tens of millions of years. Yet, suddenly and mysteriously, they died out. Horses, big cats, elephants, mammoths and mastodons, camels, giant beavers, peccaries (American pigs), sloths and the glyptodont, an armadillo the size of a pick-up truck – all of them disappeared. In all, thirty-three out of forty-five families of large mammals became extinct, leaving most of the animals in North America no bigger than a turkey. Even the beavers and bears that survived became dwarves in comparison to their ancestors. Today's North American bison are the smallest that have ever lived. In all, experts reckon that more than 70 per cent of America's large-animal population disappeared within about a thousand years.

Pretty much the same thing happened in Australia, which lost thirteen species of large mammals, although the extinctions there started earlier. Victims included the giant kangaroo, the giant horned tortoise, the rhino-sized wombat and its relatives, the diptorodonts, as well as the fierce marsupial lion. In the end, nothing larger than today's kangaroo survived. Yet in North Africa, Europe and Asia, even as the glaciers retreated and the seas rose, most of the large mammals survived: elephants, horses, camels, wolves, big cats – they all made it through.

What on earth was going on? Why did so many animals in Europe and Asia survive when those in the New World and Australia suffered dramatic and sudden extinctions?

Some experts think that the climate was to blame. As the temperatures rose, large animals were at a disadvantage because their big bodies meant it was harder for them to keep cool. These creatures may have died of heat exhaustion. Yet large mammal species had survived many previous interglacial periods when the temperature was warm, and what about the African elephants, lions and tigers? How did they survive?

Another theory is that some mysterious disease swept over the New World, devastating its animal populations. But how could such a bug target only the big animals, leaving the smaller ones and humans as survivors?

## *Humanity makes its first major mark*

The most popular theory was first put forward by American scientist Paul Martin nearly forty years ago. He put it down to the arrival of *Homo sapiens*. In both America and Australia these mass mammal extinctions followed shortly after the arrival of the first humans. In Australia they began about 40,000 years ago, in the Americas about 13,000 years ago. According to Martin, because animals in these continents had never come across humans, they were vulnerable. Read the diary of any explorer who encounters a natural habitat where no man has ever been, for example Charles Darwin on the Galapagos Islands, and you will find that they always comment on the lack of timidity of the wildlife. It's still like this today in the few parts of the world which have no humans living near them.

So when the first human wanderers arrived, flint weapons, bows, arrows and spears in hand, the animals they came across were fearless. They may have looked on with curiosity at these half-hairy, two-legged apes clambering ashore, but chances are that the horses would have just munched on. Even the lions, provided they weren't too hungry, would probably have just fallen back to sleep. Thus they were easy prey for hunter-gathering man with his sharp spears – so much so that in less than a thousand years most of the big game had been slaughtered, and many species were on the verge of extinction.

The theory also explains why in North Africa, Europe and Asia many similar animals survived the presence of mankind. Animals here had evolved alongside human species for over two million years, and had grown used to their appetite for meat and hunting. The experience of their ancestors had evolved into a well-honed instinct that allowed them to survive in sufficient numbers, avoiding contact with humans by running away and hiding. This meant that the mass extinctions seen in Australia and the Americas simply never occurred.

# Homo Sapiens

So, the theory goes, in just a few years *Homo sapiens* single-handedly deprived nearly half the world's land masses of all their large creatures by hunting them to oblivion.

Recently this theory, called the Pleistocene Overkill, has itself come under attack. For example, it doesn't explain why some species not generally eaten by humans, like sloths, became extinct, while others that were hunted, like bison, survived. Mass slaughter by humans also doesn't explain why beavers, bears and bison all became so small.

The best theory seems to be one that blends the arrival of humans with the effects of natural, cyclical climate change. It goes like this: when humans first arrived on the virgin continents of Australia and the Americas, they indeed found big game easy prey. Many of the key predator species, such as lions, tigers and wolves, were killed off in massive numbers by the two-legged hunter-gatherers. At the same time temperatures rose rapidly, causing the glaciers to melt and the seas to rise. What had once been a rich American landscape of parkland trees and pastures gave way to huge stretches of arid inland savannahs with dried-up waterholes that turned into thick conifer forests near the much wetter coasts.

Because humans killed off so many of the larger, carnivorous predator species, the populations of these animals' prey – herbivores such as bison, deer, sloths, horses and camels – grew uncontrollably because there was nothing to eat them. They became so numerous that there simply wasn't enough food to go around. Combined with the changes in vegetation caused by rapid climate change, the effect was catastrophic. Herbivores were wiped out in their millions through starvation because the landscape couldn't support them any more, and only small species which could endure long periods consuming little food and water survived.

The intensive overgrazing of these huge overpopulations also contributed to climate change, accelerating the transition from parkland to grassland, making the landscape even less suitable for supporting future generations of large animals.

# What on Earth Happened?

How fragile are nature's ecosystems. Add a new bit of something over here (humans), and see them remove something else over there (lions and sabre-toothed tigers). Now throw in a bit of random climate change, and devastation sets in on a massive scale. The role of humans in the annihilation of the large herbivorous marsupials and placental mammals of Australia and the Americas between 40,000 and 12,000 years ago – at the beginning of the last second to midnight on the twenty-four-hour clock of earth history – was humanity's first big impact on the earth's fragile, changing natural environment. It was not the last.

## Artificial selection

Mankind had begun to make its mark. But the reckless slaughter of carnivores, its full consequences yet to play out on the stage of human and earth history, was matched by the start of another revolution that wove together the fate of humans and the earth's living systems as never before.

Starting from about 12,000 years ago, history begins to reveal the first attempts by people to control and adapt natural evolution to suit their own needs. It starts with the beginning of farming – the artificial breeding of animals and the intensive growing of particular plants, or crops, for food.

Natural selection changed life on earth over billions of years, from simple single-celled microbes into everything from fruiting fungi to jumping jerboas, and slimy slugs to venomous vipers. These changes were caused by small genetic differences between generations that increased a species' chances of survival in the earth's many constantly changing environments. But about 12,000 years ago, when humans first started to cultivate the land and tame wild animals, they hijacked the process. They began what is now called artificial selection. Instead of nature selecting the most successful specimens in the wild, humans started to choose, breed, protect and grow those that suited them best.

Artificial selection allowed people to settle – to live permanently in one place – because all the food they needed could be sourced in one spot. They started to build houses and to live in villages all year round, which then grew into towns, which then grew into cities, which grew into states, and which, ultimately, turned into civilizations. With the advent of farming came the first sedentary lifestyles, and with them massive increases in human populations, the re-sculpting of the earth's landscape to suit food production and the beginnings of modern diseases, almost all of which originate from humans living in close proximity to domesticated animals.

The change to farming also marks the beginnings of all those jobs that aren't associated with food production because, for the first time ever, there was usually enough food to support people who weren't directly involved in its provision. Farming also meant that people could have more offspring, as they no longer needed to carry their children with them. They could store their food in granaries and afford to give birth every two years, if not more often. There was the added benefit that living in a village or small town meant that there were more people around to help look after young children, encouraging families to grow.

As the populations of villages and towns increased, those not involved in farming could become artisans – skilled workers – who made artefacts like pottery, jewellery and clothes for settled people. They could also explore new technologies such as wheels, chariots and armour made from pliable raw materials, which they learned to extract from the ground in the form of copper, bronze and iron.

Then there were merchants, who began to trade the products that artisans manufactured, along with any surplus food left over from the farms. Trade meant travel, ships, writing, accounting and money. Other jobs for non-food-producers included making sure that the village or town stayed on the right side of the gods, giving the best possible chance of good harvests and fending off evil events. These early priests or holy men eventually helped give birth to many of the major religions of the world.

Growing numbers of settled populations required new forms of organization and control. The world's first kings and emperors emerged, with their aristocracies and bureaucrats, whose jobs were to collect taxes, issue laws and administer justice for all to see. Kings could afford to protect their power with armies because, thanks to farming crops and animals, it was now possible to feed thousands of troops using stored grain made into bread, or tamed animals that could be milked, eaten or used for pulling carts or carrying soldiers into battle. Farming permitted campaigns of attack to glorify and expand these new urban cultures, which soon began to spawn all over the ancient world.

## An experiment with farming

Common sense suggests that humans didn't take up farming because they wanted to. Compared to the easy life of the hunter, with plenty of game around, and where one decent kill could feed a family for a week, the lot of a crop farmer was painful and arduous. For a start, crops could be harvested only at certain times of the year, so arable farming was certainly no substitute for the traditional fast-food culture of meat on demand.

Planting, weeding, digging and harvesting were just a few of the miserable tasks that had to be endured long before a single loaf of bread could be baked. Seeds from barley, wheat and rye, which were the first crops cultivated by man, had to be collected by hand from the stalks of the grasses and ground up into flour using the most primitive of food processors, a pestle and mortar.

And these weren't the seeds we are used to today. They were

natural and wild, not the product of generations of artificial selection. For good reason, nature had designed them to be as light as possible, loosely attached to the stalk so that wind power had the best chance of blowing them far and wide, spreading them to other areas, where they could germinate and reproduce in the wild. But, as any arable farmer will tell you, small seeds that fall easily from the stalk are a bread-winner's nightmare. A large quantity of this type of wheat is needed to make bread, not to mention the back-breaking task of picking up all the loose seeds that tumble irritatingly to the ground. Unpredictable, unpleasant and just plain hard work – that's what farming crops was like 12,000 years ago. Skeletons of early farmers tell the story: twisted toes, buckled, arthritic knees and in some cases lower backs that are completely deformed due to the exhausting task of grinding grain into flour between slabs of stone.

A single word can explain the reasons for the rise of agriculture: stress. The cause 12,000 years ago was exactly the same as it is in many parts of the world today, and probably will be for many generations to come.

The most recent Ice Age was at its coldest 22,000 years ago. As the glaciers melted over the course of thousands of years, rising sea levels caused massive flooding all over the world. The big melt increased global temperatures by more than 7°C and was probably caused by cyclical changes in the earth's rotation. It reached its peak about 14,000 years ago. At that point the oceans rose by a massive twenty-five metres in just 500 years after a huge ice shelf collapsed into the rising seas. By about 8,000 years ago the major melting was all but over, and the seas were at nearly the same level as they are today. One of the last areas to flood was the English Channel, cutting off Britain from the rest of Europe for the first time in more than 100,000 years.

Such dramatic and rapid changes in the natural environment were bound to have profound effects on living things. For mankind it meant that many traditional hunting grounds simply sank beneath the oceans. Regions of the world that were once rich forests, ideal for hunting and gathering, were reduced to barren deserts as patterns of rainfall and weather systems rapidly changed. In many parts of the world people were forced to move up into the hills or closer to freshwater lakes and rivers. In some areas the traditional lifestyle of moving from place to place became just too risky. There was either too little good hunting ground, or the land was too dry to sustain sufficient vegetation.

One example of how climate changes forced people into a new lifestyle can been seen in what is called the Fertile Crescent, the area that extends from upper Egypt, down the Nile to lower Egypt, Israel and Syria as far north as central Turkey, and then down towards the Gulf along the Euphrates Valley, through the ancient land of Mesopotamia (modern Iraq and Iran). Fourteen thousand years ago this was a rich land, with forests of oak and pistachio trees, plentiful rainfall and nutritious vegetation. It wasn't at all like the dry, barren land we are familiar with today.

At about that time people called the Natufians settled near the water's edge around modern-day Lebanon, because the sea provided them with a good source of fish for food (see plate 5). Others went higher up into the hills, where the soil was richer and where wild grasses grew. In fact, they found that this land was so rich in resources that it wasn't necessary to be on the move all the time. In some seasons they would hunt for wild animals, such as gazelles; in others they would settle in small villages, where they lived in round mud and clay huts for some or all of the year. Several Natufian sites have recently been discovered and excavated in Lebanon, Syria and northern Israel.

What happened next was a freak of nature. It's one that scientists predict could happen again, perhaps soon. Instead of temperatures continuing to rise as they had for the previous 8,000 years, the climate suddenly plunged into another Ice Age. In less than fifty years most of the world reverted to a state of deep freeze. This spell, called the Younger Dryas, lasted for about 1,300 years beginning approximately 12,700 years ago. Such dramatic and rapid climate changes had probably never been experienced in all human history.

## A female revolution

The effect, particularly on people in Europe and the Mediterranean, was catastrophic. For those living in the Fertile Crescent, not only had their hunting grounds been drowned by rising sea levels following the Ice Age melt, but now, thanks to this sudden climate change, a severe drought set in and much of their remaining rich and fertile woodland was transformed into barren scrub.

Wild grasses were an important part of the staple Natufian diet, but in the now sweltering scrubland they simply withered away. Some experts think this is what may have led Natufian women to experiment with sowing seeds themselves and deliberately clearing the land to make it suitable for cultivating grasses such as wheat, barley and rye. In the face of starvation, these women stored the best seeds they could find, the biggest, sweetest and most easy to harvest, to sow on specially prepared land as a crop for the following year.

Was it their handiwork – an agricultural insurance policy – that triggered a chain of events that eventually led to the spread of crop farming all over the Middle East, Europe and northern Africa? Seeds are easy to store and transport. Natufian crop cultivation seems to be the earliest known to history. Evidence of their inventiveness comes from the discovery by modern archaeologists of farming tools, in the form of picks and sickle blades used for harvesting cereal crops. Alongside these ancient farming implements are pestles, mortars and bowls, all essential instruments for gathering and grinding seeds.

Archaeologists have painstakingly sifted material excavated from one Natufian site called Abu Hureyra in modern-day Syria (see plate 5). What they have found suggests that here was a culture that had learned to domesticate wild crops by selectively sowing the best-looking seeds. As the wild grasses that people relied on for food died out, they were forced to start cultivating the most easily grown seeds in order to survive. From the location of seed finds, it seems they planted them on slopes where moisture collected naturally. They then actively managed these hillside terraces and slopes by keeping the weeds and scrub at bay, so giving their crops the best possible chance of producing a good yield.

Natufians were also among the first people known to have started domesticating animals – in their case wolves. Choosing the tamest grey wolves, they eventually bred them into domestic dogs which could help them hunt other animals that lived in the regions nearby – in particular wild sheep, boar, goats and horses. With the help of dogs, it was a relatively small step to tame these other wild animals and breed them in one place for their meat and milk.

Natufian people loved their dogs. Graves have been found in which they and their dogs are buried side by side. Their graves also reveal another telltale sign of early animal domestication: a high infant mortality rate. One third of all Natufian graves unearthed so far contain the skeletons of children under the age of eight. Were these victims of the first diseases to mutate from animals and jump across to humans? If so, it points to the beginnings of a new type of human selection – people naturally more vulnerable to these new diseases died more often than those less susceptible. As generations passed, people who lived in close proximity to domesticated animals gained a greater immunity from the diseases they spread (for consequences in human history see page 237).

Once the Younger Dryas period ended, about 11,400 years ago, the climate recovered its previous balminess, and within the space of just a few years people in the Fertile Crescent were once again living in a land of plenty, with enough rainfall to support rich, diverse vegetation. But now there was a big difference. These people were equipped with a raft of potent new technologies, in the form of breeds and seeds, that gave them the opportunity to live in a radically different way of life.

### From farms to cities

From about 9000 BC permanent new human settlements began to appear throughout the Middle East. These Neolithic farming people were now able to live in larger communities thanks to an abundance of stored food, gained from a knowledge of farming and the benefits of domesticating animals for their meat, milk and pulling power. Hunting and gathering was for some now becoming a tradition of the past.

Jericho is one of the oldest Neolithic towns (see plate 5). It is up to eight times larger than earlier Natufian sites, and is thought to be one of the first to have protective walls. Excavations have revealed rounded houses, many with more than one room, and open spaces for domestic activities such as cooking and washing. These early buildings have stone foundations, cobbled floors and walls made of mud/clay bricks. Every site has its own stone or clay silo for storing grain and other food, a sure sign that, for these people at least, the days of living on the move were now long gone. Necessity had forced them to adapt nature to their own needs, resulting in a new way of life.

Walls were erected on Jericho's western side – not, as once believed, to defend the city from attack by jealous neighbours, but as a means of protecting it from mud flows and the flash floods that frequently swept in from the still-rising seas. This was another sign that here the human spirit was newly focused on trying to control and tame nature.

That these people were in touch with other emerging cultures is beyond doubt. Obsidian is a form of natural glass which forms when volcanic lava cools quickly. It was a highly sought-after material because it made the sharpest, most effective arrowheads. Obsidian occurs naturally in the rocky hills of central Turkey, but has been found hundreds of miles away in Neolithic Jericho, showing that long-distance trade routes were already well established. Why not exchange glass for precious seeds, already modified to be excellent to eat and easy to harvest, the fruits of more than a thousand years of special selection and hard graft? It is not difficult to imagine how, once under way in one place, agricultural know-how, seed supplies and domesticated animals quickly diffused throughout Europe, the Middle East and beyond.

# Part 3
# Ancient History

## (5000 BC–1521 AD)

*How farm animals and crops led to the growth of a range of different human civilizations*

# 6

# The First Civilizations

## (5000–c.1500 BC)

### *How the art of writing ushered in an era known as 'history'*

THE DIFFERENCE BETWEEN history and prehistory can be summarized in a word: writing. Writing allowed people to keep records of what happened and when. It meant they could pass on stories to other generations without change or error. With writing came the beginning of what is called 'recorded' history. Everything before is prehistory, or prehistoric.

Recorded human history really begins at the same time as writing first appears – and that happened in the earliest human civilizations of the Middle East about 5,000 years ago, which takes us to within a tenth of a second to midnight on the twenty-four-hour clock of earth history.

No one knows who actually invented writing. It is highly unlikely that any one person did. People may have begun to experiment with the first scratches and scribbles as long as 10,000 years ago as a way of keeping track of the cycles of the moon and stars. However, it was only about 5,000 years ago that the first clear use of written symbols by a settled civilization appeared, initially as a way of keeping commercial records and accounts. Merchants of the Middle East drew simple pictures on clay tablets to identify particular goods. Next to them they scraped counting marks to show a quantity. These tablets were baked in ovens to make their marks permanent, creating an unchangeable set of records showing exactly who had received what goods. Writing helped people manage their accounts of trade and exchange.

But making drawings on clay was a time-consuming and laborious business. It made more sense to come up with a shorthand code to speed the process up. Over time, wedge-shaped strokes replaced the pictures because they were easier and quicker to mark on to the tablets. These strokes were made using a kind of pen made out of reed in the shape of a modern-day cutting knife. This style of writing is called cuneiform and it forms the basis for three of the oldest written languages: Sumerian, Assyrian and Babylonian.

## *Mesopotamia, and a once-in-a-lifetime discovery*

Sumeria was located in the heart of modern-day Iraq, close to the Persian Gulf (see plate 5). It was one of the first regions where mankind's new itch to control nature extended into the business of building artificial worlds in the form of cities and states. It is also where experts believe writing emerged.

Sumeria was a perfect place for early settled communities of humans. By 10,000 years ago sea levels had risen by nearly 130 metres from their low point, and in this part of the world the climate was wetter, and therefore better for growing crops, than it is now. It is only in the last 5,000 years or so that temperatures have increased and rainfall has fallen to make the Middle East the sandy, barren land we know today.

A wetter climate was ideal for growing crops such as wheat, barley and grapes that need winter rainfall. And just the right kind of wild animals – those perfect for domestication, such as goats, sheep and oxen – lived on the slopes and hillsides of the region. Such animals could be used as a source of food, as power for pulling ploughs and carts, and to provide raw materials for making clothes, bottles and leather goods.

The ancient region in which the first Sumerian cities emerged is called Mesopotamia. In Greek this means 'between the rivers'. The Euphrates and the Tigris were used to supply water to the nearby land through systems of man-made irrigation channels, dykes, reservoirs and dams. These meant people could purposely flood their fields to provide just the right conditions for their artificially chosen crops to thrive. The river valley also provided two large, long, flowing superhighways to carry people and their possessions from one riverside city to the next.

Thanks to a remarkable archaeological discovery made in the 1840s by a young amateur British archaeologist named Austen Layard, it is now known that a writing system developed in ancient Sumeria about 5,000 years ago. Rather than stick around in London to practise law, as he had been trained to do, Layard decided to head off for a life on the island of Ceylon, now Sri Lanka, off the southern tip of India, which was then under British rule.

Layard never got to Ceylon. He stalled in the Middle East, in Persia, where he became fascinated by the history of the region, and in particular by a strange large mound near the town of Mosul, on the banks of the Tigris. He was so curious about this odd-looking man-made hill covered in dust and sand that he persuaded the British ambassador in Turkey to pay for an archaeological dig to see what lay beneath it. On 9 November 1845, Layard, with a team of local tribesmen, started excavations. Within hours their brushes and spades revealed the walls of an ancient palace covered with stone slabs, each one tightly inscribed with a curiously shaped form of unknown ancient writing.

This wasn't just a fancy royal palace with a few old graffiti marks that Layard had stumbled across. After a series of excavations, two palaces and a huge royal library were unearthed on the site, which turned out to be what remains of the ancient biblical city of Nineveh (see plate 5). Layard uncovered a staggering 20,000 clay tablets, including king lists, histories, religious texts, mathematical and astronomical treatises, contracts, legal documents, decrees and royal letters. They provide a fascinating insight into ancient times that has transformed our understanding of when and where the first civilizations emerged, and what they were like.

Probably the most famous tablets from the Nineveh hoard are those that tell of the adventures of an early King of Sumeria called Gilgamesh. He ruled over one of the first Sumerian cities, called Uruk, situated on the east bank of the Euphrates in what is now southern Iraq. At its height as many as 80,000 people lived in Uruk, making it then the largest city in the world.

## Life in ancient Sumeria

The *Epic of Gilgamesh* and the other stories found inscribed on the clay tablets tell us a great deal about how the Sumerian people viewed the world. They give us, for example, some of the first written evidence of religious beliefs.

The Sumerians believed that the gods met each New Year's Day to decide what fateful events would happen in the coming year. Their decisions resulted in all manner of disasters, such as droughts and floods, as well as unexpected good fortune like bumper harvests and military success. Aside from these annual decisions, everything else was, they believed, predetermined by the stars.

The Sumerians and their successors in Assyria and Babylon believed that the world rested on a flat disc, surrounded by water on all sides. Above the sky was a tin roof punctured with small holes through which the celestial fires of heaven could be seen.

# The First Civilizations

They studied these holes (the stars), and watched them rotate each night along a predictable path. They discovered that five large stars behaved in a different, unexplained way. They believed these were the stars of the gods – we know them today as the five planets visible to the naked eye: Mercury, Venus, Mars, Jupiter and Saturn. The Sumerians dedicated one day to each of the five randomly moving stars, which, with the sun and the moon, made the seven days of the week. The names we use in English, derived from the Latin later used by the Romans, show the legacy we still owe to the Sumerian system: Saturday (for Saturn), Sunday (for the sun), Monday (for the moon). The link is clearer in French for the other weekdays: *mardi* (Mars), *mercredi* (Mercury), *jeudi* (Jupiter) and *vendredi* (Venus).

The Sumerians constructed towers, called ziggurats, so they could be closer to the heavens. These were terraced pyramids built from sun-baked clay bricks. The top of each tower was flat and on it was built a shrine or temple to a god. Only priests were allowed inside them, since these were believed to be the dwelling places of the gods.

It isn't just our seven-day week that we owe to these ingenious people. They were also prodigious mathematicians. Amongst the clay tablets found by Layard is evidence of complex arithmetic, with different combinations of vertical strokes and V shapes used to represent the numbers one to nine. The Sumerians developed a system of mathematics based on the number 60, because there are so many ways of dividing it up (by 2, 3, 4, 5, 6, 10, 12, 15, 20, 30).

Their genius for astronomy and mathematics was matched by their inventiveness at making things with their hands. These people are credited with inventing the wheel. Wheels were first used for making clay pots – pottery turntables. It didn't take long for the wheel to be adapted as a device for transporting goods. Tamed asses were used to pull the first carts. Solid wooden wheels were later replaced by spoked wheels, which could carry more weight, making them ideal for war chariots.

Like all human civilizations, even the ingenious Sumerians could not survive for ever. They learned that living in one fixed location, rather than moving from place to place as hunter-gatherers do, came at a considerable price. After many generations of intensive farming the land became less fertile, owing to increasing levels of salt, which spread across the fields through artificial irrigation. To start with they responded by switching from growing wheat in favour of barley, which could tolerate higher salt levels, but before long even that crop just withered away as the soil turned sour. By about 2000 BC the land around the mouths of the Euphrates and Tigris had become impossible to farm, and cities like Ur and Uruk fell into permanent decline.

Their misfortune was another's opportunity. The mighty Assyrian King Sargon the Great (ruled c.2270–2215 BC) built one of the world's first empires around Akkad, a city located hundreds of miles further up the Euphrates, where the land was still rich and fertile (see plate 5). A seventh-century BC clay tablet describes how Sargon's mother cast him off as a baby in a basket of rushes. Eventually, in a striking resemblance to the story of Moses in the Bible, he was found and cared for by the King's water drawer, Akki, and reared as his son.

As the southern Sumerian cities declined they fell victim to Sargon's conquests, becoming part of his enormous new domain, which stretched from present-day south-west Iran to the Mediterranean coast. Cultures diffused two ways. While the Akkadian language gradually started to replace Sumerian cuneiform, the Sumerians' knowledge of craftsmanship and technology spread far and wide across the vast Akkadian empire.

By evolving a system of writing, the Sumerian civilization allowed recorded history as we know it to begin. The written word meant that knowledge could be transferred, without error or change, from one part of the world to another, and from one generation to the next. It was one of the most potent tools for organizing the construction and administration of man's first artificial worlds.

## The power of the Pharaohs

No human so far in our story has ever claimed to be a god. Holy men of the hunter-gathering peoples venerated the spirits and the gods of the earth, sky, beasts and woods, but there is no suggestion that they ever thought they themselves were divine. Rather, these ancient people were so in awe of the gods that they sensed their presence all around, from the pinpricks in the tin roof of the heavens to the awesome forces of floods, thunder, lightning, sunshine, moon, rivers, woods and war. So, to make the leap from seeing the gods as other-worldly to regarding them as real, living, breathing, walking and talking humans is a big one. What power and magnificence would be bestowed on the person who managed to convince others that he was a god on earth!

According to one early human civilization one member of *Homo sapiens* could indeed be a living god, possessing that most precious gift so fruitlessly craved by King Gilgamesh – divine immortality. They called him Pharaoh. He ruled a stretch of North Africa which we now call Egypt through a succession of more than thirty dynasties lasting about 3,000 years. He was thought to be a living god because of the absolute command he could exert over his people. Such supreme authority came from a unique combination of natural advantages.

Pharaoh was all powerful. His people created for him extraordinary monumental buildings in the forms of palaces, temples and tombs – the only survivor of the famous seven wonders of the ancient world is the Great Pyramid of Giza, built as a tomb for one of the earliest pharaohs, called Khufu (known as Cheops in Greek), who died in 2566 BC. This monumental construction originally towered skywards a massive 147 metres – that's over fifty metres taller than Big Ben. It still contains more than two million blocks of stone, each one weighing more than a pick-up truck. Hundreds of thousands of people worked to build structures like this. Modern experts are still at a loss to explain how the ancient Egyptians could have cut, transported and hauled into place so many huge blocks of stone, raising them into the sky from the flat, sandy desert in defiance of everything natural around.

The Egyptians were the first example of a human civilization whose rulers amassed extreme wealth and absolute power over men. Their unprecedented riches and glory were underpinned by the belief that when they left this world they would join the gods in heaven for all eternity. Those who curried sufficient favour could be taken along too, if Pharaoh so chose, entering into a blissful life of everlasting peace.

From about 6,000 years ago nature gave these aspiring all-powerful human rulers a big helping hand in the form of a river and some strategic changes in the climate. Together they transformed the north-eastern tip of Africa into one of the most fertile and best protected lands on earth.

Unlike the rivers of Mesopotamia, the Nile naturally floods once a year, bringing with it a supply of fresh, nutrient-rich sediment – perfect for growing crops. With a natural supply of nutrients and a fresh deluge of water each year, there was no risk of salt poisoning here. Following the end of the Ice Age 11,000 years ago, North Africa was a verdant land of rolling grasslands dotted with trees and vegetation. Over the years, hunter-gathering tribes established themselves near the Nile, settling into small villages and communities. They learned to domesticate the wild cattle, goats and sheep that grazed the savannah, providing them with plentiful supplies of milk, wool and leather. Over time, knowledge about farming crops such as wheat, barley, grapes and flax reached them via nomadic traders from Mesopotamia and directly from people like the Natufians. These river dwellers were now ideally placed to grow into a rich and powerful civilization.

They also had another advantage. About 6,000 years ago the land around the upper Nile began to dry out – partly as a result of cyclical changes in the earth's axis that redirected rainfall patterns and partly because new human activities such as growing crops and herding animals reduced natural water levels. By 4,000 years ago what had once been a landscape full of crocodiles and hippos wallowing in plentiful streams of water had become the arid land we know today as the Sahara Desert.

The encroaching desert was good news for these people because it provided them with an almost impenetrable barrier to invaders. There was no need for city walls, towers, castles or elaborate military installations here. From about 2000 BC the only way other people could disrupt the ancient Egyptians' way of life was either to cross hundreds of miles of barren desert or to come by sea, which was an equally daunting challenge due to the natural defences of the boggy, reedy marshlands of the lower Nile delta. Thanks to these natural barriers, the Egyptian people lived in relative peace and security for much of their history, able to develop their own way of life with little outside interruption.

The Nile brought another gift too – one which helps explain why it was here that such powerful rulers were able to rise and take for themselves the title of god. The river provided a two-way highway that allowed easy passage up and down the country. The current arrangement of the earth's tectonic plates means that the prevailing winds across Egypt blow north to south – in the opposite direction to that in which the river flows. A vessel could simply float downstream, then raise a sail for the return journey. What could be better for controlling a kingdom than a well-protected fertile valley with an easy-to-navigate two-way river system? Nowhere on earth had as many helpful natural ingredients to aid the growth of an advanced human civilization as did Egypt 5,000 years ago.

## *The miracle of the Nile*

Legend has it that in about 3150 BC a King called Menes united the lands of Upper and Lower Egypt. It was he who began the 3,000-year-long reign of the Pharaohs, during which time the Egyptian way of life changed remarkably little. The ruler's governors imposed taxes on the people in the form of food, not money. The idea was that if the weather turned bad or the river floods were weaker than expected, there would still be plenty of food kept in a central store to support the population. It wasn't hard for a population to worship their ruler as if he were a god when it was he who provided their only insurance in the event of a run of poor harvests.

Pharaoh had to have somewhere to store all this food, hence the need for some of his taxes to be paid in the form of manual labour to build huge granaries and storehouses. The Nile's floods meant that the farmland all round the river was underwater for at least three months a year – usually from late June until the end of September. During these months hundreds of thousands of peasant farmers could sail downstream, construct for their Pharaoh some of the most magnificent buildings ever made by humankind, and then head home on the favourable winds.

All this helped make Pharaoh – in the popular mind – a living god on earth. It therefore followed that everything possible should be done to make sure that when their god departed this world, his soul should pass as effortlessly as possible into the next life. Here Pharaoh could continue to protect the people from other gods and disasters such as war, drought, famine and disease.

Awesome tombs were constructed for the pharaohs, their families and friends, initially in the form of pyramids, the largest of which are just south of modern-day Cairo, at a place called Giza. More than a hundred pyramids were built during the Old Kingdom, but only three massive structures survive to this day – the biggest being the one built by the Pharaoh Khufu. This pyramid took twenty-three years to build and used the labour of more than 100,000 slaves and farmers. Originally, it was cased in brilliant white limestone and topped off with a gold cap. The purpose of this massive monument was to provide an everlasting structure in which to store Pharaoh's body so he could use it again in the next life.

Dead bodies were preserved using a process of mummification, learned over many generations, which typically took as long as seventy days to complete. All the body organs were cut out and placed in a series of canisters called canopic jars, including the brain, which was pulled out of the head through the nose using a special instrument with a hook on the end. The heart was the only organ left in the body – so it could be weighed in the next life by the gods to help judge if the person had lived a virtuous life on earth.

The body was dried out with salty crystals and then stuffed, covered with oils and ointments and finally wrapped in bandages. The completed mummy was packed inside a coffin, which, in the case of a Pharaoh, was placed at the heart of the pyramid in the King's burial chamber. Surrounding the body was everything that the dead Pharaoh could possibly need in the afterlife: food, drink, pets (mummified, of course), games, toys, crowns, tableware, daggers, spears, clothes, books, pictures, magic spells ... The tombs of important people contained teams of servants called *shabti*. These were dolls, sometimes carved out of wood, sometimes of semi-precious stone. Their purpose was to come to the assistance of the dead soul whenever he or she needed help.

Many of the ancient Egyptians' most sacred beliefs were encoded in *The Book of the Dead*, a collection of magic spells and stories, often illustrated with scenes from this world and the afterlife, written by the living for the benefit of the dead. Verses from the book were placed on scrolls inside tombs to help the souls of the dead pass through the dangers of the underworld and into an afterlife of bliss.

By the time of the New Kingdom (starting in about 1550 BC), the capital of Egypt had been moved upstream, from Memphis to Thebes.

Here the burials continued, but with one important difference. Now the Pharaohs, along with their families and friends, placed their tombs in secret locations underground. This was to protect against looters, who had taken advantage of the occasional interludes in Egyptian history when central power broke down, such as when the Hyksos invaded on their chariots from the north and overran the lower part of the country between about 1674 and 1548 BC.

Hundreds of tombs have been discovered in the Valleys of the Kings, Queens and Nobles, near Thebes. Even though they were underground, many have been looted in the intervening years. But, remarkably, some have survived almost completely intact. Massive temples, built by the rich to glorify the gods, still stand to this day, such as the one at Karnak.

## *The original Indiana Jones*

On 4 November 1922 a British archaeologist who had been searching the valleys near Thebes for more than fifteen years stumbled across some steps leading to an unknown tomb. What Howard Carter discovered was the burial chamber of a little-known Pharaoh called Tutankhamun, who died when he was only about nineteen. For a long time it was thought he had been murdered, because his mummy shows a mysterious bump on the back of the head. But it is now thought that this young ruler died from gangrene after breaking his leg, probably while out hunting. The discovery of the tomb transformed our understanding of Egyptian civilization. A huge hoard of treasure was packed inside the chamber; the most famous object of all was found bound to the head of the mummified boy-king: his funeral mask, made out of solid gold.

Ancient Egypt was so well endowed with natural resources and protective barriers that it had little need to develop military technology in the same way as other nearby civilizations. Why bother protecting yourself when nature has so kindly managed your defences in the form of surrounding desert and marshes? Why bother going on the attack when staying put along the banks of the Nile provided more than enough natural resources? In the end, this contributed to Egypt's downfall. After 3,000 years of almost uninterrupted dynastic rule a wave of invasions swept over the empire, starting with the Assyrians in 671 BC, the Persians in 525 BC, followed by the Greeks in 332 BC and the Romans in 30 BC. By this time ancient Egypt as a separate, distinct civilization had reached its end.

### Fertility, trade and equality in the Indus Valley

Not many people can genuinely claim to have discovered a lost world. But one day in 1827 a British spy called Charles Masson had the privilege of becoming one of them. He left his army base in Agra, India, site of the world-famous Taj Mahal, and headed west with a fellow soldier on some unknown errand – it is even possible he was deserting. On his journey he stumbled across the ruins of an ancient city at a place called Harappa, now situated in north-east Pakistan, which included what looked like a castle on top of a hill. Lying on the ground he found jewels, bangles and arm rings, as well as the remains of three ancient chariots. Masson knew he had found something extraordinary, but it wasn't until a hundred years later that professional excavations revealed the full extent of this lost civilization, hidden for thousands of years beneath the mud, sand and dust.

Serious archaeological excavations began in the 1920s. They revealed that Harappa was one of the largest cities in what is now called the Indus Valley Civilization. More than 2,500 different sites have since been discovered. These settlements were established at about the same time as the first towns and cities of ancient Egypt and Sumeria – that is, starting from about 3300 BC. Over about 1,700 years people living here developed what many experts consider to be the most advanced and impressive society on earth at the time. Then, quite suddenly, they vanished, seemingly into thin air. To this day no one knows exactly why or where they went.

The people who lived at Harappa arrived from an ancient settlement called Mehrgarh, located near a town called Sibi in modern-day Pakistan. From about 2600 BC the landscape dried up as the climate changed and these people moved north to the more fertile river valley of the Indus. By the end of the second millennium BC people living in the Indus Valley had built a number of stunning cities. They contained many of the features we associate with modern living, making them unique in the world at that time.

These people were brilliant town planners. Their streets were laid out in convenient, well-measured grid patterns, like a modern American city. Each street had its own sewerage and drainage systems, which were, in some people's opinion, more advanced than many found in modern-day Pakistan and India. Excavations have unearthed a series of large public buildings, including assembly halls and a meeting place for up to 5,000 citizens. Public storehouses, granaries and bath houses were surrounded by colonnaded courtyards. Indus Valley builders even used a type of natural tar to stop water from leaking out of what is almost certainly the world's first ever artificial public swimming pool. One house has the remains of what looks like an under-floor heating system, pre-dating the famous Roman hypocaust system introduced more than 2,000 years later.

Each house had access to a well, and waste water was directed to covered drains, which lined the main streets. Some houses opened on to inner courtyards and small lanes, and for the first time houses were built on more than one level. The people wove cotton, fired exquisite pottery and crafted copper and bronze into jewellery and statues. Metal workers lived here in abundance. Evidence of at least sixteen copper furnaces has been uncovered in Harappa alone.

Unlike Egypt and Sumeria, there is a noticeable absence of royal tombs. There are no ziggurats, pyramids, temples or big palaces characteristic of a rich, dominant ruling class. What makes the Indus Valley Civilization so interesting is that it suggests a way of life which was organized and efficient but above all egalitarian. Most people, it seems, shared their wealth and lived in comparative equality.

This civilization was based on trade, because it needed access to raw materials such as copper and tin from other places. One Indus Valley city, called Lothal, featured a massive artificial dock with a dredged canal and loading bays for filling and emptying ships.

Everything about the Indus Valley Civilization seems to have been far before its time – from the sanitation of its streets and the central heating of its houses to the fabulous dockyards and meticulous works of art. Craftsmen and women were on a par with farmers, tradesmen – even priests. They all seem to have worshipped what is known as a mother goddess, which accounts for the hundreds of female figurines, including an exquisite small bronze dancing girl, found in sites throughout the region.

Plenty of evidence suggests that until about 4000 BC, and in some areas until 1600 BC, much of Europe and the Near East lived in a similar way.

## The Age of Stonehenge

Remarkable remains have been found buried in the graves of Neolithic farming people across Europe, who lived from about 8000 to 3000 BC, which is when the first bronze tools and weapons appear, and what is known as the Bronze Age begins. Mostly, people were buried together, men and women equally, in large communal graves called barrows. Studies of their bones have shown that these people did not generally die as a result of violence.

More than 10,000 tombs and barrows are known about in Western Europe alone. These are called megalithic because huge structures are often to be found near these graves, usually built from large blocks of local stone. Many were set upright in circles, like the sites in England at Stonehenge and Avebury. Elsewhere they were constructed as temples, with altar tables at one end or in the centre. Famous examples such as Hagar Qim and Mnajdra survive on the island of Malta.

Many thousands of megalithic structures still stand as monuments to the farming people who spread out from the Near East with their domesticated animals and seeds from about 7000 BC. Mostly they travelled along the coasts by sea, and up river valleys such as those of the Danube and the Rhine, fertile areas with rich soil and plentiful moisture for their crops. Some skirted the Mediterranean coasts, establishing themselves on islands such as Malta. They then travelled north and west, settling in Portugal, northern Spain and Brittany before reaching England, Ireland, Wales and as far up as the Orkney islands off the coast of Scotland, where some of the best-preserved structures and stone houses still remain.

These people deliberately changed the natural environment around them to support their new agricultural lifestyles. Between 6000 and 3000 BC millions of trees were cut down all over Europe to make way for fields. Large areas of open moorland such as Dartmoor and Exmoor in the West Country of England were formerly ancient forests, cut down by Neolithic farmers to provide open areas to grow crops and graze livestock. They needed to do this so they could settle permanently in small villages and towns – with some communities as large as 500 inhabitants.

There is no evidence to suggest that these people were violent. As at Harappa, there is no trace of a dominant ruling class. Objects buried alongside dead early Neolithic people were typically figures of goddesses, not axes, arrowheads or spears. The absence of violent death, fortifications and weapons of war suggest that these were peaceful times. Villages were built along fertile valley floors, not on the tops of hills, implying that territorial aggression, invasion and terror were little known.

Like the population in the Indus Valley, early European Neolithic farmers were sophisticated and technologically advanced. They too had a distinctive form of written symbolism. Objects covered with swirling whorls and spiral shapes have been found at more than a hundred megalithic sites across Europe. It is likely that these inscriptions were some form of communication between the people and their gods and goddesses in the world beyond.

## The worship of the Mother Goddess

Some experts believe megalithic societies were matrilineal, with women placed at the apex of society – not as rulers, but as birth-givers. Perhaps a line can be traced from the Natufian women of Lebanon (see page 95), or even as far back as the Venus of Willendorf, that 24,000-year-old statue of a pregnant woman found in Austria (see page 81). After all, women were the original seed gatherers while men went out to hunt. It was they who probably developed the most expertise in agriculture, using a mixture of instinct and common sense to select the best seeds for the next year's crops, unwittingly instituting what we now call artificial selection.

The mother goddess took a variety of forms. Sometimes she was a snake, or a vulture, or the moon. Each symbol represented a cycle of death, birth and regeneration: the snake hibernates, then wakes up and sheds her skin; the vulture recycles dead flesh by eating it; and the moon dies and is reborn every twenty-eight days, mirroring the feminine menstrual cycle.

Moon worship was highly advanced in megalithic times. It has recently been recognized that temples such as Stonehenge were originally built to glorify the moon as well as the sun. Every month shafts of moonlight line up perfectly with gaps in the massive stones, the architects having positioned them precisely to accommodate the subtly shifting patterns of the moon's varying rising and setting cycles, which repeat themselves exactly every 18.6 years. The full moon has had historic and religious significance going back thousands of years, since it was by the light of the full moon that many hunter-gathering tribes hunted, providing the best opportunities for a good catch.

## The matriarchy of Minoan Crete

Europe's mother goddess culture came to its climax on the Mediterranean island of Crete in the second millennium BC. Here it also survived longest. Crete thrived on trade routes that linked the Mediterranean with the rest of megalithic Europe and North Africa. The flowering of the island's Minoan civilization coincided with the growth of the Indus Valley Civilization, from c.3300 to 1700 BC. Homer, a Greek poet who wrote in the eighth century BC, claimed there were as many as ninety cities on Crete, and archaeologists have found a number of 'palaces', including the largest of all at the island's capital, Knossos.

The discovery of this ancient island civilization was chiefly the work of Sir Arthur Evans, an eccentric but meticulous Victorian archaeologist. As soon as he set foot on Crete in 1894, Evans rigorously pursued the mystery of the mythical King Minos, who, legend has it, ruled from a fabulous palace at Knossos which housed an appalling monster, the Minotaur. Half-man, half-bull, this beast lived in an impenetrable maze and feasted off the flesh of still-living virgins.

Minoan Crete was like a heart pumping at the centre of the Bronze Age trading system. Its trade links stretched as far as Mesopotamia in the east and Spain in the west. Tin and copper were traded for smelting into bronze, while luxury crops such as bright-yellow saffron were grown in the island's fields and exported as flavouring for food.

Evans discovered that the people who lived on ancient Crete followed the megalithic tradition. Women and men had equal rights. Wall paintings from the palaces of Knossos and Phaistos show that women were able to express themselves freely. They are depicted as bare-breasted, wearing short-sleeved shirts open to the navel and long, flowing, layered skirts.

Statues, vases and wall paintings show images of sporting contests where women competed equally alongside men. The island's favourite sport was the impossible-sounding bull-vaulting. An acrobat (sometimes female) would grab the horns of a bull and somersault on to its back. Then, in a second somersault, she would leap off its back and land upright with her feet back on the ground. No wonder Minoan women were the first people known to have worn fitted garments and bodices – essential prerequisites, you would think, for a sport like this.

Women did not dominate society, but they did oversee it. Frescoes at the palace of Thera, on the island of Santorini, a hundred kilometres north of Crete, show women standing on balconies overseeing processions of young men carrying an animal for sacrifice. Most priests on Minoan Crete were female. Under Minoan law women retained full control of their property. They even had the right to divorce at pleasure. It was a tradition too that a mother's brother was responsible for bringing up her children. Customs such as these, which seem strange to us today, lingered long in the Mediterranean mind.

Minoan palaces were not mighty and dominant like those in Egypt or Sumeria. Rather, they functioned as the region's communal administrative and religious centres, providing a place of work for craftsmen, storage spaces for food and temples for goddess worship. One look at a reconstruction of the palace at Knossos and you can understand why Greek invaders might later imagine that the corridors and irrigation channels resembled an impenetrable maze.

Like the traders of the Indus Valley and other European megalithic people, the Minoans had their own form of symbolism, which shows that their civilization was culturally and technologically advanced. In 1903 archaeologists excavating the palace of Phaistos, on the southern side of the island, found a disc thought to date from some time between 1850 and 1600 BC. It contains forty-five unique symbols arranged in a spiral shape, resembling the swirls found on vases at Knossos. No one really knows who made the disc, or what the symbols mean, but it does show that the people of Minoan Crete were artistic, prosperous and highly ingenious.

Following excavations at a site called Akrotiri in 1967, the Minoans are now known to have spread to the island of Santorini. There, archaeologists have discovered the remains of a vast, ancient island city which had been buried for thousands of years under thick layers of volcanic ash. Although only the southern tip of the town has so far been examined, houses three storeys high have been unearthed with fine wall paintings, stone staircases, columns and large ceramic storage jars, mills and pottery. Minoan Akrotiri even boasted a highly developed drainage system, featuring the world's first known clay pipes with separate channels for hot and cold water supplies.

A distinct pattern is discernible from the evidence that has been left by these early civilizations. Stretching from the ancient Indus Valley, right across the mountains of Anatolia (modern-day Turkey), to the islands of the Mediterranean and as far as the topmost island of Orkney in Scotland, what emerges is a series of like-minded civilizations whose temples and graves bear witness to a lifestyle of peace and a veneration for mother nature. Their common belief in the continuous cycle of birth, death and regeneration is personified by their worship of a mother goddess in all her forms: snake, vulture, pregnant woman or moon. Excellence in craftwork, technical skill and exquisite art are some of their legacies, along with a spirit of natural equality.

It was not to continue. During the second millennium BC the last of these early civilizations fell. New power in the form of military might was in the process of sweeping across Europe, the Middle East and Asia. Warriors had by now worked out how to live off the profits of others, ushering in an age when human elitism, ruthlessness and terror had their true beginnings.

# 7

# Oriental War and Peace

## (2000–200 BC)

*How powerful and enduring human civilizations arose in the Far East*

IF AN OLYMPIC GOLD medal were to be awarded to the largest, most robust human civilization ever to have existed on the earth, there would only be one serious contender – China.

Modern China is awe-inspiring. It is home to 1.3 billion people, more than a fifth of the world's population. It has the fastest-growing economy in the world, and can arguably take the credit for cradling more inventions and discoveries that have made a real difference to people's lives than any other country in history. The list includes the blast furnace, paper, gunpowder, the compass and printing and competitive examinations (see pages 191, 198, 200, 203).

Most impressive of all is its age. China is as ancient as any of those early civilizations that grew up around the Fertile Crescent of the Middle East, all of which have long since collapsed or been subsumed into other encroaching cultures and empires. Yet the foundations of modern China, both politically and culturally, were laid down more than 3,000 years ago. This land of fiery dragons and giant pandas (there are still a few left) is humankind's most remarkable survivor, and, quite possibly, it is now this civilization more than any other that holds the key to the future of both mankind and the overall health of the planet earth herself (see page 292). What was it that made this great power so different and so special, and has enabled its ancient culture to survive to this day?

## The rice age

By about 2000 BC, two distinct civilizations were emerging in China along the banks of its river systems, the Yellow River to the north and the enormous Yangtze, located further south (see plate 6). Roaming hunter-gathering tribes probably began cultivating crops as early as 7000 BC along the banks of the Yangtze, the greatest river system in east Asia. With its source in the glaciers of Tibet, this mighty river flows west to east, then, after twisting and turning over the course of some 4,000 miles, it finally spills its muddy load into the East China Sea.

By about 3000 BC the frequent flooding of the river and its 700 tributaries made this an ideal place for growing rice, an almost magically productive and nutritious source of food which has the best record of any crop on earth for supporting large, intensive human populations. Today India and China are the most populous human civilizations largely thanks to their early production of rice, which can under natural conditions feed more humans per hectare than any other staple agricultural crop.

Rice is highly nutritious and remarkably resistant to pests. Flooded paddy fields provide ideal habitats for water-loving creatures such as frogs and snakes that feed off insects which otherwise spoil crops. Water cover is also perfect protection from the threat of self-sowing weeds, significantly increasing the chances of a successful crop. Nutrients flow freely around the waterlogged soil of paddy fields, renewing them just as the nitrogen-rich mud revitalized lands flooded by the Nile each year, giving the ancient Egyptians their head start thousands of miles to the west (see page 108).

But growing rice is hard work. Each plant has to be sown individually and expertise in irrigation is necessary to ensure flooding at the right times of the year. Thankfully, the abundance of a suitable natural workforce in the form of water buffalo meant that people here learned early on how to harness animal power for ploughing, puddling and harrowing the fields.

The rich allure of rice didn't go unnoticed by the people living further to the north, along China's other river system. The Yellow River Valley wasn't suitable for cultivating rice because the climate wasn't wet enough. Instead, the people there had their own staple crop, in the form of millet, which they made into noodles. Although nutritious, millet seed cannot be made into leavened bread, so it never really caught on in Western civilizations, which have tended to use it as birdseed instead of eating it themselves.

## How eastern fortunes were woven in silk

The Yangshao people, who lived between 5000 and 2000 BC along the Yellow River Valley, are thought to have been the first ever to have practised China's most lucrative long-term secret – silkworm cultivation.

Silk is extraordinary stuff. It is entirely natural. It reflects the light, making it look shiny and glamorous, and above all it is amazingly strong. In fact, silk is the strongest natural fibre known to man. Insects manufacture silk as a kind of miniature binding rope to protect their larvae. Gradually, as the larvae hatch, they gnaw through the silk rope to emerge out of the cocoon as butterflies or moths. Some adult insects, such as spiders, use silk for other purposes, such as making webs for catching prey.

Legend has it that the magical properties of silk were first discovered by Leizu, wife of the Yellow Emperor, who is recorded as having reigned from 2697 to 2598 BC. While out for a walk she is supposed to have noticed something wrong with the Emperor's mulberry trees. She found thousands of caterpillars munching their way through the leaves, causing a great deal of damage. She collected some of the cocoons from which the caterpillars came and then sat down to drink a cup of tea. While she was taking a sip a moth larva accidentally dropped into the steaming water and a fine thread started to unwind itself from around the cocoon. Leizu found she could wrap this fine, strong cord around her finger. Inspiration struck. She persuaded the Emperor to plant a whole grove of mulberry trees, following which she worked out how to harness silk by reeling it into long threads that could then be woven into shiny pieces of precious cloth.

The practice of what is now called sericulture, which is the deliberate farming of a type of caterpillar called *Bombyx mori*, brought enormous wealth and prosperity to China. For as long as 3,000 years Chinese farmers and tradespeople have profited by trading silk with other civilizations who marvelled at its shimmering appearance. Plastic man-made alternatives, in the form of satin, nylon and acrylic, weren't concocted until the Second World War (see page 263).

Silk was the primary cause of the development of a series of overland trade routes that later become known as the Silk Road (see plate 6). By the time of the Roman Empire (44 BC–476 AD), silk was in huge demand by Mediterranean people. Its fine texture and semi-transparent shimmer made it one of the great luxuries of the ancient world.

## The power of iron

Chinese people probably weren't the first to discover that iron was a cheaper and more effective metal than bronze for making tools and weapons. The Hittites of central Turkey are known to have mastered the technique of smelting iron ore and were hammering on the first blacksmiths' anvils by about 1400 BC, which is when the European and Mediterranean Iron Age is said to have begun. The iron they first used probably came from meteorites. But Chinese smiths from the region of Wu on the banks of the Yangtze were the first to work out how best to harness the iron found inside the ores of the earth's rocks. The manufacturing techniques they developed for casting iron were so advanced that they weren't matched in Europe for another 1,500 years.

Iron is a natural gift of the earth and almost as essential to the development of modern human civilizations as oxygen is to animal life. Iron is by far the most common metal in use now – about 95 per cent of all metals used today are based on it. Without it, modern civilization would be very different indeed. Iron and steel, its derivative, are the materials of choice for making everything from cars to ships, pipes to forks, and computer disk drives to guns and skyscrapers.

Unlike copper, though, iron is not found in a pure form. Other elements like to react with it – for example, oxygen – making compounds such as red iron oxide. To get the iron out requires effort and a little know-how, something the Chinese had attained by about 500 BC, which is when they built the world's first blast furnace. When iron ores are heated to about 1,450°C a liquid forms. It can then be poured into moulds to make implements of any shape and size. As it cools, the metal becomes strong and rigid. The first iron implements were almost all used in agriculture. Iron ploughs were a magical technological leap forward because they could cut through the hardest of clay soils, turning huge areas of land from scrubby waste into high-yielding fields of rice. The more food, the more people could be fed. The more people, the stronger a government could become by creating well-nourished, easily supplied, permanent standing armies.

Knowledge of how to smelt iron spread rapidly. By the time of the Hàn Dynasty (206 BC–220 AD), Chinese metalworking had become established on a scale not reached in the West until the eighteenth century. The Chinese government built a series of large blast furnaces in Henan Province, each one capable of producing several tonnes of iron a day.

While iron and rice were initially the preserve of the southern Chinese people, those from the silk-weaving north were determined not to be left behind. These were the people who provided the initial impetus to centralize, consolidate, conquer and combine the whole area into a single civilization. For rice, silk and iron read food, wealth and war. It is not hard to see why such deep knowledge of how to exploit the natural world to human advantage became a magnet around which a single powerful civilization eventually arose, uniting the people of the two great river valleys.

### History, bones and characters

The Shang Dynasty (1766–1050 BC) was the first to leave tangible archaeological traces in its wake. Archaeologists excavating a site called Yin in the 1920s uncovered eleven royal tombs and the foundations of a palace. Tens of thousands of bronze, jade and stone artefacts were found. They show that this was a highly advanced culture with a fully developed system of writing, ritual practices and impressive armaments that helped its people conquer and rule lands for miles around. Human sacrifices were common. Many members of the Shang royal family were buried with a complete household of servants, including chariots, horses and charioteers – all thought essential for protection in the afterlife.

Defence against enemies wasn't the only concern of these early Chinese Kings of the north. Just as important was the strongly held belief that Kings alone provided a critical link between the gods and mankind. Unlike any other rulers we have seen so far, Chinese Kings took it upon themselves to perform detailed and highly technical fortune-telling rituals.

This was done in a most bizarre and ingenious way using turtle shells or the bones of an ox. A heated rod would be pushed into the shell or bone, causing it to crack. Like a modern-day palm reader, the King would interpret the length and direction of the lines to reveal the answers to questions which were important to him and his people. *When will it rain? Will we win the next battle? Will we have a bumper harvest this year?* Sometimes these questions would be inscribed on the shells themselves, using a form of symbolic writing that has been easy for modern historians to decipher since it resembles modern Chinese writing so closely. This in itself is testament to how today's China has its roots sunk deep in the past and that its culture represents by far the longest-surviving pattern of continuous civilized human behaviour.

Hundreds of thousands of oracle bones with ancient writing on them have been found in recent times. Most oracle bones have now been traced back to the tombs at Yin, where more than 20,000 were found during the excavations of the 1920s and 1930s. They form the earliest significant body of Chinese writing yet to have been discovered.

## Warring states and the first great philosopher

The first thousand years of recorded Chinese history, from about 1200 to 200 BC, is a story of consolidation and conquest, largely thanks to the combined impact of rice, silk and iron. The kings of Shang, and then the Zhou, who took charge in 1046 BC following victory at the Battle of Muye, used the Yellow River as their main corridor of power (see plate 6). They claimed that their power came directly from heaven. They meant it. Their rule was symbolized by an axe, usually embellished with hungry smiles and devouring teeth.

In the end, their capital Hào (near the present-day city of Xi'an) was sacked by barbarian invaders, and in 722 BC the Zhou had to move their headquarters further east to Luoyang, in the present-day Henan Province. Central authority rapidly disintegrated and a series of smaller states, some with rulers calling themselves Kings, emerged to fill the gap. By 500 BC these states had been consolidated into seven major powers, each vying for the prize of a united China, with its promise of almost infinite supplies of food, wealth and power. Over the next 300 years it was the military struggle for supremacy between these states, known as the Warring States Period, which finally created the platform for uniting China.

During this period a number of different philosophies evolved, called the Hundred Schools of Thought. Wise men and thinkers wandered from court to court, advising kings and nobles on how they might live justly, rule wisely and advance the progress of their kingdoms. One such man was Kongzi, later known to the Western world as Confucius. Tradition says he lived from about 551 to 479 BC. His legacy lives on in societies across the Far East, from Japan and China to Korea and Vietnam.

Kongzi was a minister of justice in the state of Lu. One day, aged about fifty-five, he decided to quit his job and go on a trek around the kingdoms of northern China to preach his message of the right way to lead a virtuous life and the best way to rule a kingdom. Confucius sought a system for living that could restore unity, because he thought that the world was descending into an abyss of power struggles and military confrontations. He taught that obedience, correct behaviour and good etiquette were ways in which order in society could be restored. A good king would set a good example to his people, and good subjects were bound to obey.

What Confucius didn't concern himself with is almost as revealing as what he actually taught. His philosophy has no place for gods, no afterlife, no discussion or consideration of a divine soul or spirit. In a way, Confucius developed the first godless theory of personal and political behaviour. Family loyalty, respect for older people and reverence for the past were his three pillars of social virtue.

A flavour of his philosophy can be captured by some of his most famous sayings. He hated war and confrontation, had a love of history and was always pragmatic: 'Before you embark on a journey of revenge, dig two graves.' 'Study the past as if you would define the future.' 'The only constant is change.' A number of great scholarly works are attributed to Confucius, although it is far from clear whether he actually wrote any of them. For almost 2,000 years Chinese civil servants, lawyers, military officers and other officials were required to study these texts, called the Four Books and Five Classics, in order to qualify to serve the state. This emphasis on education, teaching, conformity and obedience is still a hallmark of the enduring society that is China today.

Confucius's concern for order and peace threatened to become lost in the noise of war and battle that overran Chinese life until the year 221 BC, when the country was unified by the triumph of the state of Qin. The story of the rise of Qin (from which 'China' comes) is as blood-curdling as it is brutal.

## The first emperor

Qin was a kingdom in the north-west corner of China, a land of horse rearing and bounty hunting (see plate 6). Selective breeding meant that larger horses were now available, allowing soldiers to ride into war on horseback, liberating them from expensive, unwieldy chariots.

The military might of the Qin was matched only by its brutality. One famous general called Bai Qi is reputed to have killed more than a million soldiers and seized more than seventy cities. In 278 BC he led the Qin army to victory against its biggest rival from the Yangtze south, the Chu. He then went on to defeat the nominal Kings of China, the Zhou, at the Battle of Changping (260 BC). After this battle he had more than 400,000 prisoners buried alive.

Civil administrators were no less harsh. One such, called Shang Yang, is credited with reforming the running of the Qin Kingdom, turning it from a disorganized tribal power into a slick, effective, military machine. With the support of the then ruler Qin Xiaogong (381–338 BC) Shang Yang was able to put into practice his belief in the absolute rule of law. For him, loyalty to the state was always superior to loyalty to the family. His reforms included stripping nobles of their lands and giving them instead to generals as prizes for victory in war. He put great emphasis on agricultural reform, so that the land could support more people and feed more soldiers. Farmers who met government quotas for supplying food were rewarded with slaves.

Shang Yang's reforms were later codified into a book of law called *The Book of Lord Shang*. Qin became the strongest state amongst the Seven Kingdoms. The climax came with the rise to power of Ying Zheng as ruler of Qin. After defeating the last independent Chinese state, Qi, in 221 BC, Ying became the first emperor of all China (ruled 221–210 BC), renaming himself Qin Shi Huang after the divine rulers of Chinese mythology.

With the assistance of his prime minister Li Si, Qin Shi Huang rewired China into an awesome centralized powerhouse. Regional rulers were sacked, and in their place he appointed loyal civil governors to each of thirty-six new civil regions. Alongside them military governors were appointed, and a team of inspectors roamed the country to ensure none of them overstepped the mark. Governors were rotated every few years to prevent any one building up a regional power base. All this was an extension of what Shang Yang had implemented across the Kingdom of Qin more than a hundred years before.

In 213 BC Qin Shi Huang ordered what is called the Great Burning of Books, suppressing freedom of speech in an attempt to unify all thought and political opinion, an ancient foretaste of the Cultural Revolution that was to come more than 2,000 years later under the communist regime of Chairman Mao (see page 284). Hundreds of thousands of books were burned, many of them originating in the philosophies of the Hundred Schools of Thought. All books were banned, except for legal works promoting the supreme control of the state. Anyone found discussing illegal books was sentenced to death, along with his family. Anyone found with proscribed books within thirty days of the imperial decree was banished to the north to work as a convict building the first Great Wall of China.

A massive canal, begun in Qin Shi Huang's father's reign and built by a brilliant engineer called Zheng Guo, was completed in 246 BC. It unlocked opportunities for rice growing further north, and provided the state with an almost limitless supply of food with which its armies and people could gain an unassailable position of strength.

Finally, the new imperial government standardized just about everything that could make running a large centralized empire easier – from the characters used in handwriting to the length of axles for carts so they would run more smoothly in the ruts of imperial roads. Edicts, some of which survive, were inscribed on the sacred Mount Taishan in Shandong to let heaven know of the new unification of the earth under a single, all-powerful emperor.

Towards the end of his life Qin Shi Huang became obsessed with finding an elixir that would make him immortal. He eventually died during a tour of eastern China in 210 BC after swallowing mercury pills which his advisers believed would give him everlasting life. For 2,000 years no one knew where he was buried. Then, one day in 1974, some well diggers struck an unusual object buried several feet underground. What they found led to one of the most incredible archaeological discoveries of all time. It was an enormous royal tomb, some three miles across, containing a terracotta army of more than 8,000 life-size soldiers, designed to defend the Emperor Qin Shi Huang in the afterlife (see plate 6). More than 700,000 workers were involved in its construction. Each soldier is an individual, hand-crafted work of art, originally equipped with bronze spears and bows and arrows. The army is arranged in battle formation, supported by 600 clay horses and more than a hundred life-size working wooden chariots.

Although Qin's dynasty crumbled only a few years after his death, thanks to the hatred which his life's work had inspired, his achievement was complete. He didn't just bring about the unification of seven warring kingdoms into the largest empire on earth, he created a top-to-bottom model for imperial administration, from the principles of its ruling culture down to the nitty-gritty plumbing needed to make it all work in practice.

Rice, silk and iron provided both the appetite for expansion and the means of conquest to create the largest and most enduring human power on earth. Supreme command over nature turned these ancient people into an ingenious and unassailably robust civilization for thousands of years to come.

## India, and the reincarnation of man

The Himalayas are a vast range of Asian mountains that helped protect the hunter-gathering people living in what we now call India from the centralizing, conquering and consolidating forces of China. But their effectiveness as a barrier decreases to the north-west, where passes permit the passage of people travelling by foot, horse and chariot. Several waves of invaders came from the north. Some of them probably originated in the steppes of Central Asia, from where, having passed through Mesopotamia, they swept into the Ganges plain in northern India. Surprisingly few archaeological remains have been found so far to help piece together the early history of these invasions. Most surviving evidence is literary.

Sacred texts called the Vedas were written in a language called Sanskrit that originated in the Middle East. These texts are thought to describe life between *c*.1700 and 1100 BC. They paint a vivid picture of the tools brought by these early invaders in the form of horses, wheels and metal. Their verses talk of noble archers engaged in duels with rival heroes, exchanging volleys of arrows while galloping across fields of battle in horse-drawn chariots. They also describe the use of tools, which were employed to clear the jungle around the Ganges Valley. This was a good place to settle. Heavy rains made for lush vegetation, allowing the growth of rice, which could sustain armies.

A superficial reading of some of the ancient texts of India might lead to the impression that these people's destiny was to be as violent as those of the emerging societies to the north, east and west. At the heart of the ancient Indian religion, Hinduism, is the Mahabharata, one of the most famous sacred poems ever written.

It tells the story of an epic struggle for the throne of the Kingdom of Kuru between two rival branches of a dynastic family, the Kauravas and the Pandavas. The tale's climax centres around what is purported to be the biggest and bloodiest battle in all history – the eighteen-day-long Battle of Kurukshetra, in which the Pandavas were ultimately victorious. The most sacred section, possibly added in about 550 BC, tells of a debate between the leader of the Pandavas, Arjuna, and the god Krishna, who had incarnated himself in human form to serve Arjuna as his personal charioteer. On the eve of battle Arjuna urgently seeks Krishna's advice as to whether or not to wage war. He has a dilemma: he knows war will mean having to kill members of his own family, who were obliged to fight against him owing to previous oaths of allegiance.

In this part of the story, called the Bhagavad gita, or Gita for short, Krishna reveals the mysterious philosophy that still binds Hindu people together and defines their reverence for nature and all living things. He explains to Arjuna that despite the inevitability of war there is no need to lament those who die in battle, because the spirit of the self is indestructible. Fire cannot burn it, water cannot wet it, and wind cannot dry it, he says. This self, says Krishna, passes from one body to another, like a person taking off worn-out clothes and putting on new ones.

## Towards a new deal with nature

Reincarnation is the belief at the heart of Hinduism that makes it different from other religions. Each living thing possesses an individual spirit (*atman*), which is part of an über-spirit (*brahman*), the universal force that binds together all life. The goal of all individuals is to liberate the *atman*, freeing it to join the *brahman* in eternal bliss. The destiny of the *atman* is to be recycled again and again in any living thing, plant, animal or human, until it reaches a sufficiently advanced state of development to attain enlightenment (*moksha*) and eternal liberation.

Individual spirits can be freed through the practice of meditation. In the Gita Krishna goes into exquisite detail, explaining to Arjuna precisely how an individual can free his or her spirit by stilling the mind of selfish desires, using as many as four different types of yoga.

The doctrine of reincarnation helped ancient Indian civilization come to terms with the waves of migration, invasion and violence that have sporadically plagued the south Asian subcontinent. A divisive social structure, known as the caste system, evolved as a response to the increasing complexity of Indian society as different cultures and traditions all piled on top of each other. Rather than each new culture blending in to create diversity, the Indian way of life evolved as a kind of multi-layered cake of people who preferred not to mix.

The idea probably originated in the first horse-and-chariot-borne and bronze-wielding invaders, who charged in from the north and west from about 1500 BC, bringing with them their priests, writing (Sanskrit) and a belief in many different gods, such as Indra, the god of war and thunder. Originally there were only four castes. *Brahmans* were priests who prayed; *kshatriyas* were soldiers and fought; *vaisyas* the farmers and artisans who worked; and finally *sudras*, at the lowest end of the scale, dealt with everything that was 'unclean'.

Mixing between these classes was never encouraged; each one therefore maintained its own identity and culture. However, the idea of reincarnation gave these people some hope that, in the next life at least, there was a prospect of joining the ranks of a higher caste.

Organizing civilization into castes provided one way of dealing with generations of immigrants without causing existing cultures to feel threatened by the dilution or extinction of their own distinctive ways of life. Each time a major new culture arrives, a new caste comes into being, finding its place above or below those already there, without radical adjustments of existing customs or habits. As a result, this divisive system has preserved many ancient cultures and beliefs for longer in India than in most other parts of the world. It helps explain why Hinduism is the longest-surviving religion in all human history.

Veneration for nature, rather than violence towards it, is a distinctive characteristic of Hindu thought. The Upanishads are a collection of ancient Hindu texts, first written down in about 500 BC, designed as commentaries to help interpret the Vedas. In them, *ahimsa* is first mentioned. It is a vow that many Hindus take to be non-violent towards nature. Vegetarianism is part of this philosophy, and for this reason as many as 40 per cent of all Indians are vegetarian to this day – that's about 300 million people. Those Hindus who do eat meat hardly ever eat beef, since the cow is venerated above all other animals as a gift from nature providing milk to drink, power for pulling ploughs and manure for nourishing the soil. For Hindus the sacred cow is a symbol of unselfish natural giving and its slaughter is still banned in almost all the states of India today.

This respectful, peace-loving relationship with the natural world was given a huge boost by four men who, between them, deeply influenced how *Homo sapiens* found out that it was possible to adapt its civilizations to live in harmony with the natural world. Two of them founded religions, the other two helped spread them around the world.

## Two princes who renounced worldly goods

The first was an Indian prince called Siddhartha Gautama. He is thought to have lived from about 563 to 483 BC, and was born in Lumbini, in modern-day Nepal (see plate 7). The only historical evidence for his life comes from texts written by his followers some 400 years after his death, so some of the details may well have merged into myth over centuries of oral rendition. His mother, Queen Maya, died a few days after his birth, leaving him to be brought up by his father, Suddhodana, a king or tribal chief who had three palaces built in honour of his newborn son. His father wanted to shield Siddhartha from religious teaching and knowledge of human suffering, thinking that this would allow him to become a strong king.

But, at the age of twenty-nine, Siddhartha left his palaces to meet his subjects. His father tried to remove all signs of poverty and suffering, but to no avail. On his first outing Siddhartha saw an old man – until then he knew nothing of the trials of old age. On further expeditions he met diseased and dying people. Greatly disturbed by what he had seen, Siddhartha fled from the luxuries of his palaces to live as a monk, begging for food in the streets. He then became a hermit and, with the help of two teachers, learned how to meditate and to still his mind.

Next, Siddhartha Gautama and five companions tried to find enlightenment by the total denial of all worldly goods, including food: at one time they ate no more than a single leaf or nut a day. After collapsing in a river and nearly drowning, Siddhartha discovered what came to be known as the Middle Way – a path towards

# Geological Time

| | ERA | PERIOD | SPECIES | EVOLUTIONARY STAGE | |
|---|---|---|---|---|---|
| ,600 | HADEAN | | | No life on earth; volcanoes; rain cools the surface; oceans form. | 00:00 |
| ,800 | ARCHAEAN | | | Methanogens (prokaryotes); cyanobacteria; stromatolites; oxygen in air. | 04:00 |
| 500 | PROTEROZOIC | | | Complex cells (eukaryotes). | 15:00 |
| 850 | | Cryogenian | | Snowball earth. | |
| 635 | | Ediacaran | | Multi-cellular creatures. | |
| 542 | | Cambrian | | Shells, bones and teeth. | 20:50 |
| 488 | | Ordovician | | Vertebrates. | |
| 443 | PALAEOZOIC | Silurian | | Primitive land plants; worms. | 21:50 |
| 416 | | Devonian | | Bony fish; tetrapods. | |
| 359 | | Carboniferous | | Amphibians; reptiles; forests; flies. | |
| 299 | | Permian | | Mammal-like reptiles; Pangaea. | |
| 251 | | Triassic | | First dinosaurs; small mammals; ichthyosaurs. | 22:50 |
| 199 | MESOZOIC | Jurassic | | Dinosaurs dominate land; pterodactyls in the air. | |
| 145 | | Cretaceous | | Last dinosaurs; social insects; flowers; birds; monocots. | |
| 65.5 | | | EPOCH | | 23:40 |
| 55 | | | Palaeocene | Mammals grow larger. | |
| 33 | | | Eocene | Whales return to the oceans. | |
| 23 | CENOZOIC | Tertiary | Oligocene | Horses evolve in Americas. | |
| 5 | | | Miocene | Monkey migrations. | |
| 1.8 | | | Pliocene | First bipeds and humans. | 23:57 |
| 0.11 | | | Pleistocene | Megafauna extinctions. | 23:59 |
| 0.02 | HISTORIC | Quaternary | Holocene | Farming; first human civilizations. | |
| day | | | Anthropocene | Globalization; rise in $CO_2$ levels. | 24:00 |

Twenty-four-hour clock

# Mammal Migrations

Without the dominance of dinosaurs, the range and diversity of mammals grew rapidly. They migrated throughout the world as the continents continued to shift and sea levels fell.

Camels migrated from North Ame: reaching Asia and South America three m.y.a.

Ancestors of today's horses evolved in North America fifty m.y.a. and eventually arrived in Asia via Alaska three m.y.a.

Primates migrated through Africa fifty m.y.a. and then rafted to South America twenty-five m.y.a., roamed to Asia eighteen m.y.a. and migrated back to Africa evolving into gorillas seven m.y.a.

Marsupials hopped across South America and Antarctica to Australia fifty-five m.y.a. when the continents were still attached

m.y.a. = million years ago

Sea cows evolved from the same
ancestors as elephants and
returned to the water fifty m.y.a.
Whales and dolphins returned
to the seas thirty-five m.y.a.

# Migrations of Man

Humanity's appetite for globe-trotting has ancient origins going back more than one million years.

*Homo erectus*: These early humans migrated out of Africa c.1.7 million years ago, travelling across Europe and Asia and reaching as far south as Indonesia, where bones have been found dating back 500,000 years.

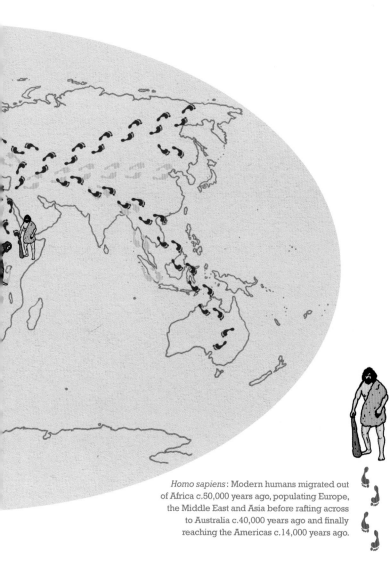

*Homo sapiens*: Modern humans migrated out of Africa c.50,000 years ago, populating Europe, the Middle East and Asia before rafting across to Australia c.40,000 years ago and finally reaching the Americas c.14,000 years ago.

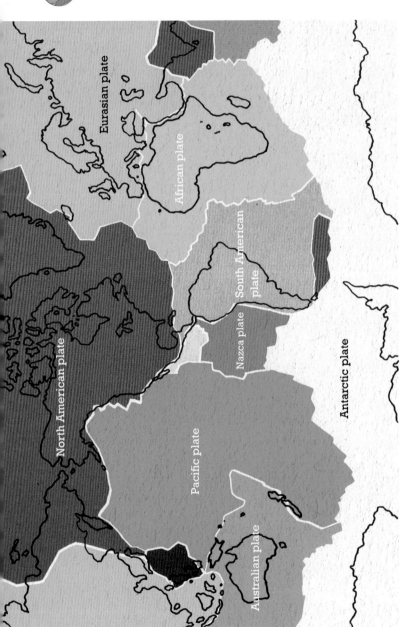

The earth's tectonic plates as they are arranged today. Earthquakes, volcanic eruptions and

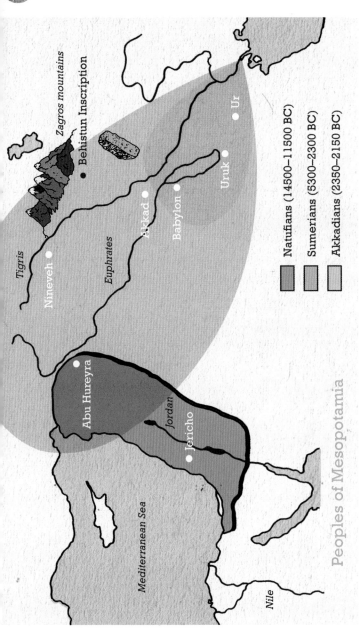

Peoples of Mesopotamia

Natufians (14500–11500 BC)

Sumerians (5300–2300 BC)

Akkadians (2350–2150 BC)

Following early attempts at plant and animal domestication by the Natufians, large-scale human civilization emerged in nearby river valleys.

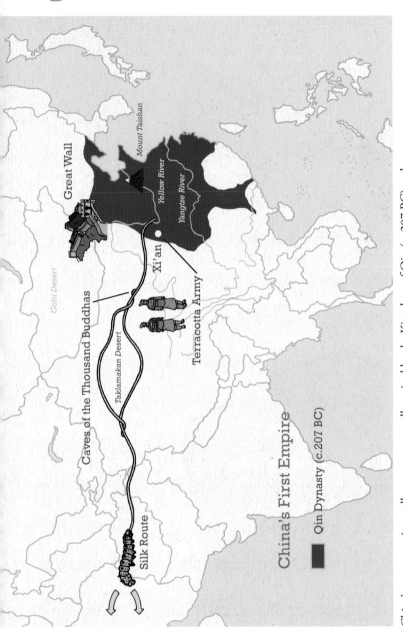

China's two great river valleys were eventually united by the Kingdom of Qin (c. 207 BC) and were made powerful through rice, silk and iron.

# The Spread of Buddhism

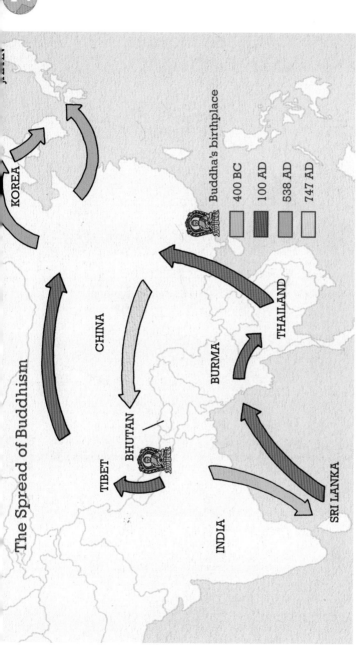

| | |
|---|---|
| | Buddha's birthplace |
| | 400 BC |
| | 100 AD |
| | 538 AD |
| | 747 AD |

KOREA

CHINA

TIBET

BHUTAN

INDIA

BURMA

THAILAND

SRI LANKA

How new beliefs based on non-violence between people and the natural world spread throughout south-east Asia.

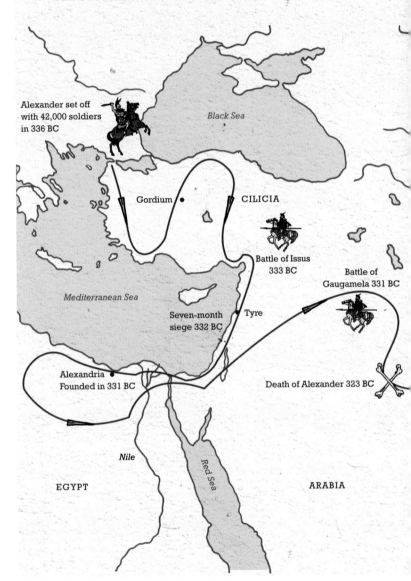

# The Epic Conquests of Alexander the Great

Alexander set off with 42,000 soldiers in 336 BC

Black Sea

Gordium •  CILICIA

Battle of Issus 333 BC

Battle of Gaugamela 331 BC

Mediterranean Sea

Seven-month siege 332 BC  Tyre

Alexandria Founded in 331 BC

Death of Alexander 323 BC

Nile

Red Sea

EGYPT  ARABIA

## 8

What was it that drove this warrior to want to conquer the world –
a desire to see the end of the earth, or an insatiable appetite for war?
In the end, Alexander's awesome adventures fuelled fusion and
friction between the different cultures of the East and West.

*Aral Sea*

Samarkand ●

**BACTRIA**

*ian Sea*

Death of Darius III 330 BC

Battle of
Hydaspes 326 BC

●IA          **PARTHIA**

● Persepolis

Bucephala ●

**INDIA**

*Persian Gulf*

*Indian Ocean*

# The Spread of Islam

The power of prayers five times a day whirled like a dervish throughout the Middle East, North Africa and some parts of Europe.

- Islamic world under Mohammed (622–632 AD)
- Territory added by the first four Caliphs (632–661 AD)
- Territory added by the Umayyad Caliphs (661–750 AD)

AL-ANDALUS

Cordoba

FRANKIA

Paris

Battle of Tours (732 AD)

MAGHREB

Rome

Tunis

Constantinople

BYZANTIUM

EGYPT

Cairo

Damascus

Jerusalem

Battle of Yarmouk (636 AD)

Battle of the Zab (750 AD)

Baghdad

PERSIA

ARABIA

Medina

Mecca

Samarkand

Battle of Talas (751 AD)

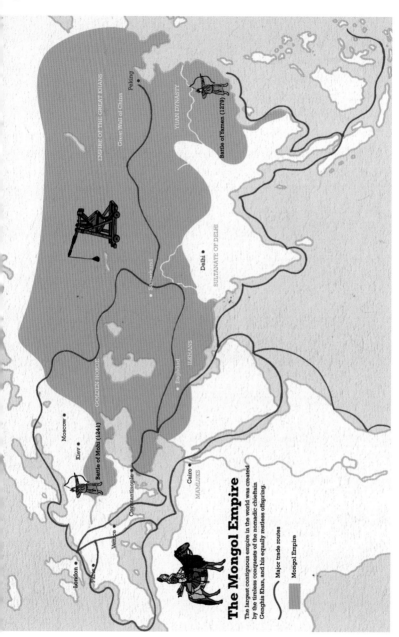

# The Mongol Empire

The largest contiguous empire in the world was created by the tireless conquests of the nomadic chieftain Genghis Khan, and his equally restless offspring.

London •

Paris •

Venice •

Moscow •

Kiev •

Battle of Mohi (1241)

Constantinople •

Cairo •

MAMLUKS

GOLDEN HORDE

Baghdad •

ILKHANS

Samarkand •

Delhi •

SULTANATE OF DELHI

EMPIRE OF THE GREAT KHANS

Great Wall of China

Peking •

YUAN DYNASTY

Battle of Yamen (1279)

~~~ Major trade routes

▨ Mongol Empire

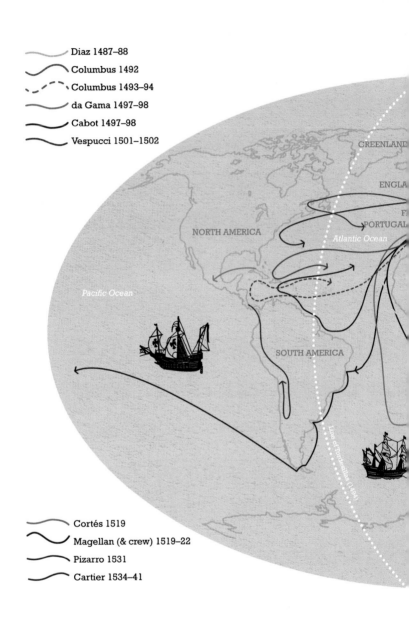

Diaz 1487–88
Columbus 1492
Columbus 1493–94
da Gama 1497–98
Cabot 1497–98
Vespucci 1501–1502

GREENLAND

ENGLA

F
PORTUGAL

NORTH AMERICA

*Atlantic Ocean*

*Pacific Ocean*

SOUTH AMERICA

*Line of Tordesillas (1494)*

Cortés 1519
Magellan (& crew) 1519–22
Pizarro 1531
Cartier 1534–41

# European Exploration

European mariner-cum-mercenaries flexed their muscles by charting the oceans and conquering previously isolated lands.

Arctic Ocean

SIBERIA

RUSSIA

CHINA

JAPAN

Pacific Ocean

ARABIA    INDIA    PHILIPPINES

:A

Indian Ocean

AUSTRALIA

e of Good Hope

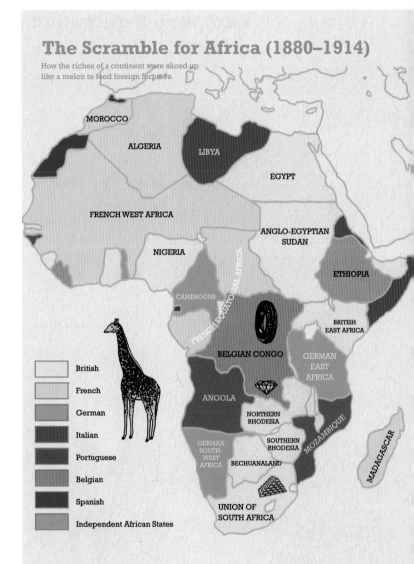

# The Scramble for Africa (1880–1914)

How the riches of a continent were sliced up like a melon to feed foreign fortunes.

MOROCCO

ALGERIA

LIBYA

EGYPT

FRENCH WEST AFRICA

ANGLO-EGYPTIAN SUDAN

NIGERIA

FRENCH EQUATORIAL AFRICA

ETHIOPIA

CAMEROONS

BRITISH EAST AFRICA

BELGIAN CONGO

GERMAN EAST AFRICA

ANGOLA

NORTHERN RHODESIA

MOZAMBIQUE

GERMAN SOUTH-WEST AFRICA

SOUTHERN RHODESIA

BECHUANALAND

MADAGASCAR

UNION OF SOUTH AFRICA

British

French

German

Italian

Portuguese

Belgian

Spanish

Independent African States

enlightenment (liberation of the *atman*) that could be accomplished without the need for extremes, whether of self-indulgence or self-denial. After receiving the gift of some rice pudding from a village girl, Siddhartha sat under a tree until he found the truth. After forty-nine days of meditation, aged thirty-five, he at last attained enlightenment, and from then on became known as the Buddha, meaning 'awakened one'.

For the next forty-five years the Buddha journeyed by foot around the plain of the Ganges River, in north-east India and southern Nepal, teaching his doctrine to a wide range of people, from royalty to terrorists and beggars. After making thousands of converts, he died at about the age of eighty, perhaps of food poisoning.

Buddha's teachings were really an extension, or popular interpretation, of many traditional Hindu beliefs. They were of enormous appeal, especially to the poor, for whom there was little hope of social or material improvement. The Buddha explained how by following his Four Noble Truths and the Noble Eightfold Path, these people could rid themselves of inner desires and free their spirits for eternal liberation without the involvement of any priest, king or other intermediary.

Another prince, who lived at about the same time as Gautama, also renounced his kingdom, and is said to have attained spiritual enlightenment after wandering for twelve and a half years in deep silence and meditation. This man was known as Mahavira, meaning 'great hero', and he became the twenty-fourth and last prophet (*tirthankar*) of the Jain religion.

Jain scriptures were written over a long period of time, but the most popular work was written by an Indian monk called Umaswati more than 1,800 years ago. In his Tattvartha Sutra, or Book of Reality, the main aspects of Jainism are set out, identifying its central belief that all life, both human and non-human, is sacred.

For Jains there is no justification for killing another, however provoked or threatened a person may be. They refuse all food obtained by unnecessary cruelty. Jains are vegetarians and avid supporters of animal welfare. In many Indian towns today animal shelters are run by Jain people. Root vegetables are avoided, as harvesting them destroys an entire plant, whereas fruit, such as an apple, is acceptable, as picking it will leave the tree unharmed. Non-violence, religious toleration and respect for nature are cornerstones of the Jain philosophy, which, like Hinduism and Buddhism, is concerned with liberating the individual's soul through enlightenment accomplished through a series of codes of conduct that involve taking five vows: of non-violence to all living things (*ahimsa*), truthfulness (*satya*), non-stealing (*asteya*), chastity (*brahmacharya*) and detachment from material possessions (*aparigraha*).

Neither Buddhism nor Jainism would have had nearly such an impact on human history were it not for the patronage of certain rulers in the secular world. By about 500 BC, sixteen different kingdoms, known as the Mahajanapadas, divided the Indian subcontinent, from modern-day Afghanistan in the west to Bangladesh in the east.

### Two rulers who spread the message of peace

Most of these kingdoms were consolidated into India's first empire by Chandragupta Maurya (ruled *c.*320–298 BC). Unlike China, India's itch to centralize was less to do with power struggles between kingdoms and more as a response to threats from outside, in the form of Persian and Greek armies that from about 500 BC threatened its borders, especially those in the north-west. By 303 BC Chandragupta is reputed to have had an army of some 600,000 men, with 30,000 cavalry and 9,000 elephants. But towards the end of his life he gave it all up and became a Jain monk. Eventually, it is said, he starved himself to death in a cave.

While Chandragupta established the Jain religion as the preferred philosophy of the most powerful ruling family in India, it was his grandson, Ashoka the Great (ruled 273–232 BC), who had the biggest impact of all. To begin with he was as ruthless and violent as any imperial monarch, controlling his empire through the threat of force. Indeed, Ashoka means 'without sorrow' in Sanskrit. But shortly after the end of one of the biggest and bloodiest wars of the time, he underwent a profound and complete conversion.

The Kalinga War (*c.* 265–263 BC) ended with the famous Battle of Kalinga, which left more than 100,000 people dead on the battlefield. The day after the battle Ashoka walked out across the city, where, as far as his eye could see, the only sights were burned-out houses, dead horses and scattered bodies. 'What have I done?' he cried.

From that moment on Ashoka is said to have devoted his life and reign to non-violence. He became a devout Buddhist and over the next twenty years dedicated himself to spreading the message of this powerful religion. Prisoners were freed and given back their land. *Ahimsa,* the Buddhist doctrine of non-violence, was adopted throughout his domains, forbidding the unnecessary slaughter of animals. Hunting for sport was banned, branding animals was outlawed, and vegetarianism was encouraged as official policy. Ashoka built rest houses for travellers and pilgrims, universities so people could become more educated, and hospitals for people and animals alike throughout India.

As many as 84,000 monuments and monasteries (*stupas* and *viharas*) were erected for Buddhists, many of them built at places associated with the life of the Buddha. Ashoka's most lasting legacies are probably his edicts. Dozens of sandstone pillars were erected throughout modern-day Pakistan and northern India. Written in the widely spoken language of the ordinary people, Prakrit, they popularized Ashoka's belief in the Buddhist concept of righteousness (*dharma*). Their inscriptions provide details of his conversion after the Battle of Kalinga, as well as his policy of non-violence towards all living things: 'I have made provision for two types of medical treatment. One for humans and one for animals. Wherever medical herbs suitable for humans and animals are not available, I have had them imported and grown ... Along roads I have had wells dug and trees planted for the benefit of humans and animals.' (Rock Edict No. 2.)

Ashoka sent missionaries to every king and court he could. He wanted everyone to know about the Buddha's message. They travelled as far as Greece, Lebanon, Egypt, Burma and Sri Lanka. The first Egyptian Buddhist colonies in Alexandria date from this time. Ashoka promoted a new notion of kingship, in which a ruler's legitimacy was gained not from the generosity of a divine god, but by advocating Buddhist ideals, establishing monasteries, supporting monks and promoting conflict resolution.

Following Ashoka's reign, Buddhism spread far and wide (see plate 7). His twin children Mahindra and Sanghamitra settled in Sri Lanka, converting its rulers and people to Buddhism. By 100 AD Buddhist monks had established a foothold in China, where their teaching fused with a similar philosophy called Taoism, founded by a philosopher called Laozi, who had lived at the time of the Hundred Schools of Thought. His book, called the Tao-te-Ching, described how violence should be avoided at all costs, and how individuals should rid themselves of strong emotions and desires through stillness and meditation. (It is ironic that in an attempt to find an elixir for immortality in c.850 AD Taoist monks discovered how to make gunpowder – see page 203.)

Ashoka's influence now looks more powerful beyond India than within it because by about 1300 AD Buddhism in India had declined into a relatively minor religion, marginalized by the resurgence of Hinduism and the onset of Islam. From China, various brands of Buddhism spread to Korea, Vietnam and Thailand. By 538 AD its message had reached the islands of Japan, and by the ninth century Borobudur, in Java, where an immense cluster of Buddhist temples remains to this day. The shrines of Angkor Wat in Cambodia were built 300 years later. Although Hindu in inspiration, they include extensive Buddhist sculptures. This religious complex, the apex of a highly religious civilization, is now buried deep in the jungle, spread across forty square miles.

The brightest modern example of a Buddhist kingship takes us back up into the Himalayas. Today the Kingdom of Bhutan, nestled high in the mountains, is home to just over 650,000 people (see plate 7). A Buddhist monk called Padmasambhava is reputed to have brought the Buddha's teachings to Bhutan and Tibet in 747 AD. Jigme Singye Wanngchuck, fourth King of Bhutan (ruled 1972–2006), stated that Gross National Happiness (GNH) is more important to his people than Gross National Product (GNP) – putting the concerns of social welfare, environmental preservation and cultural protection above economic growth. In a unique echo of Ashoka's edicts, the small, spiritual society of Bhutan is still today attempting to place material and spiritual well-being alongside the preservation of the natural environment.

# 8

# **The Classical World**

## **(4000 BC–476 AD)**

*How Bronze Age weapons, domesticated
horses and wheeled chariots ushered in
a new age of violence and inequality*

**THERE IS NO FIXED** date when the Bronze Age can be said
to start. It began at different times in different places. The earliest
known bronze artefacts may have been made as early as 4000 BC
in Mesopotamia, where the alloy was used by artisans for making
objects such as the Indus Valley dancing girl (see page 115). From
about 2000 BC nomadic chiefs living in central Anatolia, an area
rich in copper and tin deposits, started to adapt bronze for making
armour, shields and weapons in the form of axes, swords and spears.
Bronze is hard. People who could craft bronze into weapons and
armour were at an immediate military advantage over those with
just stone implements or wooden clubs.

Nomads transported precious bronze-making raw materials such
as tin and copper from places as far-flung as Cornwall and Wales
in the west to the Caucasus mountains in Asia Minor (modern-
day Turkey) and beyond to the Middle East and India. Once these
traders became expert at making bronze weapons it was a short
step to invade, conquer and subjugate the many settled farming

communities along their various trading routes between the markets and civilizations of Europe, the Middle East and Asia.

Just as significant was the conquest of a wild animal that revolutionized the nomad's ability to travel long distances. From as far back as about 4000 BC, people travelling around a region of southern Russia called the Pontic Steppe began to discover how to domesticate the wild horse.

Wild horses called tarpans roamed the Pontic Steppe near the edges of forests. These herd animals were tamed, bred and broken in as slaves for humans. Originally more the size of ponies than thoroughbreds, tarpans are now extinct: the last known specimen died in a Moscow zoo in 1875. No one knows exactly when the first tarpans began to be bred in captivity, nor who first managed to mount one, but since they were small the first breeds were better suited to pulling carts and carrying loads than transporting people.

Chariots had begun to appear in Mesopotamia by 2600 BC, according to a beautiful painted box called the Standard of Ur discovered by British archaeologist Leonard Woolley in the 1920s. This box, now on display at the British Museum, includes a graphic image of 'War', with Sumerian spearmen following a four-wheeled chariot pulled by what look like horses, cows or oxen.

Nomadic traders from the Russian steppes were probably the first to possess the triple combination of domesticated horses, wheeled chariots and bronze weapons. They also learned to increase the loads that their horses could pull by using spoked rather than solid wheels, making their chariots lighter and more manoeuvrable in battle.

Gradually from about 3500 BC their way of life spread across Europe, eventually reaching Britain, Ireland and Spain, imposing a new order ruled by a more aggressive, male-dominated society built on controlling horses and making metal weapons. Traces of this cultural shift can be seen in fragments of a style of pottery found all over Europe, originating from the Pontic Steppe. These pots were made in the shape of an upturned bell and were probably used by well-off families to contain mead or beer. This is why theirs is known as the Bell Beaker Culture.

Speed, height and extra strength gave people with domesticated horses a huge military advantage over those without. Horses provided a means of transport at least five times quicker than any other known at the time. Reconnaissance, fast communications and the precious element of surprise were now at a rider's discretion, powerfully exacerbating the potential for terrorism, blackmail, subjugation and war.

Thanks to the unsavoury combination of wheels, horses and bronze, from about 1800 BC until 500 BC Mediterranean Europe and the Middle East were in constant turmoil. Wave upon wave of horsemen wielding bronze and iron weapons availed themselves of each and every opportunity to conquer and invade.

### The Age of Heroes

The period between 1400 and 1100 BC set the stage for some of the most epic military struggles of all time including the legendary Trojan Wars, supposedly fought between a confederation of small Greek states and the people of Troy, a city in western Asia Minor. Accounts of the wars are contained in the Greek poet Homer's *Iliad* and *Odyssey*, which, although partly mythological, provide a vivid account of the chaos and violence of the late Mediterranean Bronze Age.

Another famous piece of literature tells of more violence and distress erupting further south, in Egypt, Jordan and Israel, at about the same time.

Like Homer's poems, the first five books of the Bible were written down many hundreds of years after the events they describe are supposed to have taken place. These religious texts are sacred to Jews and Christians, some of whom believe every word they contain to be literally the true word of God. As a piece of history, however, they are as confusing as they are vivid. The most dramatic historical events in these early books are the exodus of the Israelites out of Egypt and the plagues sent by God through Moses to punish the Egyptian Pharaoh for enslaving his chosen people. No one really knows quite when these events are supposed to have happened. Estimates range from 1650 BC to about 1200 BC, which is when the first archaeological evidence of the Israelite settlement of the Promised Land of Canaan (now Israel) can be traced.

The scriptures tell how the Jewish people were descended from Abraham, a nomadic herdsman from the Mesopotamian city of Ur, who was instructed by God to travel to the land of Canaan. In return for being worshipped as the only true God, he gave this land to Abraham and his 'seed' for ever. The scriptures go on to say that Abraham had two sons by two different women. Ishmael was his first, born to a servant girl called Hagar. Then came Isaac, born to Abraham's wife Sarah. One of Isaac's children, Jacob, had twelve sons, each of whom became leader of one the twelve tribes of Israel from which Jewish people claim their descent.

After the Jewish people settled in their Promised Land (from c. 1000 BC) a series of conflicts ensued with neighbouring civilizations including the Assyrians and Babylonians, the end result of which was the sacking and burning of both Jewish capitals – Samaria (722 BC) and Jerusalem (586 BC) – following which the surviving Jews were enslaved in Babylon. At this point it looked as if the chosen people of God might leave the books of history for ever. But just seventy years after their eviction from Jerusalem they were saved by a Persian emperor called Cyrus, one of the first rulers in recorded history that posterity has since called 'the Great'.

## Religious tolerance in Persia

Cyrus's Persian Empire was remarkable for its respect for other cultures and religions. Local rulers, called satraps, were installed as the governors of conquered lands. After capturing Babylon,

Cyrus allowed the Jews to return to Jerusalem and ordered the building of a new temple 'with the expense met out of the King's household'. As a result, Cyrus is the only non-Jew to be honoured in the Bible as a messiah, a divinely appointed king sent by their one god Yahweh.

The Jews, almost driven to extinction twice, were determined to lay claim to their Promised Land once and for all. The stories of the Old Testament – called the Tanakh in Hebrew – were written down by scribes, edited and finally canonized as the official word of God in about 500 BC. Anyone dispossessing them from now on could do so only against a background of prescribed historical illegitimacy and absolute divine displeasure.

Meanwhile, Cyrus had trouble back up north, where nomads from the steppes were threatening the borders of his empire. In 529 BC an offshoot of the Scythians called the Massagetae were in revolt at the head of the Tigris River. They were led by Queen Tomyris, who supposedly had one of her breasts cut off so she could fight more effectively. According to the Greek historian Herodotus, Cyrus's troops began the battle well, killing both of the Queen's sons and many of her troops. But events swung against them as the battle wore on and eventually Cyrus was slain. So bitter was the Queen at the death of her sons that she had Cyrus's head chopped off and his skull made into a goblet from which, it is said, she drank fine wine until the day she died.

Despite Cyrus's death, the Persian empire he created thrived for the next 200 years. Darius I (also called the Great) ruled from 522 to 485 BC and is credited with reorganizing the empire and building a magnificent new capital called Persepolis, in modern-day Iran, with walls twenty metres high and ten metres thick. Darius also dug the first Suez Canal, allowing ships to pass from the Mediterranean to the Red Sea through a channel which, according to Herodotus, was wide enough for two triremes to pass and took four days to navigate.

However, like Cyrus, Darius was plagued by perpetual incursions and invasions by northern nomadic tribes, who, unbeknown to the Persians, were themselves being pushed west by other nomads eager to find wetter lands for grazing their animals. Continual harassment in the end dragged Persia into what became the biggest and bloodiest conflict yet to take place in human history, one which ultimately led to the collapse of the once proud Persian Empire and precipitated the rise of the Greeks.

## The beginnings of a rift between East and West

In a bid to put a permanent end to the trouble from the Scythians, Darius took a huge army north in about 512 BC, crossed the Bosporus, the short stretch of sea that divides Europe from Asia, and pressed on into what is modern-day Greece. He marched as far as the Danube intending to attack the Scythians from the rear. Unfortunately, thanks to an incorrect understanding of the geography of the region, Darius missed his intended target altogether and instead attacked and subjugated the people of Thrace and Macedonia in northern Greece.

This pre-emptive attack badly backfired. Proud, independently minded Greek cities such as Athens and Eretria encouraged a revolt against Persian rule in western Turkey, led by the Greek Ionians. Darius counter-attacked in 492 BC, but was defeated at the Battle of Marathon two years later, an event which sent shock waves throughout his empire. It was the moment that signalled the beginning of Greek independence from mighty Persia. Greek city after Greek city now declared itself free from foreign rule. Instead of having a buffer zone against the nomadic tribes of the western steppes, the Persians had unleashed a new foe, led by the increasingly powerful maritime city of Athens.

Darius died soon after Marathon. In 480 BC his son Xerxes prepared to put an end to this new European menace and sacked

Athens, burning it to the ground. However, the citizens of the city had escaped to a nearby island, from where they watched as the flames from their homes lit up the night sky. The final act commenced in September, when the Greek and Persian navies clashed at Salamis. The Persians' large triremes proved too clumsy against the more manoeuvrable Greek ships and their navy was ignominiously destroyed.

Europe and Asia were now truly at war. Conflicts between the Persian cultures of the Middle East and the European cultures of the West invariably meant that the Jewish people got caught up in the middle. How little some things have changed.

### Athenian democracy

Signs of a distinctive, new and eccentric pattern of human behaviour began to occur in what became the most famous of all the Greek city states – Athens. Long before the Persians razed the city to the ground in 480 BC this city had become a laboratory for experiments in novel human behaviour. In c.594 BC a poet called Solon won a victory for the city by capturing the nearby island of Salamis. He used the considerable power and prestige gained from this triumph to seize political control.

Solon's reforms involved redistributing political power so that it wasn't just the most powerful families who participated in politics and the judicial process. He created a system that can now be recognized as the first attempt to create a democratic government – one in which the population at large had a say. Nobles remained the city's magistrates, but Solon introduced juries into almost every social dispute, and so, for the first time, involved ordinary citizens in the deliberations of justice.

Part of the reason Athenians could afford to spend so much time in political and judicial deliberation was the highly nutritious olives that grew in groves tumbling down to the Mediterranean shores.

Because they were so easy to grow, preserve, transport and trade, these fruits afforded the Greeks riches in the form of spare time with which to experiment with new ways of life and observe how the natural world works.

## Greek science

At just about the same time, the beginnings of what was soon to become a revolution in scientific and religious thought were emerging just across the narrow stretch of sea separating Europe from Asia – the Bosporus.

Miletus, on the west coast of Turkey, was home to a man called Thales (born *c.*640 BC), who became famous for correctly predicting that a solar eclipse would take place on the afternoon of 28 May 585 BC. Thales demonstrated that the movements of the planets could be predicted using a set of astronomical tables originally compiled by holy men in Babylon and Egypt. The invasions of Darius the Great had brought such knowledge, stored on clay tablets, into western Turkey. When these fell into the hands of someone like Thales, with a keen eye for numbers and mathematics, patterns began to emerge that could then be extrapolated to predict events like a solar eclipse.

Anyone who could make an accurate prediction of something as dramatic as a solar eclipse was bound to make quite a stir in a world where such events were traditionally believed to be caused by the arbitrary whims of all-powerful gods. Thales' reputation spread fast, far and wide. The discovery of a set of rules that governed the movement of the planets in the heavens also led some people to wonder what else in nature worked on similarly predictable lines. Thales' lifelong quest for a set of universal laws to explain nature was taken up by other philosophers, many of whom lived in Athens.

# What on Earth Happened?

## Greek philosophy

Socrates (470–399 BC) was a famous Athenian philosopher who also believed in a set of natural universal laws. Like Buddha (see page 136), Socrates thought a man's soul could be improved over time, but not through mastering stillness of the mind – rather the opposite. For Socrates the path to enlightenment involved the application of problem-solving reason, high-powered discussion and heated debate.

By about 460 BC debate, argument, rhetoric and oratory had become the chief virtues of civic life in Athenian society. For Socrates, these skills were at the core of his philosophical method. Nothing that he actually wrote has survived, but we know a great deal about him and his ideas thanks to his pupil Plato, who also became one of the most influential philosophers of all time.

Plato's most famous philosophical work, *The Republic*, features a debate about the best way to rule a human society. Plato also believed that what underpinned the universe was a reality that didn't originate from the traditional ragbag of Greek gods like Zeus, Apollo and Aphrodite, who inflicted their fancies on an unsuspecting world. Instead, Plato believed that the truth could be revealed through philosophical reasoning and contemplation. Therefore, in his description of an ideal society, it was philosopher-kings who ruled society, sharing the wisdom of their insights with their subjects.

## A Spartan experiment

One notion proposed by Plato was the suggestion that if man could successfully control nature by selectively breeding plants and animals then why shouldn't society apply the same techniques to humans? 'The brave man is to be selected for marriage more frequently than the rest so that as many children as possible may have such a man for their father.'

This radical idea was put into practice by the southern Greek city of Sparta, which from 431 to 404 BC led a league of city states locked in a vicious war against the growing power of Athens and her empire. The secret behind the power of this city, which eventually overthrew mighty Athens in 404 BC, was a prime example of how mankind was beginning to organize itself in experimental new ways. Sparta was a totalitarian military society at its most pure and powerful.

Lycurgus (*c.*700–630 BC), its legendary founder, decreed that baby boys born too weak to become soldiers should be abandoned and left to die on the desolate slopes of Mount Taygetos. All the others were sent off to a military training camp at the age of seven to learn to become fearless warriors. Boys were initiated into the camp only after running the gauntlet of older youths, who would flog them with whips, sometimes causing the weakest to die on the spot, thus furthering the selective breeding principle. Instead of being fed, the boys were encouraged to steal food. They were punished if they were caught – not for stealing, but for being clumsy enough to have been spotted.

Spartan soldiers, called hoplites, were expected to put the welfare of the city above duty to their families. They were trained in the discipline of the phalanx – a highly effective form of warfare in which troops were linked together into a human wall. Rectangular formations of tightly packed soldiers, at least four lines deep, with shields and spears locked closely together, were trained to march towards the enemy to the beat of pipes and drums, breaking into a run just before battle commenced. A phalanx required total loyalty and depended on every man in the fighting force. Just one drooping shield, like a weak link in a chain, could expose the whole formation to failure. The force with the strongest, most fearless soldiers, who pushed hardest from the rear, invariably won. Young soldiers were rewarded for military victory by being given the opportunity to couple with as many as twenty Spartan women, providing a powerful incentive to be brave in war. Failure on the battlefield was not an option. A hoplite returning from battle alive but without his shield was disowned by his family and sentenced to death.

Spartan society impressed not only some ancient philosophers like Plato but later ideologies such as the Hitler Youth Movement of the 1930s, where children were taught that their duty to the state was of greater importance than to the individual or the family (see page 279).

Spartan women were given a higher status in society than anywhere else in ancient Greece. By cultivating beauty, intelligence and strength in their females, the Spartans believed they could succeed in producing a master race. Men and women, both naked, trained for athletics championships alongside each other, with the women even participating in flogging contests to see who had the most endurance, an ordeal known as *diamastigosis*.

## The origin of the Olympic Games

With Greek social structures so completely based around physical fitness, selective breeding and military victory, it is no wonder that an athletics championship should have been established to test the limits of human physical prowess in a competitive context. By the fifth and sixth centuries BC the games had come to have enormous importance in Greek society. Each city state fielded its best athletes in the hope of winning the ultimate accolade in civic pride. Winners were immortalized with poems, statues and, the most prestigious honour of all, a crown made of olive leaves.

Like all empires, Sparta's dominance eventually waned. Its experiment in human engineering ultimately failed through a lack of popular support and a dwindling supply of willing and able males to keep its armies big and strong. But by about 380 BC another force was already marshalling itself to the north of ancient Greece – one which, although it put an end to the independence of the city states, proved instrumental in spreading across the world their various templates of how human civilizations could engage with nature, through the debates of democracy, the systems of science or the traumas of totalitarianism.

## Aristotle, the great Greek teacher

Greek philosophers were edging towards the radical idea that there were no gods or God who controlled the destiny of life on earth from some detached mountaintop; rather, it was man himself, who, thanks to his own brainpower, could decipher the laws of the universe to become master of all nature.

Supreme amongst such thinkers was Aristotle (384–322 BC), the scope of whose works was truly immense. They covered everything from speculations on the nature of the human soul to the physics of the universe, from city politics and personal ethics to the history of plants and animals, and from public speaking and poetry to music, memory and logic.

Aristotle combined what he considered the best of what he had learned from his teacher Plato and other Greek philosophers like Thales with everything he observed in the natural world. It led him to a single, profound conclusion: underneath all reality there was indeed a fundamental set of universal natural laws that explained everything to do with life, the universe and everything from human politics to the weather. To understand these rules of nature was to understand reality. The key was careful observation of the universe and its systems by good use of the human senses, and then using human reason and intellect to uncover the truth.

The question that Aristotle's scientific, rational view of the world provoked was this: in a mechanistic universe governed by rules, what place was there for old-fashioned, whimsical gods? His answer was simple. The rules of nature themselves were the very essence of all that is divine in the universe: 'For God is to us a law, impartial, admitting not to correction or change, and better I think and surer than those which are engraved upon tablets.'

Aristotle gave mankind the confidence to explore, discover and learn. But such insights would be useless hidden in the mind of one brilliant man, or stored in a rich patron's library. To fulfil their potential, these ideas needed a force to scatter them far and wide, giving as many human cultures as possible the chance to exert the power of human brains over nature's brawn.

## Alexander, the great Greek conqueror

As luck would have it, Aristotle's pupil the young Prince Alexander of Macedon was just the right man at just the right time. Quite possibly it was his great teacher's passion for the natural world that fired Alexander, impregnating him with a feverish determination to see everything in the world for himself, conquering whatever empires lay en route.

Alexander ascended to the throne of Macedonia in north Greece at the age of just twenty, in 336 BC. For the next thirteen years he led an army of 42,000 Greek soldiers on an extraordinary military adventure across Persia, Egypt and even into India (see plate 8). On his way Alexander famously undid the impossible-to-untie Gordian knot by slashing it with his sword and routed the Persian Emperor Darius III at the Battle of Issus in 333 BC. He then marched down the Mediterranean coast, laying siege to the city of Tyre, which he eventually took after seven months, clearing the way towards Egypt, where, thanks to the decline of Persian power, he was welcomed as a liberator and pronounced Pharaoh in 332 BC. Here Alexander founded the most famous of all the cities named after himself, Alexandria, establishing it as the main sea port linking Egypt with Greece, the maritime axis of a new and increasingly powerful Hellenic empire.

Eighteen months later Alexander left Egypt, marching back

to Persia, where again he defeated Darius, at the Battle of Gaugamela (see plate 8). This time the Persian King fled from the battlefield only to be murdered by his own troops in the mountains of Media. The way was now open for Alexander to conquer all Persia, first marching on Babylon, then Susa, the ancient Assyrian capital, and finally Persepolis, the magnificent royal home of the Persian Kings.

With the death of Darius and the submission of Egypt and Persia, Alexander's military goals had been accomplished. But still the warrior in him could not be controlled. Having sent many of his Greek soldiers back home, he now paid mercenaries to fight for him in a new imperial army, and set off on a three-year campaign to subjugate Scythia and Afghanistan before reaching the River Indus in northern India.

Despite Alexander's determination to cross the sacred River Ganges and march into the heart of India, his men had reached their limit. Eventually Alexander and a company of soldiers made their way back to Persia across deserts and plains. On the afternoon of 10 June 323 BC in the palace of Nebuchadnezzar II in Babylon Alexander died, probably of malaria. He was one month short of his thirty-third birthday.

Many historians have devoted their professional lives to the study of this man, yet no one really knows what drove him to try to conquer the world. Whatever his motivation, his conquests caused the Greek language to become the lingua franca of the entire Middle East and Egypt. Thousands of Greek people, some soldiers, others merchants, artisans, scientists and philosophers, moved abroad, taking with them their experimental world views. Of the seven wonders of the ancient world, five were Greek constructions – each one an awesome monument to these people's confidence in man's power over the natural world.

Roman love for all things Greek was particularly focused around the personality and career of Alexander, who after his death became antiquity's greatest role model. Roman emperors came to regard Alexander as the epitome of bravery, strength and courage.

## The Roman supremacy

Rome's rise and fall was like a human weather system as destructive as nature's most violent hurricanes. This enormous whirlwind was powered by three essential ingredients: grain, booty and slaves. Once the storm was over the landscape of Europe looked quite different, while the legacy of what made the ferocious ancient Roman Empire so powerful helped shape the rest of European history to come.

Roman legends give a clue as to what made these people tick because there is so much similarity between them and the mythological tales from Greece. The Romans were brilliant copycats. Infantry tactics, mythology, art and architecture came from Greece, while their heavy cavalry and expertise in horses came from Persia. When the Romans wanted to attack the most powerful maritime city in the region, the Phoenicians' Carthage, they simply captured one of its ships and within the space of about two months built themselves an entire fleet of more than a hundred similar ships from scratch.

An early threat to the rise of Rome came in the form of a famous Carthaginian general called Hannibal, who in 218 BC marched an army of mercenary soldiers and African war elephants all the way up Spain and across the Alps. His surprise attack from the north led to several victories, the most famous being at the Battle of Cannae (216 BC) near Apulia in south-east Italy, where Hannibal's cavalry encircled the massed ranks of Roman infantry, cutting them to pieces. In the end, though, Roman persistence paid off. Knowing that Hannibal didn't have the equipment to breach the walls of the city of Rome itself, the Roman forces just waited, shadowing his armies, watching his tactics, but always avoiding battle. Meanwhile, another Roman army, under the leadership of a young commander, Scipio, defeated the Carthaginian forces in Spain and crossed the short stretch of sea to Africa, where they marched towards Carthage itself. Hannibal had no choice but to return home to try to save his own city but there he was defeated at the Battle of Zama in 202 BC.

By this time the Romans had become a highly efficient war machine, expanding their frontiers all round the Mediterranean and adapting their tactics to incorporate cavalry and ships. With each conquest they brought home huge hoards of booty in the form of treasure and prisoners of war who they turned into slaves. Plunder paid for a fabulously rich lifestyle for Rome's citizens, while imported slaves provided free labour in their homes, on the farms, in the city streets and on the many enormous construction projects that quickly turned Rome into the most advanced artificial world on earth.

By 146 BC a succession of military victories had brought Greece into the Roman Empire, followed in 129 BC by Asia Minor. From here the Romans had the perfect bridgehead to launch a series of campaigns in the Near East, conquering Armenia, Lebanon, Syria and Judaea by 64 BC under the leadership of the general Pompey, each time adding further riches to their economy in the form of gold, silver and slaves. To the south the Roman general Octavian, who later became the Emperor Caesar Augustus, added the jewel in the crown – the conquest of Egypt in 30 BC. With its almost limitless supplies of grain from the Nile Valley, the Egyptian bread basket provided the perfect finishing touch, supplying unlimited quantities of food throughout the Roman Empire.

But at the centre of the Roman grip on power lay an intractable problem. What does a civilization that is built on military conquest and financial growth do when it finds that, for various reasons, it cannot expand any more? Gaul (modern-day France) had been brought under Roman control by Julius Caesar in 46 BC and Britain was finally subjugated after the failed revolt of Boudicca at the Battle of Watling Street in 61 AD. But further expansion towards Scotland proved profitless and eventually the Romans built a wall to keep out the violent Picts. In the north-east the Romans were forced to post several legions along the natural border of the Rhine/Danube Rivers in an effort to contain Germanic tribes such as the Goths and Vandals, who, despite numerous attempts, they found impossible to bring under control. To the east a new Persian Empire had overthrown the Greek dynasties which succeeded Alexander. Their *Azatan* knights successfully held the Romans back from the rich lands of the Middle East. Then there were nature's barriers. To the west, after Spain, there was the edge of the world – the apparently endless Atlantic Ocean. To the south, beyond Carthage and Egypt, there was just dry, barren, lifeless desert.

The story of the later Roman Empire is the tale of how a human civilization fixed on violence and growth managed to hold itself together despite reaching expansion's elastic limit. Thanks to a variety of ingenious and often brutal strategies the ruling Roman oligarchy was able to sustain its luxurious standard of living for an impressive 300 years *after* the major phase of expansion ended.

Imperial Rome's first survival tactic was political. Tyrannical rule was necessary to force through a rapid succession of reforms needed to hold this violent society together. At least 40 per cent of the capital city's massive population were slaves. They made a doomed attempt at breaking the grip of imperial and dictatorial government when a leader called Spartacus, an escaped Greek gladiator, rallied them to rebellion in 79 BC. After some initial successes they were eventually routed by the general Marcus Crassus in southern Italy. More than 6,000 were crucified, their crosses set up along the 130-kilometre stretch of road from Capua to Rome. Crassus ordered that their bodies never be removed. There they remained as rotten carcasses for many years, a gruesome memorial of what happened to slaves who disobeyed their masters.

Other strategies were also deployed by Roman rulers to keep the huge population of their capital city under firm control. One tactic was to divert the poor and enslaved into building projects to provide improved amenities for the well off. With this policy the Roman Empire rapidly became the fountain from which mammoth engineering works were undertaken all over its conquered lands. Many of its ruins survive today across Europe, North Africa and the Near East.

Exploiting labour from slaves and the poor gave birth to Europe's first comprehensive road network – essential infrastructure for keeping order and control in an empire that at its biggest, in about 100 AD, covered over five million square kilometres. Slaves, supervised by soldiers, built more than 85,000 kilometres of road, most of it in straight lines, making man's first long cuts of bricks, cement and concrete into Europe's supple surfaces. Everything that got in the way, from forests to farms, was razed to the ground.

Spectacular forms of mass-market entertainment were another part of the system for keeping the overpopulated Roman capital governable. Riches won in suppressing a Jewish revolt against Roman rule that began in 66 AD financed the cost of building Rome's giant Flavian amphitheatre (the Colosseum), which was constructed under the Emperor Vespasian.

When it was opened in 80 AD, this theatre could seat more than 50,000 spectators – comparable to many large modern sports stadiums. A new Emperor, Titus, celebrated the opening of this temple to entertainment by giving the people of Rome a hundred days of spectacular drama in the form of mock battles, gladiator fights, animal hunts and executions. According to the contemporary historian Dio Cassius, more than 11,000 wild animals were killed in these games. Many of them, such as lions, crocodiles, elephants, giraffes, panthers, leopards, hippos, rhinos and ostriches, were imported from outside the Empire. Attendance was free. The

Emperor came to the games so his people could admire him in all his glory. He was only too happy to see the most violent of the Roman underclass gratified and in one location, safe under the watchful eye of imperial troops.

## Jesus, the subversive Jewish carpenter's son

In the midst of this hurricane of indulgence, exploitation and violence there was a miraculous moment of calm. As if it were the eye of the imperial storm, almost exactly halfway through Rome's dominance of the Mediterranean world, a son was born to a Jewish carpenter and his wife in a place called Bethlehem, a town situated just south of Jerusalem. His name was Jesus.

Like the Buddha some 500 years before, Jesus was an enlightened charismatic who made a virtue out of poverty and lectured on the benefits of non-violence. His message was simple. Be peaceful. Love your neighbour as yourself. If someone strikes you on one cheek do not hit back but offer them the other. Do not worship false idols such as money or material possessions and, above all, be humble – for one day the meek will inherit the earth.

Jesus's followers saw him perform miracles and came to regard him as the earthly incarnation of God as prophesied by Isaiah and others in the Jewish Torah. One of the most deeply held Jewish beliefs was that at the time of the covenants between God, Abraham and Moses the Israelites were identified as God's chosen people. Yet here was a man whose followers claimed he was King of the Jews and who offered the prospect of eternal salvation to anyone and everyone who believed in him, regardless of their colour, race or creed!

Jesus was given over to the Roman governor of the province of Judaea, Pontius Pilate, as a heretic, and despite Pilate's misgivings was condemned to die on a cross like a common criminal. His body mysteriously disappeared three days after being placed in a tomb and his disciples began to see visions of him. They wrote about these miraculous events, which they called the Resurrection, and believed it was their divine mission to spread the good news about the son of God coming down to earth and dying on a cross so that everyone who believed in him might have everlasting life. They set about establishing a religion in his name.

## How Christianity was adopted by Rome

The early Christian Church developed a huge popular following because it filled a spiritual vacuum inherent in the materialistic, brutal and unequal society of the Roman Empire. Its main appeal was to non-Jewish poor people, women and slaves. Everyday life in the Roman Empire was proof enough for these people that the pantheon of Greek/Roman gods had nothing much to offer in terms of spiritual nourishment or hope for the future. The idea that the son of God had come to free them and offer them eternal salvation in his Kingdom of Heaven sounded a lot more promising.

Another community attracted towards Jesus's teaching were those keen to establish a new hierarchy to resist the seemingly infinite power of Roman society. Greek thinkers who followed the idea of a universal force of nature first put forward by Socrates, Plato and Aristotle found the concept of a single universal God who was open to all people rather compelling. The biggest problem for them was how to reconcile this all-pervasive divine force with a carpenter's son from Galilee whose followers claimed he was the incarnation of God.

The problem wasn't finally settled until after Christianity was legalized in the Roman Empire by the Emperor Galerius in 311 AD in a desperate bid to contain the increasing threat the new religion posed to Rome's imperial authority. In the end the idea of the Trinity provided the answer. It combined the Jewish God of the

Old Testament as the Father with the person of Jesus Christ as his Son and the divine platonic or natural force pervading all things as the Holy Spirit. The Father, Son and Holy Spirit make up the Trinity that still marks out Christianity as distinct from other religions. This doctrine was finally ratified and codified into an official creed at the Council of Nicaea in 325 AD, under the auspices of the first truly Christian Roman Emperor Constantine.

In 330 AD Constantine established a new capital for the eastern portion of the Empire, which became known as Constantinople (now Istanbul). Here he promoted Christianity by building churches and forbade pagan temples. Despite this, most of his imperial staff remained pagans, showing that whatever his own personal beliefs Constantine, like the Persian Cyrus the Great, was a tolerant ruler.

But Roman religious understanding was not to last long. One of this empire's final legacies was to throw out all notions of religious freedom and instead adopt Christianity as a compulsory state creed. This act, sanctioned by Emperor Theodosius I (ruled 379–95 AD), turned the brief light of toleration into a fury of indignation against all non-Christian faiths. Under the influence of Ambrose, Bishop of Milan, Theodosius outlawed all variations of the Christian faith except for the Trinitarian beliefs set down in the Nicene Creed. Bishops who disagreed were expelled, many of them fleeing to the more tolerant Sassanid regime in Persia. Traditional Graeco-Roman paganism was outlawed too. The eternal flame in the Temple of Vesta in the Roman Forum was extinguished and the Vestal Virgins disbanded. In their place came the Christian world's first law against witchcraft. Finally, in 393 AD, Theodosius abolished the highly cherished Olympic Games, since, he claimed, they were a relic of the pagan past.

The Roman Empire finally collapsed due to a variety of destabilizing forces including invasions by Germanic tribes, the arrival of the Huns from the Mongolian steppes and resistance by the early Christians. Historians usually date its fall to 476 AD, when the Germanic chieftain Odoacer deposed the last Emperor of the Western Empire, Romulus Augustus.

What made Roman civilization so remarkable in the classical world was its ability to survive so long, despite its addiction to the constant economic growth needed to feed the insatiable appetites of its rich ruling class. It ruthlessly suppressed the poor by enlisting them as soldiers for its armies or slave labourers for its engineering projects. It controlled its huge populations through mass-entertainment programmes and propaganda. It exploited the earth's natural mineral resources when further military expansion proved impossible, and it hijacked a minority religious sect to incorporate a new state religion with a fierce intolerance for anything its leaders deemed as heresy.

Such tactics became powerful templates for the future. They were subject to repeated reincarnation in various guises, initially across the fractious lands of Europe and the arid deserts of the Middle East, but later throughout the entire world. Thanks to the rise and fall of the Roman Empire, the relationship between human civilizations and nature lurched into a new phase that helped set the stage for the beginning of the modern world.

# 9

# Natives and the Americas

## (1500 BC–1521 AD)

*How people living outside civilizations
maintained their veneration for
nature, while others in the Americas
grew dependent on maize*

DESPITE THE MAYHEM and violence of the Mediterranean
world and the massive rise of urban human populations around
the Mediterranean and in India and China, human beings in much
of the rest of the earth were still carrying on much as ever they
had. One estimate suggests that of the 200 million or so people
living 2,000 years ago, roughly seventy million still had a Stone
Age lifestyle. Most of these people lived outside Europe and Asia.
Their beliefs were based on nature as the essence of everything that
mattered for their well-being and lasting survival.

Living within nature is historically mankind's most robust form of
existence (see page 83). The art was learned over millions of years of
cohabiting with animals in the forests. The most resilient and ancient
of all human societies have lived this way. Typically, they are not based
on fighting nature or harnessing its forces to improve material standards
of living. Nor do they tend to rely on over-exploiting the natural

world. Today, it is only at the very edge of human civilizations that a few of these ancient systems hang on, mostly as fragments, but at the time of the fall of the Roman Empire in about 476 AD, many of them still flourished.

One of the most ancient natural human habitats is in Australia. We know *Homo sapiens* arrived there more than 40,000 years ago, thanks to the discovery of Mungo Man. This poorly preserved skeleton, found at the bottom of a dry lake in New South Wales on 26 February 1974, is of an old man, about five feet seven inches tall, lying on his back. He had been sprinkled with red ochre, showing the existence even then of elaborate burial traditions.

Exactly what route humans took to Australia is hotly disputed. Land bridges are known to have connected Australia and New Guinea during the last Ice Age, although recent genetic evidence suggests that people came from a broad arc stretching across Africa, India, Japan, eastern Russia and even North America, as well as the closer Polynesian islands. These people believed that all living things shared a common spirit, a belief which has been called dreamtime since the beginning of the twentieth century. Animals were the ancestral beings of mankind, and their movements even shaped the earth itself. The Aboriginals' creation story, called the dreaming, explains how the land was formed. All things, animate and inanimate, share the same dreamtime spirit. There are literally thousands of dreaming stories in Aboriginal folklore, covering all aspects of their relationship with nature and other living things.

Although the Aboriginal way of life was mostly untouched for thousands of years, archaeologists have recently discovered that by 500 AD some changes had begun to creep in as a result of contact with other encroaching civilizations. For example, the dingo, the Australian wild dog, was introduced from about 1500 BC by traders from New Guinea. These dogs had a significant impact on Australia's ancient ecosystem, and are thought to have been responsible for driving several species of marsupial carnivores to extinction. The Aboriginals adopted them as companions, domesticating them to help them hunt. The introductions of eel traps, fish hooks made from shells and the development of smaller, more intricate stone tools, also help account for an overall growth in population, perhaps to as many as a million people by the time of the arrival of the first European settlers in 1788 (see page 268).

It is highly likely that the Australian Aboriginals' deep respect for all life and the sacred earth helped them survive a series of enormous climatic changes during their 40,000 years of history. One important survival strategy was to divide small Aboriginal clans into different groups, with each one revering a particular animal or plant as its defining totem. A series of non-contact taboos between men and women of the same clan evolved, ensuring that marriages occurred between groups rather than within a single group, thus avoiding potentially disastrous incestuous matches. Reverence for specific natural resources also meant that in times of scarcity it was less likely for any one species to be unwittingly hunted or gathered to extinction. In this way Aboriginal people maximized their chances of survival in extreme conditions, and through marriage ties between groups established a network of obligations between clans to care for others and share precious resources.

Totems and taboos were not limited to native Australians. Across the Pacific Ocean, amongst the jungle tribes of the Amazon in South America, a system of living with nature evolved that was every bit as ingenious and resilient. The Huaorani were an Amazonian tribe whose responsible use of forest resources has few modern parallels. Their success was founded on an extraordinary expertise in carefully using animals, plants and trees to support a simple forest hunter-gathering way of life.

For these people the animals of the forest had a spiritual as well as a physical existence. They believed that when a person died, his spirit was challenged by an enormous python which guarded the domain of the dead. Victims were returned to the world as animal or insect spirits. Such beliefs gave these people a deep respect for non-human living things as previous human incarnations. Their diet was based on hunting only certain types of animals, such as monkeys and birds, leaving the rest of the ecosystem balanced, with sufficient predators and prey to avoid the overpopulation or extinction of other species.

The belief that animals and plants as well as humans have souls is known as animism. It is striking how common and how widespread such beliefs were before the major monotheistic, people-centred religions of Judaism, Christianity and Islam took root. Animistic beliefs account for a great deal of the considerate and often cautious relationships between man and nature found throughout most indigenous peoples still living in the world today.

## About the interconnectedness of all things

Animism includes the belief that all forms of life and other natural materials are inextricably connected by an invisible force or spirit. A vast trove of detailed information about indigenous societies and their animistic beliefs was the subject of *The Golden Bough*, written around the turn of the twentieth century by a Scottish scholar called Sir James Frazer (1854–1941). This massive study of myth and religion caused outrage when it was first published because it compared the Christian story of Jesus as the Lamb of God, and the timing of Christian festivals such as Christmas, Easter and All Saints' Day, with heathen festivals.

Frazer gathered evidence from hundreds of missionaries and officials throughout the British Empire who were working with, or ruling over, many native tribes. The book is packed with examples of animistic beliefs – an all-encompassing ideological glue that once stretched across the entire globe, from the Celtic druids of Europe to the Aboriginals in Australia, with Asian, American, African, Middle Eastern, Polynesian and even Arctic tribes echoing a similar belief in the one spirit force that touches all nature.

On the Polynesian island of Timor, in the South Pacific, it was sometimes deemed necessary for one tribe to wage war against another – perhaps for self-defence, or owing to a dispute over resources. When a tribe's victorious warriors returned home the leader of the expedition was confined to a specially prepared hut, where for two months he would undergo thorough bodily and spiritual purification. During this time he was forbidden to visit his wife or feed himself – food had to be put into his mouth by another person. Sacrifices were offered to appease the souls of their dead enemies, whose heads had been taken as a means of communicating with their spirits. Part of the ceremony consisted of a dance accompanied by a song, recorded by Frazer: ' "Be not angry," they sang, "because your head is here with us; had we been less lucky our heads might now have been exposed in your village. We have offered the sacrifice to appease you. Your spirit may now rest and leave us in peace …" ' It was through elaborate customs and taboos that violence was usually limited to being a last resort and, thanks also to such taboos, the chances of its escalation were minimized by the necessity of an expedition leader undergoing the laborious process of purifying his body and soul.

Tribes living so close to nature ensured that nothing ever went to waste. The Sami are a people who still live in northern Europe, on the fringes of the Arctic in Finland, Norway and Sweden. At the end of the last Ice Age they moved northwards from central Europe, pursuing herds of reindeer which dwelt in the forests that had replaced snow and ice. By 500 AD the Sami had learned how to domesticate reindeer to supply them with just about everything they needed for survival – from dragging sleighs to providing meat and milk. Clothes and tents were made from their skins, arrowheads and needles from their bones.

Sharing resources between all living things, animals or people, was central to the lives of animistic people. Some of the most common taboos didn't prohibit things at all – rather they prompted obligations of generosity. The Penan tribe belongs to the Dayak people of Borneo. They are thought to have been part of the Austronesian expansion which took place about 1000 BC, eventually leading to the populating of Polynesia. A distinctive element of their culture is the requirement of always sharing wisely. This is called *molong*, a word meaning 'never take more than necessary'. To *molong* a sago palm is to harvest the trunk with care, ensuring that the tree will sucker up from the roots. *Molong* is climbing a tree to gather fruit rather than cutting it down, or harvesting only the largest fronds of the rattan, leaving the smaller shoots so that they reach their proper size in another year. Whenever the Penan *molong* a fruit tree they mark it with a knife – a sign that means 'Please share wisely.' The greatest taboo in Penan society is *see hun* – a failure to share.

The tougher the living conditions, the more generous the human spirit. In Timbuktu, a city in present-day Mali that lies on the southern edge of the scorching Sahara desert, there's an ancient tradition that still survives amongst some camel herders. It demands that any guest be given what he needs – even if it means slaughtering the last goat whose milk feeds the nomads' children, or sharing the last drop of drinking water.

Some cultures venerated trees as much as animals, and for them the forests were the holiest of holies on earth. They were the sacred places of Celtic European pagans long before the onset of Christianity gave them a new, more abstract God to worship. The pagan beliefs of the Nordic people, who came from southern Scandinavia, the Netherlands and northern Germany, led them to worship their gods in woods, not temples.

Wyrd, from which the modern English word 'weird' originates, was an animistic concept of fate common to pagan beliefs. It explained the interconnectedness of all things, linking past actions to future events. Yggdrasil is a gigantic mythological ash tree that connects the nine worlds of Nordic cosmology. Its trunk forms the axis of the world. Beneath one of its roots lies the sacred Well of Wyrd, next to which reside the three Norns who engrave the Wyrd on the bark of the tree and look after it. So revered were trees that it was customary to offer sacrifices (both human and animal) to the gods by hanging them from tree branches.

Evidence of such rituals emerged in 1950, when a well-preserved body, now known as Tollund Man, dating back to the fourth century BC, was discovered in a Danish peat bog. A rope made of two twisted leather thongs was drawn tight around his neck and throat and then coiled like a snake over his shoulder and down his back. Copious quantities of a hallucinogenic fungus called ergot were found in his stomach, leading some experts to believe he was strung up in the branches of a nearby tree as part of a ritualistic sacrifice before being buried in the mud.

Animism was mankind's natural global system of beliefs. Oral taboos gave human societies that did not dabble with agriculture sufficient strength, resilience and adaptability to survive the harshest of natural disasters. Tribes that believed in what most modern people consider magic or superstition fostered a spirit of resourcefulness, conservation and a hatred of waste that modern societies are only just beginning to appreciate should be, at the very least, second nature.

## Civilizations in the Americas

Imagine an alien scientist looking down on his latest and greatest experiment – planet earth. More than three billion years have passed since he first sowed the seeds of life, wondering what on earth would happen and how they would take root. Now, literally millions of different life forms have emerged to sustain and take advantage of the planet's living systems. So far, so good.

# Natives and the Americas

Right at the end of this epic horticultural experiment, just a tenth of a second before midnight when seen on the scale of a twenty-four-hour clock, he notices that in one part of the world a certain species, a biped ape called *Homo sapiens*, has made a rather sudden and dramatic change of lifestyle. By mastering the art of mass food production, this species has started to build enormous new nests, in the form of cities and civilizations, and in the process has been clearing vast tracts of natural forests for fields in which to cultivate crops and keep animals. What's more, his experiment with agriculture has led to an explosive growth of populations which shows no sign of abating. As a result, a great deal of innovation, aggression and killing has emerged in a vicious competition for resources and power. Perhaps, thinks the alien, it would be a good idea to conduct a control experiment on the other side of the planet, just to see if the same thing happens there ...

Some 5,000 years after adverse climate conditions caused the Natufians and others in the Fertile Crescent to dabble with agriculture (see page 95), hunter-gathering people in the Americas were just beginning to reap their first annual harvests. They had absolutely no idea that people on the other side of the world were building huge civilizations based on crops such as wheat, barley and rice, and farm animals like pigs, sheep, cows and goats. Thebes, Jerusalem, Jericho and Babylon were completely unknown to people in North, Central and South America.

For thousands of years these people lived by sharing in the state of nature. Native American people faced several challenges that made their attempts at civilization like no others. In south-central Mexico, where the river valleys provided the right soils for cultivation and the climate was conducive to growing annual crops, the only grass capable of domestication was a rather weedy and unappetizing wild bush called *teosinte* which grew along the banks of the Balsas River. In this part of the world there was no wild wheat, barley or rice.

171

# What on Earth Happened?

To begin with *teosinte* had just five to ten seeds, each of which was encased in a hard shell designed by nature to survive the most acidic of animal stomachs. By choosing those plants with abnormally numerous seeds and those with the softest shells, the patient people of Central America eventually engineered the crop we know as maize or corn. It took as long as 5,000 years of painstaking artificial selection to convert unappetizing *teosinte* into a nutritious cob suitable for harvesting on an annual basis.

By 1100 BC a few Native Americans in central Mexico had begun to start their own experiment in living in a settled society. Stores, houses and fixed settlements were followed by terraced fields, annual harvests and seasonal cycles. Enough food was produced to allow former hunters and gatherers to become priests, rulers and artisans, freed up to worship, administer and trade.

The enormous and lengthy struggle to come up with easy-to-cultivate crops reaped huge rewards for these people, as it has for posterity. The labour of these New World agriculturalists eventually produced: chillies, sunflowers, pumpkins, peanuts, peppers, squashes, beans, courgettes, marrows, aubergines and avocados. Perhaps more significant today are tomatoes, potatoes and cacao beans for chocolate (the word comes from the Aztec *xocolatl*). Between them these crops, all of which originate in Central and South America, account for over half of all food grown throughout the modern world.

Early Native American agriculturalists also cultivated non-food crops like cotton, which they used to construct fishing nets and to make clothing. These were also the first people to extract latex from rubber trees, used to manufacture items that played an important role in their religious rituals. None of these crops spread outside Central and South America until Europeans arrived in the early 1500s.

The first settled people in the New World that have any kind of recorded history came from Mexico. They are known as the Olmecs, meaning 'rubber people'. At first, their civilization looked very similar to those of other early settlers in Egypt and Mesopotamia. Indeed, their achievements were almost identical. Like the Egyptians and Babylonians, Olmecs developed a passion for arithmetic, driven by their desire to know when was the best time to plant and harvest crops. They used base 20 as their standard for counting. It was the considerable achievement of these Olmec people that they made the world's first ever known use of the integer zero, allowing any number to be expressed simply by placing figures in a series of rows, with zero as a place holder.

The sky was their clock and, like the people of Mesopotamia and Egypt, the Olmecs believed that the planets were driven by gods. Everything in their world moved in cycles depending on the sun, moon and planets, especially the bright morning star of Venus. Their annual calendar of 365 days (which had twenty months of eighteen days each, and five special days left over) was the most precise in the world, and the Olmecs are now thought to have been the first people to develop writing in the New World. Recently, road builders found a stone block in a pile of debris which shows sixty-two symbols of an ancient script, some of them representing animals, plants, insects and fish, which probably dates back as far as 900 BC.

Giant stone heads were hewn out of volcanic rock. Seventeen have been discovered to date, most near San Lorenzo and La Venta. Nearly four metres high and weighing up to forty tonnes, these were the Olmecs' equivalent of the Egyptian Sphinx. The gods the Olmecs worshipped were based on representations found in nature and are not so different from the jackal-headed Anubis, Egyptian god of the dead. There was the feathered serpent and the rain spirit, represented in later Central American civilizations as Quetzalcoatl (Aztec) and Chaac (Mayan). Snakes were highly symbolic because it was believed they represented an umbilical connection between the earth and the spirit worlds.

# What on Earth Happened?

## *Of Mayans and maize*

The first Mayan settlements emerged in about 1000 BC, south of the Olmecs along the Yucatán Peninsula. Large-scale towns and cities, such as Tikal, Palenque, Copán and Calakmul, rose between 200 BC and 800 AD, rivalling settlements in the rest of the world both in size and sophistication.

The story of this civilization remained completely hidden from the modern world until 1839, when an American traveller and writer, John Lloyd-Stephens, went in search of ancient ruined cities that Mexican locals claimed lay buried deep in the jungle. With his English architect companion Frederick Catherwood, he discovered a number of ancient Mayan cities, including Copán and Palenque. Thanks to their accounts, historians have since been piecing together evidence of the people who built these cities, and what it was that made them tick.

Unfortunately, the task has been made a lot more complicated than it should have been. Although as many as 10,000 texts have been recovered from stone engravings and buildings, tens of thousands of precious books, written on paper made from the bark of fig trees, have been lost. The zeal of Christian Spanish invaders in the early sixteenth century, who regarded all Native American writing as the work of the devil, means that only three of the many original paper texts (called codices) now survive. One priest, Friar Diego de Landa, personally oversaw the destruction of hundreds of books and more than 5,000 precious works of art at a ceremonial bonfire on 12 July 1562. He later wrote about the event and the effect it had on the native people: 'We found a large number of books ... and, as they contained nothing in which were not to be seen as superstition and lies of the devil, we burned them all. Which they [the natives] regretted to an amazing degree, and which caused them much affliction.'

One of the most precious surviving documentary sources, the

# Natives and the Americas

*Popol Vuh*, was fortuitously written down by an unknown Spanish missionary in the 1540s. It sets out native beliefs that had been passed down orally over many generations. It reveals how crops lay at the very root of Mayan beliefs about how the world was created. Three divine creators in the form of water-dwelling feathered serpents decided to create humans to keep them company. First they tried to make them out of mud, but that didn't work. Next they used wood, but that also proved unsuccessful. Finally, 'true people' were modelled out of maize, their flesh made of white and yellow corn and their arms and legs of corn meal.

This creation myth reveals why Central American civilizations evolved in very different ways from those on the other side of the world. The survival of their peoples depended completely on crops like maize, for the simple reason that they had no large domestic mammals. Since the arrival of humans at the end of the last Ice Age, nothing much larger than a turkey had survived (see page 86).

There were no pastoral nomadic people, like those on the Eurasian steppes, whose lives were built on tending domesticated herds of animals while constantly moving from place to place. The constant harassment such people inflicted on the settled civilizations of the Middle East, Europe and Asia never occurred in the New World of the Americas. There were no major military imbalances here – no haves versus have-nots – because no one had the ability to travel quickly on horseback to use the tactical advantages of surprise, height and speed in battle.

Carts were never invented, because there were no large animals suitable for domestication to pull them. No one had any use for the wheel, which although it has been found in Native American toys, was never deployed in real life. No wheels meant no gears, no pulleys or other civil engineering tools like treadmills, used by the Greeks and Romans to build their massive lighthouses, waterwheels and aqueducts, all of which were designed to make their worlds less vulnerable to the unpredictable forces of nature.

Without the arms race between nomadic and settled people that caused wave upon wave of war and destruction across Europe and Asia, these people never discovered how to smelt iron. Nothing so strong was necessary. Gold and silver were theirs in abundance, and copper too. These metals' softness and suppleness made them ideal for crafting long-lasting jewellery and other artefacts for religious worship and ornamentation.

The effects of these differences between the New World and the Old became more profound as the centuries rolled by, not that Native Americans had any inkling that they were militarily inferior to others until Spanish explorers arrived in the early sixteenth century (see page 235). Without horses, chariots, roads and wheels, the relationship between these civilizations and the natural world travelled on a unique trajectory. Perhaps the history of Central America represents what might have happened to the Egyptian civilization were it not for the invasion of the Hyksos in 1674 BC, which dragged those ancient people reluctantly into the wheel world (see page 112).

## Desperately seeking rain

For many years historians regarded Native Americans as essentially peaceful peoples because archaeological evidence suggests that until about 1000 AD most towns and cities in Central and South America were unfortified. It is now apparent that there was a much darker side to their way of life. Unable to rely on the enormous benefits of animal power, these people were totally dependent on their annual harvests of maize and other crops. Traditionally it was the king's duty to convince the gods to bring sufficient rain. Government policy was therefore fixed on finding effective ways of contacting the spirit world to curry its favour.

The Olmecs came up with a unique form of dialogue with the spirit world which also dates the historical origins of competitive sport. It was constructed around a ball game called *ulama*. Dozens of prehistoric ball courts dating back to 1400 BC have been excavated in ancient cities all over Central America. The oldest yet discovered is at Paso de la Amada. It is approximately eighty metres long and eight metres wide.

Ancient rubber balls have been found perfectly preserved in swampy sacrificial bogs alongside other religious offerings, suggesting the game had a religious purpose. The object was to score by bouncing the ball through one of two vertical stone rings up to six metres above each end of the court. Two teams of between two and five players would try to accomplish this using their hips, thighs, forearms and heads, but without touching the ball with either their hands or feet. Hip belts, knee pads, headdresses and protective masks were all part of the players' kit, and were often adorned with symbolic figures and pictures of the gods.

Although the game was sometimes played for fun, championships were usually held during religious festivals, when contests between rival kingdoms and states would be fought, quite literally, to the death. The members of the losing side were ritualistically sacrificed to the gods, their bodies buried underneath the court and their skulls sometimes turned into cores around which new rubber balls could be crafted. For the Mayans and their successors the Aztecs, this game symbolized a battle between the lords of the underworld and the peoples of the earth.

Kings and their priests gambled everything on their efforts to please the gods to ensure there was sufficient rain for their crops. The lengths to which they would go were horrifically revealed by a series of excavations that began in 1895. In that year the American archaeologist and diplomat Edward Thompson purchased, for seventy-five dollars, a Mexican plantation that he knew included the ruins of the sacred Mayan city of Chichen Itza.

The focus of his attention was the Sacred Cenote, a ninety-metre-long sacrificial pool that the Mayans believed provided a portal to the spirit world, possibly because the Yucatàn Peninsula is composed of porous limestone, which makes naturally occurring lakes and pools extremely rare.

Between 1904 and 1911 Thompson and his team recovered more than 30,000 objects from the pool, first by dredging it and then by donning diving suits and fumbling in the pitch dark twenty metres below the water's surface. Among the thousands of objects recovered were knives, sticks, bells, plates, jugs, figurines, jewellery and ornaments.

Among Thompson's discoveries was a sacrificial knife with a handle carved into the shape of two writhing rattlesnakes, which was used to gouge out the still-beating hearts of human victims. A gold plate dating to *c.*900 AD shows a Toltec warrior wearing an eagle headdress sacrificing a Mayan captive. His costume signifies a descending bird of prey. In his left hand he holds the sacrificial knife, while in his right he grasps the freshly extracted heart of his victim. Four assistants can be seen splaying the victim over the sacrificial stone slab. One looks directly outwards towards you – the witness.

Thompson found the bones of more than forty-two victims in the small lake. Half of them are estimated to have been younger than twenty when they were sacrificed, and fourteen were probably under twelve. The Mayans believed that the younger the victim, the more pleased the gods would be, because younger souls were considered purer. By the time of the Aztec dominion (*c.*1248–1521 AD) child sacrifice was especially common in times of drought. If sacrifices were not given to Tlaloc, the Aztec god of water, the rains would not come and the crops would not grow. Tlaloc required the tears of the young to wet the earth to help bring rain. As a result, priests are said to have made children cry before their ritual sacrifice, sometimes by pulling out their nails. The Mayans' desperation for rain lay at the heart of the reason why, by about 900 AD, their civilization had fallen into decline. Increasingly severe droughts, exacerbated by the effects of deforestation, soil erosion and intensive farming, led to starvation, invasions and violent contests with neighbouring people over scarce natural resources.

## The rise and fall of the Aztecs

In 1428 the Aztecs formed an alliance of three city states – Tenochtitlan, Texcoco and Tlacopan – centred in the valley of Mexico. This was the final native Central American civilization before European invaders arrived in the 1520s. It stretched from coast to coast, except for a small area to the south-east called the Kingdom of Tlaxcalteca. This state allied with the Spanish in 1521 to help destroy the Aztec King Moctezuma, bringing the history of independent indigenous American civilizations to a close (see page 238). Better access to remaining resources was at the heart of the Aztec triple alliance, which redoubled its efforts to get the gods on side by increasing the number of human sacrifices to prodigous levels. Aztec rulers such as Ahuitzotl (1486–1503) even went to war with neighbouring states specifically to acquire additional prisoners to use as fodder for sacrifices – conflicts known to history as the Flower Wars.

New buildings were erected in the magnificent Aztec island capital Tenochtitlan, which rose out of an enormous lake and was connected to the mainland by a giant retractable causeway. This remarkable metropolis lay on the site of the current Mexico City, although the lake has now been drained to make way for modern buildings. Little remains of the ancient city, which was destroyed by Spanish invaders in 1521 (see page 238).

The Aztecs believed that the sixty-metre-high Great Pyramid they built at the heart of the city would ensure that Tlaloc, god of rain and fertility, and Huitzilopochtli, god of war and the sun, looked more kindly on them. Each god had its own temple on top of the giant stepped structure. Consecration rituals for the Great Pyramid's two gods in 1487 were reported to have involved several thousand human sacrifices in the hope of persuading the gods to send more rain.

## From Nazcas to Incas

Other civilizations appeared along the coastal regions of South America because living by agriculture in the heavily forested interior was simply too difficult. Early Peruvian cultures such as the Nazca (*c.*300 BC–800 AD) and the Moche (*c.*100–800 AD) shared many cultural habits with the Central Americans further north. Gold and silver were panned from rivers flowing down from the vast Andes mountains and traded for Mexican maize. Commercial contact led to the exchange of similar systems of religious belief.

The Nazca were responsible for what are still regarded as almost superhuman depictions of their animal gods. On a 500-square-kilometre plateau these people created hundreds of perfectly straight lines and geometric patterns by painstakingly brushing the arid sand and grit to one side. Look down on the landscape from an aeroplane and more than seventy enormous pictures of animals, insects and humans reveal themselves, some of them as much as 270 metres long. Look at them from the ground, and nothing can be seen but paths in the dust. How on earth could these people have constructed such art (called geoglyphs) without being able to see what they were creating from above? It's one of history's big mysteries.

The most likely reason why the Nazca created these enormous images is that, as for the peoples of Central America, communicating with the gods was at the heart of everything that mattered. The night sky was their audience chamber and the arid ground their advertising board. Pictures of monkeys, spiders, hummingbirds and lizards were all gifts to the gods, offered in exchange for sufficient quantities of water so their crops could grow.

The Moche people lived at the same time as the Nazca. They were farmers who left an excellent record of their way of life via the vivid pictures painted on their pots. Scenes of hunting, fishing, war, punishment, sexual acts and elaborate religious celebrations are all clearly illustrated. Pyramids consecrated with the remains of human victims have also been found – yet more attempts to secure divine approval.

The apex of South America's ancient coastal civilizations came with the rise of the Incas. Once just a tribe in the area of Cuzco, they rose to dominance during the twelfth century AD. Strong leadership and a cult that worshipped their rulers as representatives of the gods on earth helped these people build a federal tribute empire in which other city states and kingdoms submitted to their overlordship in return for protection and assistance during times of trouble.

Unlike the Central American peoples, the Incas benefited greatly from a domesticated mammal large enough to be useful – the llama. The presence of this pack animal caused them to build an extensive network of more than 20,000 kilometres of roads and trails, some of them crossing the Andes at heights of up to 5,000 metres. There were no carts or wheels, but human runners, posted at intervals of approximately twenty-five kilometres on each main trail, meant messages could be sent quickly by relay, covering distances of more than 200 kilometres in a day. Instead of paper, parchment or clay, these runners carried pieces of rope which bore messages encoded in an elaborate series of knots that represented numbers and even phonetic sounds. This has still not been fully deciphered.

The roads built by Inca emperors converged on their capital city, Cuzco, regarded as the navel of their world. In 1438 the Supreme Inca, Pachacuti ('world-shaker'), mounted an ambitious expansion programme, and with the help of his son Tupac brought most of modern-day Peru, Ecuador and Chile under Inca rule. They divided the empire into four main regions, each with its own governor. Most people accepted Inca rule willingly, since it provided them with a range of powerful paternalistic services to bail them out when times got tough.

No one ever went hungry in the Inca Empire, and there is no evidence of poverty. If roads were damaged or houses fell down, the region's governor would immediately send troops to repair and rebuild them. A national workforce was manned by males between the ages of fifteen and twenty, who were obliged to spend five years serving the state and its people. State storehouses were kept in every major town and city, and were opened to the people in times of emergency to provide food and clothing. People were able to pay their taxes in kind by weaving cloth or providing food. Each village had a record keeper whose job it was to monitor the production of goods by the inhabitants, some for use locally, some for dispatch to central stores.

Marriages took place at village festivals. It was the responsibility of neighbours to build newly-weds a small house in which to live. Married couples enjoyed a year without having to pay tax, to help them get off to a good start. When they had children they were entitled to another two years of tax-free living. Older citizens paid less tax as their productivity waned, and when they could no longer provide for themselves they were given food, help and clothes from the state's central stores.

Inca Emperors were fastidious about their bloodline, insisting that male heirs marry their sisters. In this way the belief in an unbroken line from the gods to the rulers could be preserved. Pretty and talented girls were chosen by state inspectors to be sent to court to join the *acllahuasi*, the House of the Sun Virgins. Maize was chewed by these virgins to help ferment a sacred Incan brew, drunk by thousands at annual religious festivals in an effort to please the gods, who they believed would then look down on them and be satisfied to see that their grateful people were happy. Apart from his queen (and sister), every emperor was allowed to choose as many wives as he wished. This meant that by the time of the eleventh Inca Emperor thousands of children had been fathered by him and his predecessors, forming a unique administrative aristocracy which tightly bound the state to its people.

As with the Pharaoh in ancient Egypt (see page 107), the Inca Emperor was a god on earth. His currency was gold, which was regarded as the droppings of the gods. Gold was divine – its colour the same as the shining sun. It was easy to craft, and unlike iron, or even silver, which eventually tarnishes, it stays pure and lasts for ever. In the end this is what attracted the sixteenth-century European conquistadors, whose appetite for other people's treasure had no limits.

Neither the religious fundamentalism, which reached its peak in the practice of human sacrifice, nor the idea of a benevolent state that looked after all its citizens in times of need survived the onslaught of the European invaders. Mayan, Olmec, Aztec and Inca beliefs rapidly diffused into a new mixed culture, while their cities were lost in the mountains and jungles. Within a generation of Christopher Columbus's discovery of what he thought was the east coast of Asia in 1492, the awesome power of both the Aztec and Inca Empires had been destroyed by just a handful of Spanish adventurers (see page 235). How these invaders crossed the world, what it was they were looking for, and why they were so quickly able to conquer these empires are some of the most extraordinary stories in modern human history. They began in one of the most unlikely, inhospitable places on earth – deep in the dusty deserts of Arabia.

# Part 4
# Modern History

**(570 AD–present day)**

*How the fate of human civilizations and the natural world fused into a global whole. Is our current way of life sustainable?*

# 10

# Islamic Globalization

## (570–1450 AD)

*How a series of visions appeared to
a merchant from Mecca,
connecting East with West*

**MOHAMMED WAS A PROPHET** and the founder of Islam, a religion and way of life that has profoundly affected the course of human and natural history. About 1,400 years ago, this merchant from the city of Mecca was seized by a series of visions in which he saw the Archangel Gabriel reveal the true and final word of Allah, the one almighty God. His family and followers then wrote down these revelations in a series of verses called the Koran. Today, with more than 1.3 billion practising Muslims, Islam is the second most popular religion in the world, after Christianity (there are an estimated 2.1 billion Christians in the world today).

Before the emergence of Islam, the Arab religion was pantheistic. The Kaaba was a shrine in Mecca, in the middle of the Arabian desert, that contained 360 different gods. Every year nomadic tribes would converge on the Kaaba in the Hajj, a pilgrimage. No violence was allowed. It was believed that the Kaaba represented the intersection between heaven and earth. Its cornerstone, a piece of sacred black rock, symbolized that link, having fallen from the gate of heaven as a meteorite. It is still located in the Kaaba, a large cubic building in the al-Masjid al-Haram mosque in Mecca.

Mohammed was born in Mecca in about 570 AD. His family business was the transportation of goods such as salt, gold, ivory and slaves using horses and camels. As a youth he gained a reputation for honesty and wisdom. It is said he successfully resolved a heated dispute during the reconstruction of the Kaaba after it had been damaged by flash floods. The four chief clans of Mecca couldn't decide which of them should have the honour of lifting the sacred cornerstone into place. It was resolved to let the next person who walked into the shrine make the decision – that person was Mohammed. Mirroring the wisdom of King Solomon, he took off his cloak, placed the stone in the middle and instructed the leaders of the clans to lift it into place jointly by taking one corner of the cloak each.

Mohammed was a profoundly unsettled man. Perhaps it was because he never knew his father, Abdullah, who died on a trading trip six months before he was born. Perhaps it was because he lost his mother, Amina, who died of an illness when he was only six. Maybe life as a merchant disillusioned him. Despite what was by all reports a happy marriage, at the age of about forty he withdrew from everyday life to a small cave on Mount Hira, near where he lived. There he had the first in a long series of dramatic and vivid visions in which the Archangel Gabriel – the same angel who is said to have visited Abraham and Mary, Jesus's mother – revealed to him the final and absolute word of God.

The angel told Mohammed that there was only one God, not many, and that he was in heaven, not on earth. He said that God had revealed his word many times before through prophets such as Adam, Abraham, Moses, Jacob, Joseph, Elijah, Jesus and more than fifty others, but that over time, partly by accident but sometimes through deception, humans had corrupted his word and leaped to false assumptions. In so doing they had constructed religions such as Judaism and Christianity, which, although based on the truth of there being only one God, had become misguided and false.

It was a mistake, said the angel, for the Jews to think they were God's only chosen people. The Arabs were also descended from Abraham – not, like the Jews, through his second son Isaac (see page 145), but through his elder son Ishmael. Christians were mistaken when they claimed that Jesus was the son of God, because God is divine and cannot be made flesh. Rather, God spoke through prophets, finishing with Mohammed, who was the last prophet. Nor will there be a second coming, when Jesus or any other Messiah (meaning a saviour or liberator of the world) comes to earth in judgement. No, there is only one God, Allah, the God in heaven, and he is the only judge.

Mohammed's visions also provided the foundations for a code that defines the Islamic way of life. The Five Pillars of Islam are a simple but powerful creed: profess faith in Allah as the one and only true God (and to Mohammed as his messenger); pray to Allah five times a day; give generously to the poor; observe all religious festivals; and, finally, make a pilgrimage to Mecca at least once in your lifetime.

## Engaging simplicity

Islam spread like wildfire. Within a hundred years of Mohammed's death in AD 632 its simple, powerful message had penetrated Egypt, Palestine, Syria and the rest of the Middle East. It spread to Persia, toppling the Sassanid Empire in 651, extending its reach as far as the Black Sea coast to the north and modern-day Pakistan to the south. By 711 Muslim warriors had crossed North Africa and moved up into southern Spain, and within five years had captured the entire Iberian Peninsula as far north as the Pyrenees (see plate 9). By 732 they were near Poitiers, in the heart of France, only to be stopped by a miraculous victory, against all odds, by the Frankish ruler Charles

Martel at the Battle of Tours. Some historians, including Edward Gibbon in his famous *Decline and Fall of the Roman Empire*, believe that had Martel not won this battle, Europe might well have become Islamic.

Meanwhile, at the other end of the Islamic world, in Central Asia, a new Islamic dynasty called the Abbasids defeated the Chinese at the Battle of Talas in 751, securing control of the area as far north as the Aral Sea. This Arab victory introduced Islam into inner and Central Asia, where it has remained ever since. Within 150 years of Mohammed's death, Islam was the largest and fastest-growing religion in the world.

After Mohammed died, disputes had immediately broken out as to who should lead the Muslim community. Since he had no agreed heir, a split emerged that still exists to this day. Sunni Muslims believe that Mohammed passed on his estate, and therefore his authority, to the Muslim community around him. It was with their approval that Mohammed's close friend and ally Abu Bakr legitimized his claim to become the first Islamic Caliph, Mohammed's rightful successor. However, Shia Muslims believe Abu Bakr orchestrated a coup d'état, and that Mohammed's cousin and son-in-law Ali, who later became the fourth Caliph, was the Prophet's true heir, owing to his blood relationship. Ever since, Sunni Muslim rulers have claimed their authority from the election or approval of senior Islamic representatives, while Shias believe political and religious legitimacy comes through direct descent from Mohammed and his family.

Rivalries burst into bitter struggles that exploded in a series of Muslim civil wars called *fitna*, shot through with coups and assassinations. Such rivalries helped spread the new word of God faster and farther. Out of Arabia came men highly charged with political ambition who scattered in all directions on horses and camels, spreading the word of Allah using whichever version of Mohammed's rightful inheritance suited their own particular claims.

The voluntary and mostly permanent conversion of millions of people to the new faith of Islam had dramatic consequences for the relationship between nature and mankind. At the heart of the religious philosophy of Mohammed was the complete removal of any concept of God on earth. The only earthly link with divinity was through the immutable, inspired written word of the Koran. Forests, animals, plants, mountains – dreamtime – none was a focus of Islamic veneration. Even the weather, thunder, lightning and other forces of nature were not considered sacred in themselves. Putting a single God in heaven, not on earth, was a trend started by the Jews. Then, barring the temporary exception of Jesus, Christianity reinforced the idea. Now the process was perfected by Islam. God was not to be found in the druidic woods of Europe or in Poseidon's stormy seas, not even in the pyramids of Egypt or on top of the ziggurats of Babylon. God was to be known on earth only through a single set of perfect and immutable rules uttered by Mohammed and later written down by his followers in their holy book.

Initially the verses of the Koran were either memorized or etched on anything that came to hand, from stones to pieces of bark. One close follower of the early Caliphs, who was ordered to compile the Koran into a single complete manuscript, protested that 'shifting mountains' would have been easier. In the end he resorted to gathering material from 'parchments, scapula, leaf-stalks of date palms and from the memories of men who knew it by heart'.

## Spreading the word

The advent of paper supercharged the Islamic world's religious lust for the written word. Until the middle of the eighth century the only people who knew the secrets of paper manufacture were from the Far East. But following the capture of a few Chinese prisoners by a gang of Arabian knights at the Battle of Talas in 751, this secret's genie was uncorked (see plate 9). The prisoners' knowledge of paper making helped establish the process outside the Far East for the first time, in the city of Samarkand, now the capital of Uzbekistan. By 794 a paper mill had been set up in the Abbasid capital of Baghdad. From there the art spread to Damascus, Egypt and Morocco, and paper replaced papyrus, silk, wood and parchment.

The first paper book known in Christian Europe was produced using paper made from a mill built by Islamic rulers in Valencia, Spain in 1151. This book, a religious document called *The Missal of Silos*, is kept in the library of the monastery of Santo Domingo de Silos, near Burgos, Spain.

The mass production of blank books made it easier for calligraphic experts to copy out the poetic verses of the Koran and for these to be distributed all across the Muslim world. From about 900 AD Islamic mystics from Baghdad, called Sufis, began to teach that the Koran could help individuals gain direct experience of divine love. The advent of paper making encouraged the Abbasid Caliphs in Baghdad to commission translations of ancient Greek, Persian and Indian scientific and philosophical texts into Arabic, in the hope of making their language and culture more acceptable to the newly conquered Persian nobility, whose rich past stretched back to the Hellenic age of Alexander the Great. Music, poetry, literature and the concept of courtly love now mingled in the Abbasid world with the ideas of ancient Greek and Roman writers on science, medicine, astronomy and mathematics.

Rulers such as Harun al-Rashid (ruled 786–809 AD) sent diplomats to Constantinople to acquire Greek texts. His son al-Ma'mun (ruled 813–33 AD) is even said to have made it a condition of peace that the Byzantines hand over a copy of Ptolemy's *Almagest*. Written in about 150 AD, this book of mathematical astronomy explained in precise detail how to predict the position of the sun, moon and planets on any given date, past, present or future. It became an astronomical gospel for Islamic rulers, who used it to determine the dates of future religious festivals, such as Ramadan, that were based on the cycles of the moon.

Thousands of other ancient texts were translated into Arabic or Persian in the Abbasids' House of Wisdom, an enormous royal library in Baghdad. Caliphs lured translators, scholars and philosophers from all over the known world to their courts and even encouraged debates on how to reconcile the works of rational philosophers like Aristotle with the divine revelations of Mohammed.

## The world of the Caliphs

The Umayyad Caliphs in al-Andalus (Spain) were determined not to be outdone by their Abbasid enemies in Baghdad. Ruling from their rival capital of Cordoba they also patronized philosophers, doctors, mathematicians and scientists, but in addition they transplanted an entire Middle Eastern culture, root and branch, to southern and central Spain. Technical experts arrived to help reshape and revitalize the country's earth and soil, bringing with them Arabic knowledge of irrigation. Thousands of miles of *qanats* – underground aqueducts – were constructed, which from *c.*900 AD transported water from mountain sources to the fields. Oranges, lemons, apricots, mulberries, bananas, sugar cane and watermelons – crops which had never been grown in Europe before – were brought over from the Middle East and successfully cultivated in Spain. They even brought rice from India, without which today there would be no such thing as Spanish paella.

Agricultural riches meant that by 1000 AD the population of Cordoba had grown to more than 100,000. In the words of one Muslim chronicler, al-Maqqari, who is widely suspected of exaggeration, the city had 1,600 mosques, 900 public baths, 213,077 private homes and 80,455 shops!

Islamic merchants brought gold and ivory from across the Sahara, and Cordoba's artisans turned them into coins, jewellery and luxury goods for the Caliph and his court. Thanks to the growing population and prosperity of this city, engineers were commissioned to build and later extend a monumental mosque, called the Mezquita. With more than a thousand columns made of jasper, onyx, marble and granite, it could accommodate as many as 40,000 faithful for their five-a-day prayers.

Islamic courts like those in Baghdad, Cairo and Cordoba acted like throbbing hearts, pumping ideas and inventions around a huge body united by a single faith and the common language of Arabic. They were responsible for fetching and carrying knowledge from as far as China in the East to France in the West, a process that eventually led to the transformation of the fortunes of Europe, helping future explorers assemble toolkits for global conquest. Sometimes ideas were exchanged through war, like the transmission of how to make paper, and sometimes through trade.

### The birth of modern arithmetic

In about 1200 an Italian merchant called Leonardo Fibonacci travelled to Algiers in North Africa to help out in his father's *funduq* – trading post. There for the first time he saw the incredible power of arithmetic written on paper rather than using the old-fashioned abacus. The idea had come from India via Baghdad, where at the House of Wisdom two scholars, al-Kindi and his colleague al-Khwarizmi (780–850 AD), had written books on the newly arrived paper that illustrated how to replace the convention of using written words to describe numbers (such as alpha, beta and gamma) with symbols ranging from 1 to 9. They showed how these could be arranged to allow fast calculation, and added the symbol 0, to represent no value, so that between these ten digits any number could be written.

After Fibonacci had seen Algerian merchants using the system, he was determined that his Italian counterparts should not miss out on its potential. *Liber Abaci*, his book published in 1202, introduced these new numbers to the Christian West. It showed how Arabic numerals could transform everything from bookkeeping to the calculation of interest and money changing. So successful was this innovation that within 200 years most Italian merchants and bankers had abandoned their old-fashioned ways and converted entirely to arithmetic using ink, pen and paper.

It wasn't just arithmetic that spread to the Christian West via Islamic scholars. Al-Khwarizmi's treatise on al-jabr (transposition) showed how a process of linear and quadratic equations could determine an unknown value. When al-Khwarizmi's work was translated in Spain, the Arabic word for 'thing' (*shay*) was transcribed as 'xay' because the letter 'x' was pronounced 'sh' in Spain. Over time this word was shortened to just 'x', which has become the symbol universally used to denote an unknown value. Thanks to the translation of this text into Latin by Christian scholars such as Gerard of Cremona (1114–87) in Toledo, the foundations of modern Western physical sciences were laid. Today algebra is an essential cornerstone of modern science and engineering projects for everything from building particle accelerators to skyscrapers.

## Science, medicine and music

Islamic scholars were just as passionate as the ancient Greeks about fathoming out how the laws of nature worked, be they biological, mathematical or astronomical. Modern medicine owes much of its inspiration to Arabic philosophers, who were influenced by ancient Greek writers like Claudius Galen (129–200 AD), a court physician in Rome. A bright young Arabic doctor called Ibn Sina, also known as Avicenna (980–1037 AD), wrote no fewer than 450 books after reading the works of Galen in the royal library at Bukhara, now in Uzbekistan. His *Book of Healing* and *Canon of Medicine*, detailing the symptoms and causes of diseases, treatments using different types of medicines and the functions of various organs and parts of the body, were standard textbooks in European universities for more than 500 years. The fourteen-volume *Canon of Medicine* included the first ever detailed description of how the human eye works and even described how to remove cataracts.

Just as important to the evolution of Western science was a man called ibn al-Haytham (965–1040 AD), who worked out the laws of optics some 600 years before Isaac Newton. Al-Haytham was educated in Baghdad, but later travelled to Spain, from where his discoveries made their way via Christian translators to the Latin West. He demonstrated how rays of light are affected by the processes of reflection and refraction. Such insights were the key for the future understanding of how lenses work. It was a Latin translation of the work on optics by al-Haytham that early Western scientists used to work out how to build a telescope.

Islamic rulers had a deeply religious reason for wanting to find ways to understand the science of navigation. Mohammed had stipulated that at prayer times all Muslims should face towards Mecca (initially the direction was Jerusalem, but that was changed after the reluctance of the Jews in Medina to embrace Islam), and that mosques should therefore be built with their prayer shrines (*qibla*) pointing in the right direction. Once Islam spread across the world, knowing in which direction the holy city lay became one of the most significant scientific challenges of all.

The astrolabe was a tool used throughout the Islamic world for precisely this purpose. Ultimately, its value to European explorers was just as great as that of the Chinese-inspired compass. The idea of designing a hand-held instrument that could track the process and elevation of the stars at night to determine one's position on the earth's surface went back to the ancient Greeks – to Eratosthenes (276–194 BC) and Hipparchus (190–120 BC). Using trigonometric tables, Persian scientist Mohammed al-Fazari (died *c.* 777 AD) built the first Islamic astrolabe, although it worked along only a single line of latitude.

Later, Andalusian scientist al-Zarqali (1028–87 AD) modified the instrument so it could be used anywhere in the world. After his textbooks and astronomical tables were translated into Latin by Gerard of Cremona in the twelfth century, they provided vital navigational resources for early-fifteenth-century Christian explorers. The first known European astrolabe was built in 1492 in Lisbon by Jewish astronomer Abraham Zacuto (*c.*1450–*c.*1510), whose astronomical tables were used by Christopher Columbus as navigational aids for his overseas expeditions (see page 233).

Warfare between the Islamic world and the Christian West conveyed other important innovations from East to West. Well-bred cavalry horses from Persia and stirrups from China were two examples picked up by Charles Martel after his remarkable victory at Tours, suggesting that the culture of the European medieval knight may have originated in Persia and then diffused via Islamic Spain into eleventh-century France.

When William VIII of Aquitaine captured a group of attractive Saracen slave girls at the Siege of Barbastro in 1064, he so loved their songs that he was moved to write his own love poetry. William later became the founder of the French troubadour movement, a group of itinerant singers and poets who enthralled crusaders with their songs about war, romance and courtly love. If troubadour songs lie at the start of Western Europe's musical tradition, their likeliest origins come from the Muslim world.

The presence of Islamic rulers in Europe, especially in Spain and Sicily, eventually provoked a furious contest between Christian and Muslim civilizations. One dispute centred on control of Jerusalem, holy to both Christianity and Islam, while there was an 800-year struggle for the return of the Iberian Peninsula to Christian rule known as the *Reconquista*.

## The spread of holy war

The idea of *jihad* was deployed with dramatic effect by Mohammed's early followers in their seventh-century firestorm raids out of the Middle East, their soldiers inspired by the words of the Koran: 'Consider not those who are killed in the way of Allah as dead. Nay, they are alive with their Lord, and they will be provided for.'

By 1095 the Muslim idea of justifying war in the name of religion had matured in the Christian West and included the forgiveness of soldiers' sins and the promise of eternal bliss for the brave, granted by Christ's representative on earth, the Pope in Rome. Once the Islamic concept of holy war had been adopted by Christian crusaders in Europe, mankind was truly launched on a new path towards global conflict.

Mohammed's fiery revolution thoroughly connected Europe, North Africa, the Middle East and China through war and trade. Like a whirling dervish dance, which originated with the Sufi mystics of Persia, the capitals and Caliphs of early Islam sent bold ideas and inventions flinging around the enormous Muslim universe and whatever else it touched in peace or war.

When European explorers eventually set out on their great adventures across the seas in the fifteenth century, their fortunes relied on a wide range of Islamic imports, most of which came from China including gunpowder, mathematics, maps, navigational aids and, most precious of all, paper.

## China and the birth of bureaucracy

It was ancient China's expertise in paper making that helped its people build the most technologically advanced civilization in the world. Perhaps the Chinese reverence for paper was a reaction against the Great Burning of Books ordered by the paranoid and obsessive absolutist Qin Shi Huang in 213 BC – the Emperor who built himself the terracotta army to defend him in the afterlife (see page 131). Shortly after his death, a new dynasty called the Hàn came to power. During more than 400 years of almost uninterrupted rule (206 BC–220 AD) its Emperors unified China around a new cultural system. At its core was the beginning of what came to be the world's biggest imperial bureaucracy, begun by Emperor Wu (141–87 BC), in which studying books became central to how people rose through the ranks of the imperial government.

Wu's reforms made it compulsory for court officials to study the classic books of Confucius (see page 129), teaching them that what mattered most was loyalty to the state. In 140 BC Wu ordered the first ever imperial examinations, whereby a hundred official appointments were to be based on performance in an academic test. Most of the candidates were commoners with no connections to nobility. For the first time poor people from the rural heartlands of China could, if they were clever enough, secure positions in government, positions that brought with them wealth, privilege and influence. Gaining a place bestowed huge honour on the successful candidates' homes, families and villages. As if to prove the point, Wu appointed several scholars from this intake as some of his most trusted advisers.

This simple idea had massive consequences for the effective government of China. By the time of Emperor He (ruled 88–106 AD), materials for writing had become essential tools of government administration. So when a bright court official called Cai Lun came up with a radically new method for making a cheap, versatile writing material, Emperor He took a great deal of notice. So impressed was he by Cai Lun's system of pulping, draining and drying plant fibres into thin matted sheets, usually made from the bark of mulberry trees, that Lun was rewarded with vast wealth and an aristocratic title.

In time the Chinese began to use this soft, cheap marvel of nature for almost everything, from wrapping up precious objects to making umbrellas and parasols. Wallpaper, kites, tea bags, playing cards and lanterns all made their first appearance in China. Even the modern habit of using toilet paper has its origins here. The first evidence of its use comes from a report in 851 of an early Arab traveller to China, who says that the Chinese were 'not careful about cleanliness, and they do not wash themselves with water when they have done their necessities, but they only wipe themselves with paper'.

Paper rescued Chinese civilization from perpetual war and civil unrest. It allowed the Tang Dynasty (618–907 AD) to expand the examination system and provide poor people with the hope of wealth, privilege and prestige – if only their families could produce sons with good brains. Emperor Wu's initial idea of cultivating a bureaucracy stuffed with scholars was revived by Tang rulers, and competition amongst poor people to succeed in imperial examinations accelerated rapidly.

Now all male citizens were allowed to apply, not just those recommended by existing government officers. Buddhist monks were paid by local communities to pray for and teach the rural poor. The curriculum was extended to include everything from military strategy to civil law, agriculture and geography. Of course, the Confucian ethic of loyalty and obedience to the state ran through everything, providing all candidates, successful or otherwise, with an effective form of cultural alignment.

### The first printed book

The spread of Buddhism from India to China went hand in hand with what some people regard as the second most powerful invention after paper – printing. Books mass-produced by a technique called block printing are known to have originated in China thanks to a remarkable discovery made by Aurel Stein, a Hungarian archaeologist who in the first half of the twentieth century travelled more than 25,000 miles by mule and foot through inhospitable deserts, plains and mountains because he wanted to find out more about the early culture of Central Asia. It was worth the effort. His finest discovery was at the Caves of the Thousand Buddhas, located at an oasis on the edge of the Taklamakan Desert in north-west China (see plate 6).

When Stein arrived at the caves, in 1907, he heard rumours of an enormous cache of ancient documents that had recently been found hidden behind a temple wall. A shy Taoist priest called Wang Tao-shih had taken it upon himself to become their guardian, and had locked up the treasures in a storeroom. When Stein persuaded the priest to show him inside the tiny room, measuring no more than nine feet square, he saw that it was packed floor to ceiling with precious manuscripts. Here, perfectly preserved by the dry atmosphere of the Central Asian desert, were thousands of untouched ancient texts, some dating from as early as the fifth century AD. After weeks of careful diplomacy Stein managed to purchase as many as 40,000 of these documents, in return for a generous contribution towards the further restoration of the caves.

The jewel in the crown of Stein's hoard, now kept in the British Museum, is the world's oldest known complete, dated, printed book. It is a Buddhist text called the *Diamond Sutra* printed with the date 868 AD – towards the end of the Tang Dynasty. It is made of seven sheets of white paper, pasted together to form a scroll of just over seventeen feet. The manufacturing technique used is called woodblock printing, in which sheets of paper were pressed on to wooden blocks intricately carved with words and illustrations. Although making books this way required advanced craftwork skills to carve the wooden blocks, once these were made the number of copies that could be printed was almost limitless.

# What on Earth Happened?

## *The wealth of scholarship*

China's golden age of innovation in science and technology took off with the founding of the Song Dynasty by Emperor Taizu, who seized the imperial throne in 960. According to the *Song Shi*, a history of the dynasty written in 1345, he spoke to his military commanders at a victory banquet in words that sound remarkably like a modern manifesto for sustainable government: 'The life of man is short. Happiness is to have the wealth and means to enjoy life, and then to be able to leave the same prosperity to one's descendants.'

One of Taizu's first acts was further to expand the concept of a scholastic imperial bureaucracy. By the end of his reign, in 976 AD, roughly 30,000 candidates per year – all of whom had already passed a pre-qualifying test (*jinshi*) – were taking the imperial administration's exams. By the end of the eleventh century this had risen to 80,000, and by the end of the Song Dynasty (1279) it reached 400,000, creating an enormous intellectual population.

Printers worked overtime, with more than 500 classic Confucian texts, dictionaries, encyclopedias and history books carved on to thousands of wood blocks to provide mass-produced study materials for candidates. At least a thousand schools were established throughout China to help prepare students for their civil service exams.

It wasn't just printing books that invigorated cultural and academic life in Song times. Thanks to an expansion of rice cultivation, by 1102 the Chinese population had more than doubled, to over a hundred million people. Traditional currency, in the form of either silk bolts or copper coins, had become difficult to carry, short in supply and expensive to manufacture. So in the 1120s the Chinese government turned to its favourite invention. It used woodblock printing to make the world's first known banknotes, called *jiaozi*. Within a decade several state-run paper-money factories had been established, employing many thousands of workers.

But in 1127 disaster struck. The ingenious Song government was rudely interrupted by a horde of horse breeders from Manchuria, the Jurchens, who double-crossed them after defeating a mutual enemy called the Liao in 1125. Their victory over the Song, using innovative siege engines to break through the imperial capital's walls, resulted in China being split between a northern region ruled by the Jurchens (who became the Jin Dynasty), and a southern region under the Song, who fled south of the Yangtze River to a new capital at Lin'an.

These events triggered an arms race of epic proportions. Song rulers challenged their best scholarly brains to come up with every conceivable way of creating technological superiority in warfare to guarantee success in the event of further attacks. Their quest led directly to the development of the world's first firearms.

## The original gunpowder plot

Charcoal, sulphur and mineral ores were first mixed into a primitive form of gunpowder by Taoist monks in the Tang Dynasty, in c.850. These holy men had been charged by their imperial masters with finding an elixir for everlasting life, but in the course of their experiments they stumbled across a combination of chemicals which, they warned, could result in disastrous consequences: 'Some have heated together sulphur, realgar and saltpeter with honey; smoke and flames result, so that their hands and faces have been burnt, and even the whole house where they were working burned down.'

Such words must have fired the hearts of those whose preference was for power over others on earth. The first known image of a firearm in actual use dates to c.950. For years the significance of a silk banner found at the Caves of the Thousand Buddhas lay unnoticed in a Paris museum until it was rediscovered in 1978. It shows an army of demons trying to distract the Buddha from attaining enlightenment. Among the weapons they use is a fire-lance – a long pole held by a demon wearing a headdress of three serpents. There is a cylinder at one end from which flames spout forth. Beneath him, to the right, is another figure with a serpent entangled in his eyes and his mouth. He is about to throw a small bomb or grenade, from which flames are already pouring out.

Brilliant minds at the court of the southern Song Dynasty (1127–1279) were able to construct an array of powerful new weapons, ranging from catapult bombs and cannon to flame-throwers.

## A new maritime perspective

The Song's shift south had other important consequences. Court officials set about commissioning China's first permanent standing navy in 1132, after realizing that the Yangtze River was now effectively their new Great Wall. Previously, in 1130, slingshots throwing gunpowder bombs had been ordered as standard on all ships. A new generation of paddle-wheel ships, powered by human treadmills, some with as many as eleven paddles on each side, dramatically increased manoeuvrability in the tight conditions of river-based warfare. By 1203 many of these warships had been reinforced with the addition of iron armour.

Naval power gave the southern Song complete control of the East China Sea, previously dominated by Hindu rulers called the Cholas, a Tamil dynasty that ruled southern India and Sri Lanka between the tenth and thirteenth centuries. Foreign trade was essential for the survival of the Song, since the mountainous terrain of southern China was less suitable for widespread agriculture than the north. With overland trading via the Silk Road firmly in Jin hands, trade by sea was essential for the survival of their civilization (see plate 6).

Such conditions led to the first known portfolio investment schemes, now so common in the modern capitalist world. Instead of putting all their money into one trading venture, Chinese merchants would collaborate in guilds and spread their money across several expeditions, so that if one were lost, it came as a complete disaster to no one (other than the crew, of course). According to one source, such arrangements proved highly lucrative: 'they invest from ten to a hundred strings of cash, and regularly make profits of several hundred per cent'.

Goods were carried on junks that sailed across the Indian Ocean and into the Persian Gulf. These vessels were waterproofed with tung oil, fitted with watertight bulkheads (which meant that if the ship was holed it would not sink) and equipped with stern-mounted rudders for improved steering. Some of them were powered by a combination of sails and oars, and were able to carry huge cargoes and several hundred men.

Their sailors took with them that most precious of all instruments for seafarers – a compass. The idea of magnetizing a needle by rubbing it against silk and then placing it inside a straw and floating this in water to make a primitive compass had been known in China since at least the first century AD. In 1044 a Song Dynasty manual on military techniques called *Wujing Zongyao* described how this knowledge was used to create a south-pointing chariot to help guide troops in gloomy weather and on dark nights (the same book also included a recipe for how to make gunpowder). The biggest breakthrough came a few years later, when court official Shen Kuo, who passed his imperial state examinations in 1061, described how to magnetize the needle of a compass and use it for navigation by stringing it up on a thread of silk. His compass is known to have been used on Chinese ships from as early as 1111.

Astonishing technological breakthroughs were made possible by an exchange of knowledge in an imperial court that promoted a sophisticated knowledge base of paper, printing and books. By now Chinese civilization had substantially enhanced man's power over nature by harnessing gunpowder weapons and twenty-four-hour navigation (in all weathers) by magnetic needles. But no dynasty lasts for ever, however ingenious its technology. Nature's cycles were probably the ultimate cause of the collapse of the Song in 1279 AD.

## The rise of Genghis Khan, a ruthless Mongol chief

Beginning in about 1200 AD, the climate began to cool. North Atlantic pack ice started advancing south towards Iceland, and Greenland's glaciers expanded. This climate change signalled the start of what is called the Little Ice Age. Cold winters and unpredictable summers continued across Europe until the middle of the nineteenth century. According to oxygen isotopes captured in Greenland ice cores, the first signs of cooling appear to have been in high latitudes.

Mongol horsemen who burst southwards between 1205 and 1225 would have been early casualties, as bitter Arctic air invaded the heart of Asia with devastating effects. Steppe lands, now populated with more animals and people than ever before thanks to years of increased rainfall, simply couldn't cope. In a cooler climate their pastoral yield was insufficient. People living in the steppes probably had only one choice if they wished to maintain their numbers and lifestyle. They had to unite and conquer new, more fertile lands. Fortunately for them, they found just the man to lead them. His name was Genghis Khan.

By 1206 Genghis had united rival Mongolian tribes (Merkits, Uyghurs, Keraits and Tatars) through a mixture of diplomacy, charisma and leadership skills. Taking climate changes into account, however, his rise to power can also be explained by his being in the right place at the right time. The survival of the Mongol population of some 200,000 people depended on a coordinated nomadic expansion.

Genghis was a brilliant military planner and a strict disciplinarian who demanded toughness, dedication and loyalty from all his men. He organized his forces into decimal units of ten, one hundred, one thousand and ten thousand. Soldiers who performed well in battle rose through the ranks. Cowardice was not tolerated. Each unit of ten had a leader who reported up to the next level. If one soldier deserted, his unit of ten was executed. If a unit of ten deserted, the whole hundred was slaughtered.

Careful planning in military councils (called *kurultai*) and excellent reconnaissance conducted on fast steeds meant success was swift. Whenever Genghis faced an enemy city he gave them a simple choice: surrender or die. He was a man of his word. To proud rulers who offered resistance, he showed no mercy. If a ruler agreed to submit, his people were spared, but total loyalty was expected in return.

By 1213 the Mongols had advanced as far as the Great Wall and within two years they had charged into the heart of northern China. In 1215 they besieged and sacked the Jin capital at Yanjing (now Beijing). Having subdued the Jin, Genghis's anger was roused by an apparently unprovoked insult from the Islamic ruler of Khwarazm, an empire that stretched from the western edge of China to the Caspian Sea. In 1219 Mongol armies massed on the eastern edge of the Islamic world. Each city was given the usual choice.

Genghis then headed north, where his forces split into two and conquered Georgia and the Crimea. On their way back to Mongolia they defeated a Russian army led by six princes, including the ruler of Kiev. As was customary in Mongolian tradition the princes were given a bloodless execution: they were crushed to death under the weight of a banqueting platform while the Mongolian generals ate their victory feast.

## *The world's largest end-to-end empire*

In 1225 Genghis returned to China, where he again fought and subdued the Jin. Shortly after, he died – no one quite knows how. Some say he fell off a horse. Another legend has it that he was murdered by a beautiful Tangut princess who, as they were about to make love, castrated him with a knife hidden inside her body, in revenge for the murder of so many of her people. At the time of Genghis's death the Mongol Empire stretched from the east coast of China to the Caspian Sea. But his children were to take it further still, establishing empires in Russia, Siberia and Central Asia. By 1241 their armies were ready to flood into Western Europe following victory over Polish, German and Hungarian forces at the Battle of Mohi, south-west of the Sajó River, in Hungary.

By this time the Mongol Empire was the largest contiguous civilization that the world had, and still has, ever seen (see plate 10). Its inexorable expansion was only halted by the death of Genghis's successor Ögedei Khan in 1242, because tradition said that Mongol leaders must convene a grand council to confirm the appointment of the next Great Khan. So they retreated, at least for a while, to approve their new leader, and Europe was spared.

As Genghis Khan and his successors swept westwards they converted to Islam, bringing with them more technologies from the ingenious Far East. Innovations such as paper making, printing and gunpowder brought west by Islamic traders, warriors and Mongol hordes lit the touchpaper for the globalization of humanity. As a result of their progression west, a suite of diverse cultures, each having its own distinctive relationship with nature, gradually began to turn towards a single world view with common access to a powerful bank of scientific knowledge and a raft of new expertise ranging from portfolio investment schemes, numerals and algebra to paper making, the compass and gunpowder. Firearms were first witnessed by Europeans in Muslim Spain, where they were used against Christians in 1342 at the siege of Algeciras. Within 100 years they were being actively deployed by Europeans in their own holy wars.

The inventiveness, scholarship, power, wealth and glory of ancient China and the transmission of its genius west by the forces of Islam was matched only by the contrast provided by the climate of desperation across medieval Europe, much of which, by 1450, was languishing in a wilting wilderness of disease, famine and war.

# 11
# Medieval Misery

## (476–1450 AD)

*How chaos enveloped Christian Europe
following the collapse of the Roman Empire*

**COULD IT BE** that the fluttering of a butterfly's wings in China set off a thousand-year-long storm, thousands of miles away, in far-off Europe? Since the start of the twentieth century scientists have been studying the idea, called chaos theory, that an apparently tiny change in one part of the world can trigger a dramatic set of events that severely or even permanently disrupts another.

Something like this seems to have happened to medieval Europe starting at about the time the whirlwind Roman Empire was in its final decline. A military victory by the Chinese Hàn Dynasty in about 100 AD over a northern Mongol tribe called the Xiongnu could well have been the butterfly.

Little evidence survives of what happened to these nomadic horsemen, who were forced west by the Hàn forces, until the arrival north of the Black Sea of an army of Chinese-looking warriors in the fourth century AD. Archaeologists have found large cauldrons buried under riverbanks, exactly like those used by the Xiongnu tribes of western China. From the accounts of early Byzantine writers, the appearance of this army's famous leader Attila suggests an Eastern origin: 'short of stature, with a broad chest and a large head; his eyes were small, his beard thin and sprinkled with grey; and he had a flat nose and a swarthy complexion showing the evidences of his origin'.

The Huns, as they were called, who charged into Europe during the fourth century AD, were vicious warriors with powerful weapons. Their small, lightweight, composite bows were legendary for their power, speed and range – ideal for use on horseback. The secret lay in the material they were made of, which generated maximum elastic thrust: the strong but flexible horn of the water buffalo, animals which pulled ploughs in the paddy fields of the Far East.

On 31 December 406 a terrifying alliance of Germanic and Asian tribes surged across the frozen River Rhine at Mainz, and into western Europe. The Huns reached as far as Orléans in France (in 451) and Ravenna in Italy; meanwhile the Visigoths from eastern Germany went for the jugular, sacking Rome itself in 410 before establishing their own empire across southern France and Spain. Next to come were the Vandals, another east German tribe, who streaked down Spain, crossed into North Africa and along to Carthage, where they built themselves a fleet. They then sailed across the Mediterranean and invaded Sicily, Sardinia, Corsica and Malta before launching their own devastating raid on Rome in 455.

Europe's misery was no temporary setback. A huge effort to restore law and order and to unify the broken territories of the Roman Empire was undertaken by the Byzantine Emperor Justinian I (ruled 527–65 AD), ruling from the new capital in Constantinople. He sent armies and generals to Spain, Italy and North Africa to reclaim lands seized by the nomadic horsemen, besides having to confront periodic aggression from the empire's age-old Persian enemies to the east. Justinian met with partial success, reforming the legal basis of the Roman Empire, ejecting the Vandals from North Africa and defeating the Ostrogoths, another Germanic tribe, at Ravenna by 552.

It didn't last long. Three years after Justinian's death another wave of raiders came down from the north in the form of the Lombards, originally a Baltic people who had settled in Germany near the Danube River. By 561 they had installed themselves as rulers of Italy, a conquest that lasted more than 200 years. Any African and Spanish gains made by Justinian were later overrun by Mohammed's warriors, who by 732 had conquered all Spain and half of France, only to be stopped from taking the rest of Western Europe by the Frankish leader, Charles Martel (see page 213 and plate 9). The Franks were early converts to Catholic Christianity thanks to their founder Clovis I (died 511 AD), who became the Pope's political protector. Clovis is considered by many modern scholars to be the founder of France.

Complete catastrophe for early Christian Europe was only just averted when Constantinople, its new imperial capital, narrowly escaped conquest by the forces of Islam. More than 80,000 Muslim warriors from Damascus descended on the city in 718, supported by some 1,800 ships. The siege failed thanks only to nature's intervention: the winter of 717–18 was the coldest in living memory.

Over the course of a few hundred years the mighty Roman Empire had been reduced to ruins. By the seventh century the population of Europe was in steep decline, falling from about 27.5 million in 500 AD to just eighteen million 150 years later. Bubonic plague had taken a major toll of European lives. The disease ravaged the eastern Roman Empire, beginning in 541–2, severely complicating Justinian's efforts to reassert imperial control. An estimated 5,000 people a day died in Constantinople, where the disease claimed the lives of up to 40 per cent of the city's population. It then spread across much of Europe, with repeated outbreaks over the next 300 years, killing, it is thought, as many as twenty-five million people in all. Fields were abandoned, forests regrew and the economy went into reverse. Outside the occasional kingly court, life in Europe between 350 and 750 AD was extremely nasty, totally brutish and usually rather short.

# Medieval Misery

## A 'holy' Roman empire

Bit by bit, hopes of a revival in central authority to help protect all Europe began to re-emerge thanks to the success of the Franks under Charlemagne. Building on his grandfather Charles Martel's victory against the Arabs in 732, Charlemagne successfully extended Frankish rule throughout France and into Italy. By the beginning of the ninth century he had repelled the Lombards and restored power to the Pope in Rome. Charlemagne was crowned Holy Roman Emperor by Pope Leo III on 25 December 800. Leo now reasserted the Pope's claim to be Christ's living apostle on earth, first established by Pope Leo I at the Council of Chalcedon in 451. Could papal spiritual supremacy backed up by political power from a newly restored Holy Roman Emperor re-establish Europe's order and balance, in the way the Song Dynasty had in China?

As if to celebrate Europe's recovery, even the weather perked up. Cold, harsh winters gave way to the Medieval Warm Period. Temperatures between 800 and 1300 AD were as mild as they are today. Grapes grew as far north as Britain and the ice sheets retreated, opening up new sea passages across the North Atlantic.

Thanks to the breakdown of the medieval economy, strong new rulers like Martel and Charlemagne had to use barter to raise troops to re-establish central rule, law and order. The milder climate strengthened their hand with a revival in agricultural wealth. Rulers were able to demand military service in return for granting land, which provided a source of income from farming. Knights like those from Persia were Europe's new shock troops, but they were expensive to equip. The cost of buying and then maintaining horses and armour meant that only those with good incomes could afford to fight in this way, hence the need for grants of land in exchange for service.

## *Knights and feudalism*

This new political fabric, called feudalism, was given a significant shot in the arm by small butterfly wings still flapping on the other side of the world. High technology for harnessing animal power, in the form of cast-iron stirrups for horses, originated in China some time in the third century AD. They are thought to have come to Europe via the nomadic Avars of Central Asia, spreading north to Baltic tribes near Lithuania and west via Islamic warriors pushing towards Constantinople, Spain and France. Once in use by the armies of the Frankish Kings of Charlemagne's time, stirrups had a massive impact on the ability of rulers and their henchmen with horses to exert a new form of social and military control.

Stirrups allowed the welding of horse and rider into a single fighting unit capable of a violence without precedent, immensely increasing their ability to damage the enemy. According to Lynn White, a twentieth-century medieval historian: 'It made possible mounted shock combat, a revolutionary new way of doing battle.' Men with horses and stirrups now became powerful rulers in their own right. Tied into armies through oaths of allegiance and into feudal contracts in exchange for land, order of a sort was restored through the power of a new class of knights-cum-landlords.

## *Traders and raiders*

From as early as the 790s Viking raiders, equipped with their own stirrups and horses, began to take advantage of improved climatic conditions, bringing with them formidable sailing skills. Viking longboats reached wherever water and oarsmanship took them.

The Vikings were the chameleons of the medieval world – one minute merchants, next pirates, and before long conquerors. For Viking adventurers, trade and raid were different sides of the same coin. By 839 they had sailed deep into the heart of Europe through its extensive networks of naturally interconnected rivers. They settled along the Danube, in Kiev and beyond, establishing themselves as the Rus, a word that is thought to come from an old Norse term, *rods*, meaning 'men who row'. Islamic sources say they then subjugated the Slavic peoples, who were traded as slaves along a network that reached across the Black Sea as far as Islamic Baghdad ('Slav' possibly comes from their being traded as slaves by the Rus).

The most successful Viking settlement in Europe was around Rouen, where they integrated into Frankish culture, chameleon-like, adopting both feudalism and Christianity. They became known as Normans (from 'Norsemen' or 'Northmen'). Their most famous ruler, William of Normandy, built an army based on feudal ties, horses and stirrups. With the seafaring expertise gained from his people's Viking ancestry, William was confident of victory in his invasion of England, which began with the Battle of Hastings in 1066.

Feudalism thrived on conquest. Kings granted newly captured lands to their knights and nobles, who in return provided arms for further conquest and war. As a way of trying to stamp his own authority in England, and to define his overall wealth from the outset, William the Conqueror, as he became known, ordered a comprehensive survey of his new kingdom – the result was the famous Domesday Book of 1086.

For years historians have pored over this unique snapshot of life in medieval England, which details the livings of more than 265,000 people, from farmers, millers and blacksmiths to potters, shepherds and slaves. Recently, conservationists have been able to use it to assess the impact of medieval agriculture on the natural landscape, since among the questions asked by William's inquisitors was how much woodland, pasture and meadowland was owned by each person. Their analysis is startling.

It seems that a staggering 85 per cent of the English countryside had already been cleared by this time, for use as pasture for domesticated animals and arable land for growing crops. To support such large-scale production, some 5,624 watermills were in use for grinding grain in 3,000 separate communities. England's remaining forests and woodlands were under tight control, with many reserved especially for royal use and hunting, further indicating that by then substantial deforestation had already taken place.

Such dramatic changes in the landscape were not restricted to Britain. In 500 AD about 80 per cent of all European land was forest, but by 1300 this had fallen to less than half.

The spread of Christianity, a creed founded on the requirement for Adam to till the ground to atone for his original sin in the Garden of Eden, accelerated this process. Pagans venerated trees – they were their shrines. Christians did not. Monastic orders such as the Benedictines (established in Italy in 529 AD) and the Cistercians (founded in France in 1098) have been described as the 'shock troops' of clearing and deforestation.

Monasteries established in England, France, Germany, Italy, Spain and Portugal not only spread the word of God but massively increased ecclesiastical wealth by felling trees and turning the land into fields for rent. Between 1098 and 1371 more than 700 Cistercian monasteries were established in Europe; each was a nucleus for clearing and farming, following a fashion championed by Charlemagne himself, who had decreed: 'Whenever there are men competent for the task, let them be given forest to cut down in order to improve our possessions.'

## The first Europeans reach America

Extra food produced extra people. By 1000 AD, the European population had risen to more than thirty-seven million, and then doubled again to seventy-four million by 1340. Such a dramatic increase in wealth, food and people meant that the need to find new lands to conquer and colonize grew ever greater.

Viking explorers provided the most spectacular examples, capitalizing on the warmer climate and less icy oceans by finding a new sea passage from Norway to Iceland, which was first settled by Ingólfur Arnarson in 874. This was followed by settlements on Greenland, beginning in 982. According to the Saga of Erik the Red he named it Greenland because he wanted to attract other people to it. The Vikings even reached North America, where in 1006 Erik the Red and his son built a small town.

This settlement, established nearly 500 years before Columbus's voyage in 1492, marks the first attempt by Europeans to colonize the Americas, although for some reason they withdrew soon afterwards. According to one Viking saga disaster struck after the settlers tried to build good relations with the natives (who they called *skraelings*) by inviting their chiefs into the new village for a convivial drink of milk. Unfortunately, owing to the absence of domesticated milk-producing mammals in America, the chiefs' lactose intolerance caused them to fall sick. Suspecting poisoning, they drove their new neighbours back into the sea.

## Onward Christian soldiers

By 1095, Popes had received repeated appeals for military help from successive Byzantine Emperors to fend off encroaching Muslim forces, following their victory over a Byzantine army at the Battle of Manzikert in 1071. In response, Pope Urban II called for a single European expedition to liberate the holy city of Jerusalem, hoping it would help him reassert papal authority over the Church of Constantinople into the bargain.

His appeal fell on fertile ground. For the previous one hundred years Christian knights had been fighting the Muslims of Spain, forcing them southwards. By 1085 the Christians had besieged and taken the strategically important city of Toledo, putting almost half of Spain back in their hands. The city's libraries contained many important Arabic translations of ancient Greek texts. Now they could be translated into Latin by the Christians, unlocking the secrets of Greek science, geography, mathematics, astronomy and philosophy that had been lost to the medieval West following the period of anarchy that swept away the last vestiges of ancient Rome. Their survival was entirely thanks to careful preservation by curious Islamic cultures, which venerated the written word.

When Pope Urban extended the promise of earthly forgiveness to all European soldiers, if only they would unite in a common cause to liberate the Holy Land from Muslim infidels, the response was overwhelming. However, no better example exists in history of how European culture finds the ideal of a united cause so difficult to put into practice, however appealing the prize. Over the next 200 years, what had started off so promisingly turned to disaster.

The successful First Crusade (1096–9) led to the recapture of Jerusalem and the massacre of its mostly Muslim population. After resurgent Muslim attacks, a second campaign (1147–9) ended up with Christian knights committing Europe's first mass extermination of the Jews. In 1187 Saladin, the Muslim Sultan of Egypt, recaptured Jerusalem, giving European leaders a reason to unite once again. In 1189 an unprecedented alliance of the Kings of England (Richard I) and France (Philip II), and the Holy Roman Emperor and King of Germany (Frederick Barbarossa), all supported by Pope Gregory VIII, marched to liberate the Holy Land once again.

It was not a success. Frederick drowned while crossing a river in 1190, and Philip fell ill with dysentery and returned to France with his armies in 1191 before they reached Jerusalem. His departure fuelled mistrust between the English and the French. Richard concluded a truce with Saladin after realizing that his forces would never be strong enough to retake Jerusalem. Then he was captured on his way home by Leopold V, Duke of Austria, who handed him over as a prisoner to the new Holy Roman Emperor, Henry IV.

Europe's flailing attempts at unity were finally torn to shreds by the crusade of 1204, when the Christian armies never even got close to Jerusalem. They turned instead on the rich city of Constantinople – inhabited by fellow Christians, who they had originally been sent to protect. What followed has often been described as one of the most shameful moments in Christian history. These supposed soldiers of Christ sacked the city, stole its treasures, raped its women and scattered its citizens.

## Famine, pestilence and disease

By 1200 the continent of Europe was militarized, antagonized and overpopulated. Efforts at re-creating a stable central authority based on the Pope's Christianity or Charlemagne's revival of imperial authority had failed. Nothing like the paper-based Chinese bureaucracy emerged here. Nothing like the Incas' systems of state aid could knit together its people (see page 182), because thanks to the kings' need for mounted warriors, precious land was bartered into the hands of knights and nobles, who wielded ultimate local power from inside their castles of impenetrable stone.

The medieval reality of a highly fragmented but deeply militarized Europe was fully evolved by 1337, when a devastating hundred-year war began, in which England's Kings committed themselves to an epic struggle to reclaim their Norman ancestors' lands in France. English knights, supported by thousands of skilful archers using powerful longbows, pushed deep into French territory, urged on by the prospect of fresh feudal grants of reconquered land.

But by then major warning signs of imminent and dreadful change were already evident. With a population now nearing eighty million, medieval Europe was under severe strain. Despite massive deforestation and the innovations of the horse, plough and crop rotation, its agriculture could supply food only for a finite number of people. A series of three wet, cold summers was all it took to bring the whole of Europe north of the Alps and the Pyrenees to its knees. Grain would not ripen, there was no fodder for livestock, and salt – the only way to preserve meat – was scarce because salt pans could not evaporate in the relentlessly wet weather. Bread prices rose by as much as 320 per cent in some places. No one but the richest landlords could afford to eat; even the King of England, Edward II, was unable to find bread for his entourage while touring the country in August 1315.

Survival was possible only by slaughtering essential draught animals and eating seeds saved for next year's crops. The consequences for morality and order were horrendous. Children were abandoned to fend for themselves (this is the origin of the Hansel and Gretel story), old people were starved to death for the sake of the rest of their families, and disease soon spread through the malnourished, weakened population. Between 10 and 25 per cent of the populations of many towns and cities perished. In 1276 average life expectancy was thirty-five; by 1325 it had fallen by a third.

## The origin of biological warfare

Worse was to come. Having been spared the horrors of plague for some 700 years, medieval Europe was now at its most vulnerable to renewed attack. Traditionally it is thought rats were to blame for the spread of the appalling Black Death that struck Europe between 1347 and 1351, but in fact humans were just as responsible. Once again, butterfly wings in China lay at the source of upheavals in Europe. Plague originated in the province of Hubei in the early 1330s, spreading to a further eight provinces by the 1350s. Mongol traders travelling along the Silk Road are thought to have carried the disease west (see plate 6).

In 1346 troops loyal to Jani Beg, commander and Khan of the Golden Horde from 1342 to 1357, had to abandon their siege of the Crimean port of Kaffa because plague had struck them. Their response was history's first and most lethal use of biological weapons. Beg's few surviving troops loaded the bodies of their many dead on to catapults and hurled them over Kaffa's walls, infecting the Genoese defenders inside. By the time the Genoese sailed home, most of their men lay dead. Just enough survived, though, to pass on the killer disease, which during the next three years claimed over forty million European lives – more than half the continent's total population. Between 1348 and 1375 the average life expectancy in Europe fell to just over seventeen years.

Survivors found themselves in a completely different world. Instead of being oppressed, peasants were now so few as to be able to demand higher wages. The peasants' revolts of 1358 in France (the Jacquerie) and 1381 in England (led by Wat Tyler) had their origins in the new dynamics between rich and poor that emerged after the Black Death. Social mobility, political representation and even a change in styles of clothing can all be attributed to the plague that wiped out so many people. The rich panicked, forcing through a series of sumptuary laws, dictating what clothes people could wear and what breeds of dogs and hunting birds they were allowed to own, to try to stop newly rich peasants from rising above their social station.

Rapid declines in population also changed the nature of medieval warfare, and caused the fabric of feudalism finally to fray. There simply weren't enough peasants left on the land to supply troops for epic struggles such as the Hundred Years War. Instead, English Kings like Henry V (ruled 1413–22) were forced to pay mercenary soldiers, or even to recruit their own standing armies. Both required money and more taxes on the people, leading to bargains in parliaments to raise funds for waging war in exchange for concessions of power, privilege and prestige.

Europe's rulers desperately needed new ways of fighting that didn't require the deployment of regiments of archers, whose skill with the longbow took years of training and enormous personal strength. Dilemmas like these provided the perfect environment for China's last but ultimately most lethal secret to be played out on the stage of medieval Europe.

### Firearms reach Europe

Gunpowder had been known in the West since 1267, when a recipe appeared in the English philosopher Roger Bacon's *Opus Majus*, but it only came to the attention of English warlords in 1342 at the siege of Algeciras when Islamic troops used primitive cannon with remarkable effect. According to one Spanish historian, 'The besieged did great harm among the Christians with iron bullets they shot.' The Earls of Derby and Shrewsbury were at the scene, and quite possibly transferred the technology to England. It was tried out for the first time against the French at the Battle of Crécy in 1346.

Within a hundred years cannon had transformed the power of those European rulers who could afford them. Soon handguns enabled unskilled peasants to kill at a distance. Desperation brought on by famine and disease gave way to a new level of catastrophe ushered in by the arrival of a black powder that could, in minutes, reduce a knight's castle to rubble.

Feudalism and chivalry were now in the process of being replaced by the rule of the gun. Meanwhile, cannon so large that they took fifty oxen to pull and a crew of 700 men to fire were being manufactured in Europe and sold to the highest bidder. Urban the Hungarian (not the Pope) was the world's first known arms dealer. Told by the Byzantine Emperor Constantine XI that his services were too expensive, he sold his technology to opposing Islamic forces headed by the Turkish Sultan Mehmed II.

Nearly 750 years had passed since the previous attempt by Islamic forces to take the great imperial city of Constantinople, guardian of rich trade routes to the Black Sea. By the spring of 1453 another force of 80,000 Muslim soldiers had gathered just outside its massive walls. The weather wouldn't stop them this time. Enormous eight-metre-long super-guns, crafted out of copper and tin, were slowly rolled across the plains of Asia Minor to a point about a mile outside the city. Giant balls of stone and marble, some plundered from the temples of ancient Greece, relentlessly pounded Constantinople's walls with such force that on impact they burrowed two metres into the ground. On 28 May the Turks finally breached the city walls and their troops flooded inside. Mehmed rewarded his men with three days of looting, as was the custom.

When news of the fall of Constantinople reached Venice on 29 June, and then Rome a week later, it stunned the Christian world. Medieval Europe was on its knees once again. Torn from within by disease, depopulation, gunpowder and war, now its most precious and historic ancient capital had finally fallen into heathen hands.

## Europe, the world's poorest continent

Emerging from the Great Famine and Black Death of the fourteenth century, Europe was the civilized world's least successful continent. With no clear idea how to stimulate its economy, it was in a desperate fix. All the available strategies for creating sufficient wealth to secure its civilizations had ended in abject failure.

The Great Famine meant that growing wealth through agriculture had suffered a dramatic setback, and the Black Death had seriously added to Europe's woes by devastating the population. Stealing wealth from elsewhere had proved spectacularly unsuccessful following the disaster of the crusades, whose biggest triumph had been the sack of Europe's most prestigious city, Constantinople, in 1204. Earning wealth through trade was an obvious alternative strategy. But, apart from its northern shores, the Mediterranean was now an Islamic lake. Yet between about 1300 and 1550, many of Europe's finest artistic and literary achievements were created by poets, philosophers, artists and sculptors such as Dante, Petrarch, Michelangelo and Leonardo da Vinci. During these years, money and wealth on a scale not seen since the height of the Roman Empire flooded into the Italian peninsula. With the rise of wealthy aristocratic patrons such as the families of the Medici, Sforza, Visconti, Este, Borgia and Gonzaga, rich city states studded the landscape across Italy, from Venice in the east to Rome in the west, among them Florence, Siena, Pisa, Genoa, Ferrara and Milan.

Here, in the toe of Europe, the reality of Europe's dependence on the success of Mohammed's world was playing itself out. Renaissance Italy was the European terminus of Islam's worldwide trading system. Precious Greek and Roman texts, lost to the Christian West, were translated from Arabic copies captured in cities such as Toledo in Spain and brought to Italy by merchant families enriched by wealth they had earned in cities such as Cairo. Artistic patrons such as the Medici, whose fortunes came from charging other Europeans exorbitant prices for wool and textiles, established banks and double-entry bookkeeping, based on knowledge of Arabic numerals brought from Islamic Tunis to Italy by the Pisan trader Fibonacci. Even Dante, the most celebrated Western poet of the period, and perhaps of all time, structured the heaven, purgatory and hell of his epic poem *The Divine Comedy* around the nine-layered Islamic view of the universe first written about by philosophers at the House of Wisdom in ninth-century Baghdad.

The concentration of such enormous wealth in this small part of Europe stimulated new thought, artistic expression and a curiosity about the natural world, which was rekindled by the rediscovery of ancient writers like Aristotle and Plato. But this Italian crucible of wealth and patronage, dependent on trade with Islam, could not in itself provide all Europe with a secure strategy for the future welfare of its people. The enrichment of a few dynastic families by virtue of their place at the end of another civilization's trading network was hardly a solid foundation for lasting security. Instead, Italian pomp just increased the jealousy of other European nations, which, stoked by the failed crusades and the arrival of gunpowder, became eager to gorge on Italy's treasures for themselves. Between 1494 and 1559 the Great Wars of Italy were fought between France, Spain, the Holy Roman Empire, England, Scotland, Venice, the Papal States and the Ottoman Empire. By the end of the period Spain had become the dominant power in Italy to the detriment of France.

## The economic grip of Islam

The Islamic conquest of Constantinople in 1453 made Europe's already desperate situation even worse. Most of the Balkans, including all Serbia and Greece, had fallen into Muslim hands, and their people were converting to Islam, which is why there are still many Muslims in places such as Bosnia today. The silver mines in Serbia and Greece, the backbone of the continent's traditional bullion supply, were now firmly in enemy hands.

As if Islamic control over Europe's chances of securing wealth through trade wasn't tight enough, in 1517 the Ottoman Sultan Selim I (ruled 1512–20) strengthened it even further by invading Egypt, cutting off a historic overland trading link to the East. His successor Suleiman the Magnificent (ruled 1520–66) invaded Hungary in 1521, and after winning the Battle of Mohacs in 1526 Muslim armies massed outside the walls of Vienna. Thanks to the fortuitous intervention of nature, echoing the salvation of Constantinople more than 800 years before, it was only the harshest of winters that saved Vienna from falling, forcing Suleiman to recall his troops.

But if the cold weather provided temporary relief for the inhabitants of Vienna, it proved fatal to another potential European route to riches. The adventurous Vikings, who had established settlements totalling about 5,000 people in Greenland, found the onset of the Little Ice Age too harsh to make survival there viable.

Plummeting temperatures led to the collapse of this pilot phase of European maritime exploration. The last ship known to have sailed from Norway to the eastern settlements of Greenland landed in 1406, apparently blown off course while on its way to Iceland. It returned to Norway in 1410. Nothing more is known about what happened to the Viking community that had survived for 450 years as Europe's most remote outpost. It is presumed that they starved to death, having over-exploited the natural resources as a result of the extreme cold.

Europe was surrounded and trapped. To the north lay ice, to the west an ocean too vast to navigate, to the east and south were the lands of Muslim rulers who traded only on their own terms and who exercised tight control over Europe's economy. By 1451 the continent was badly in need of a miracle. Unfortunately, at precisely the moment Christ's long-promised return to save his blessed kingdom on earth was needed most, his ambassador on earth, the Pope, had been found wanting ...

## Papal misdemeanours

For centuries the Roman Popes had directly controlled lands in central Italy, called the Papal States, which had been secured for them back in the eighth century, in the time of Charlemagne's father Pippin. The justification for giving such earthly power to a supposedly spiritual representative of God on earth came from an ancient document called *The Donation of Constantine*. According to this text, soon after his conversion to Christianity the Emperor Constantine I was stricken with leprosy, but thanks to his new faith he was miraculously cured by the then Pope, Sylvester I (314–35 AD). In gratitude, Constantine entrusted his Western Empire to the Papacy in Rome. For centuries Popes used *The Donation of Constantine* to justify not only direct control of the Italian lands they had acquired through Pippin and later his son Charlemagne but everything from their right to raise their own private armies and to levy taxes all across Western Europe, to anointing not just their own chosen bishops, but kings and emperors as well.

Then, in an essay written in 1439–40, a linguist from Florence named Lorenzo Valla proved conclusively that the Pope's precious document was an elaborate fake. Valla demonstrated beyond doubt that the Latin words used in the document came from a later period, probably the ninth century, at about the time when Pippin ceded the first territories to the See of Rome. Desperate to cover up the truth, the Papacy did everything it could to prevent the formal publication of Valla's essay, but in 1517 this explosive evidence of papal fraud finally made it into the hands of Christian Protestants. Mass-produced by the recently invented printing presses, it was available for all the world to see.

It wasn't just this fraud that undermined the authority of Christ's representative on earth. Popes of the Italian Renaissance were notorious for their appallingly debauched and corrupt way of life. The most flagrant example was Pope Alexander VI (1492–1503), who among several claims to fame enjoyed a string of mistresses who produced a number of illegitimate children. His love of parties and dancing reached a climax with the infamous Banquet of Chestnuts hosted by his son Cesare Borgia at the Vatican, seat of papal authority in Rome, on 30 October 1501. After dinner, the guests, who included members of the clergy, were invited by fifty specially selected prostitutes to take off their clothes and crawl around naked on the floor picking up chestnuts. Following this bizarre ritual an orgy took place in which, in the words of the master of ceremonies, 'prizes were offered – silken doublets, pairs of shoes, hats and other garments – for those men who were most successful with the prostitutes'.

With such unholy representatives, it is hardly surprising that hopes for deliverance for Europe were not forthcoming from divine intervention via the Papacy.

# What on Earth Happened?

## Searching for new routes to riches

Medieval Europe was politically fragmented, at war with itself both physically and ideologically, and surrounded on all sides with no obvious means of escape. In such times even the most eccentric ideas were bound to attract the interest of at least some rulers. So when one Portuguese dignitary expressed an interest in going on a grand treasure hunt to find the source of Islam's west African gold, he was listened to with great attention.

Born into the Portuguese royal family, Prince Henry (known as Henry the Navigator), third son of King John I, spent most of his life trying to find treasure. His interest was first aroused when his father's navy captured the important North African trading port of Ceuta in 1415. For years Muslim pirates had been raiding the Portuguese coast, stealing villagers to be sold in the lucrative slave markets of North Africa. Ceuta was the African terminus for gold transported by camel caravans across the Sahara. If only, thought Henry, a way could be found to get to that gold without having to cross the desert, perhaps new wealth could be accessed without most of it ending up in the pockets of Muslim traders.

Henry's quest led him to establish a settlement later called Vila do Infante (Town of the Prince) on the southern coast of Portugal, where explorers could plan maritime expeditions. He soon discovered that light, manoeuvrable ships called caravels worked best for coastal exploration and that by using a triangular lateen sail, common on Arab boats, it was possible to tack successfully against the wind, allowing his ships to sail other than where the wind blew them.

Henry's goal was to reach the far side of the Sahara Desert by hugging the west African coastline and sailing south. With each voyage, he made and updated maps to act as guides for future expeditions. Lagos, a small natural harbour, now a popular tourist destination on the Algarve coast, was his base.

# Medieval Misery

The first major challenge was to navigate south of Cape Bojador, a headland just south of modern-day Morocco, which was until then the most southerly point known to medieval Europeans. It took ten years and fifteen separate attempts to successfully pass this point, which because of its fearsome currents and strong winds became known as the place where sea monsters dwelt. Finally, in 1434, one of Henry's captains, Gil Eanes, discovered that by sailing far out to sea, beyond the sight of land, more favourable winds could be picked up which would propel boats further south down the coast.

By 1443 Portuguese sailors had reached the Bay of Arguin, on the Atlantic coast of modern Mauritania, where they later built a powerful fort. By now they were south of the Sahara. From 1444, dozens of vessels left Henry's port of Lagos each year, bound for sub-Saharan Africa. In 1452 came the first real results, in the form of slaves and gold delivered directly across the seas by Europeans without reliance on overland Muslim middlemen. Their arrival permitted the minting of Portugal's first ever gold coins, aptly called *cruzados*.

Was this the beginning of a new strategy that could perhaps provide an answer to desperate Europe's desire for wealth? Could the enterprise of a prince from the south-western edge of the continent really offer deliverance from the tyranny of Islam's traders? If gold and slaves could be acquired from just down the coast of west Africa, what other riches lay out there in the unknown world across the deep blue seas?

Here we stand at the threshold of the last 500 years in our world's story, such a tiny fragment of time that it represents just a hundredth of a second to midnight on the twenty-four-hour scale of all earth history. In that tiny speck of time terrible tales of disaster lay in wait for the world and its populations of human and non-human beings, mostly as a result of just a few determined European adventurers whose lust for treasure pushed them headlong into mankind's biggest ever global challenge. Soon the new strategic vision that had dawned in Portugal spread like a virus throughout Europe's fledgling states. Whichever of them was to become predominant, one thing was certain: the best prospects for future success lay in becoming mistress of the sea.

# 12

# European Conquest and Revolt

## (1450–c.1800 AD)

*How a few maritime explorers accidentally found a New World, and European nations discovered how to exploit the world's riches*

POTOSÍ IS THE HIGHEST city in the world. Located in the mountains of Bolivia, at 3,967 metres above sea level, it should be a paradise of clean air and fresh mountain springs. But today this once-idyllic mountain retreat is one of the most polluted places on earth. Its water has turned to acid, its land is sterile, crops cannot grow and the mountainside is littered with highly toxic waste including cadmium, mercury, chromium and lead.

Towering over the town is the peak of Cerro Rico, known locally as 'the mountain that eats men'. Inside were once the world's richest silver mines, dug out by thousands of African and Native American slaves imported by Spanish explorers, who founded the place in 1546. The slaves came from anywhere that labour could be snatched – locally from the south in Peru, or from as far away as the west coast of Africa or even the islands of the Pacific. Their feet trampled powdered silver ore with deadly mercury into a brew of poisonous metallic slime. Then the mercury was burned off, releasing clouds of lethal vapours that eventually dissolved into the mountain streams, turning the water toxic. Between 1556 and 1783 more than 45,000 tonnes of pure silver were extracted from the mountain using this process, much of it shipped directly to Europe. No one knows how many men, women and children died from asphyxiation, poisoning and overwork in this godforsaken place, although the total has been estimated at a staggering eight million.

The pity of Potosí came about because between 1450 and 1650 Europe's treasure hunters struck lucky. The arrival of Henry the Navigator's booty in the form of African slaves and gold transformed Portuguese opinion about the best strategy for gaining new wealth. Investment in expeditions down the west coast of Africa yielded astonishing results. On one such voyage, in May 1488, the explorer Bartholomew Diaz was the first European to see the tip of Africa (see plate 11). He realized that here was a previously unknown sea route to the spice-rich lands of India and the Far East. Already flush with the profits from African gold and slaves, King John II of Portugal christened this new headland the Cape of Good Hope.

King John assembled the best scholars, mathematicians and map makers in his kingdom, and commissioned a series of expeditions in a climate of absolute secrecy. One, led by Duarte Pacheco Pereira, is thought to have revealed an unknown land to the west (Brazil). Much mystery still surrounds how much the court of John II knew about Brazil and the distances between Portugal and India via the eastern and western routes. This is partly because the information was regarded as top secret, but also because many court records were lost in a devastating earthquake that destroyed much of Lisbon in 1755.

### Columbus, and the European rediscovery of the Americas

Such secret knowledge is what may have led King John to reject the overtures of a boastful Genoese seaman called Christopher Columbus, who came to his court in 1485 and again in 1488 claiming to be able to reach the East by a westward route across the Atlantic. He demanded to be appointed 'Great Admiral of the Ocean', to become governor of any lands he discovered, and to receive one tenth of all the revenues derived from his quests.

Columbus's confidence that a route to the riches of the Far East could most easily be found by sailing west across the Atlantic was founded on a basic miscalculation. After studying the works of ancient Phoenician explorers and Arabic map makers, he concluded that the distance to Asia from the shores of Europe was just 3,600 kilometres (the actual distance from Spain to China, sailing west, is about 24,000 kilometres). Columbus had good reason to want the journey to appear reasonably short, since no patron would support a venture whose sailing time would make it impossible to provide sufficient food and water to sustain the crews of its ships.

In 1492 Columbus's quest for financial support for his mission at last met with success. In that year the Spanish rulers Ferdinand and Isabella finally ousted the Muslims from Granada, thus turning all Spain into one Catholic kingdom. With Spain no longer able to rely on gold tributes from the Moors of Granada, and with gangs of armed Christians hungry for lands to conquer, the idea of overseas exploration was enthusiastically received. Most important of all was the Spanish government's desire to find a new route to the riches of the East, not only to destroy the stranglehold of Muslim merchants but to rival Portuguese exploration along the Gold Coast of Africa.

Columbus is widely thought of as the most successful of all the early European overseas explorers and the discoverer of what is now North America. In truth, he was neither. None of his four expeditions discovered gold or silver in any great quantities, and the only mainland he reached was a stretch of Central and South America on his fourth and last voyage (see plate 11).

Columbus's voyages were significant in at least two respects, however. To begin with, he cracked the code of the Atlantic winds, which allowed European sailing ships to cross the ocean by sailing north-west and then returning by heading due east. Second, his discovery of land to the west began an epic rivalry between Spain and Portugal to explore the entire globe until it had been completely charted and mapped. In 1494 the two nations signed the Treaty of Tordesillas, which, incredible as it sounds today, divided the world into two halves along a north–south line drawn 370 leagues west of the Cape Verde Islands in the Atlantic. Everything discovered to the east would belong to Portugal, everything to the west to Spain (see plate 11). This was the first clearly articulated globalization strategy entered into by two European nations, explicitly designed to secure control of the whole world for their own exclusive benefit. To seal the deal Pope Julius II even sanctioned the arrangement with divine approval by publishing a papal bull in 1506.

### From discovery to slavery

Transporting and selling slaves, mostly from Africa, had been a profitable enterprise of Muslim merchants for centuries. However, European Atlantic explorers very quickly discovered a new use for slaves – as an agricultural labour force. In 1419 two Portuguese sea captains in the service of Henry the Navigator discovered the unoccupied Atlantic island of Madeira. It was Henry's idea to extract wealth from this place by planting sugar cane – then so rare as to be considered a spice – which had been introduced into southern Spain from South-East Asia by the Islamic Caliphs of Cordoba (see page 193).

Growing sugar is especially labour-intensive because the canes must be planted by hand. Henry's plentiful source of cheap African slaves meant that by the 1450s sugar production in Madeira provided a new model for creating wealth: valuable crops grown in the right climate tended by unwaged labour proved very lucrative indeed. It wasn't long before every explorer serious about making his venture financially viable adopted the practice. Columbus himself introduced sugar cane to the Caribbean on his second voyage, the same trip on which he began to enslave the natives.

News of Columbus's adventures travelled fast. Other countries began to sponsor their own expeditions, including Henry VII of England, who sanctioned a trip by Genoese navigator John Cabot, financed by merchants from Bristol.

Meanwhile, Vasco da Gama was the first Portuguese navigator to reach India, arriving at Calicut on 14 May 1498 (see plate 11). His voyage proved that the route round Africa was the quickest and easiest maritime passage to the East. Portuguese explorers soon established settlements along the coasts of the Persian Gulf, India and Indonesia, even reaching Japan.

Just as significant was the Portuguese (re)discovery of Brazil by Pedro Cabral, on 22 April 1500. By the 1530s sugar cane plantations cultivated by indigenous and imported slaves had become the Portuguese colonialists' richest sources of wealth, reinforcing the new trend of crops grown on one side of the world for transportation to the other.

## The Spanish invaders

Further north, soldiers from Spain, fresh from victory over the Muslims of Granada, were eager to increase their fortunes through overseas conquest. Using settlements established by Columbus on Hispaniola and Cuba as their bases, Hernán Cortés and Francisco Pizarro were responsible for Europe's most devastating conquests of all – adventures that resulted in the complete annihilation of the Aztec and Inca Empires of Central and South America (see pages 179, 183).

How did just a few hundred men and horses from Spain manage, within only a few years of landing on the American coast, completely to overwhelm empires that between them comprised an estimated twenty-five million people? It seems that for Cortés and Pizarro and their men success came from a lethal mixture of luck, cunning and forces of nature which stacked the odds heavily in their favour.

# What on Earth Happened?

When Cortés arrived off the Yucatàn Peninsula in the spring of 1519 with eleven ships carrying about 110 sailors and 530 soldiers he had the good luck to chance upon a Spanish sailor who had been shipwrecked on an earlier expedition. Gerónimo de Aguilar had been captured by the Aztecs and had lived among them as a slave for the previous eight years, learning their language and customs. Cortés also captured a beautiful native woman, called Malintzin, who spoke both Nahuatl – the language of the Aztecs – and Mayan, which was spoken by people living on the peninsula. Using them as translators, Cortés could now make himself understood by just about anyone he might encounter on his quest for gold. Malintzin later became Cortés's mistress and was baptized as Doña Marina. She bore Cortés a son, who became one of the first mixed-race Americans, mestizos. Today she is regarded by Mexican people as both the embodiment of treachery and a mother figure.

With the vital asset of easy communication Cortés was able to negotiate a military alliance with two native civilizations, the Totonacs and Tlaxcalans. Climate change was at least partly responsible for why these people were ready to help the Spanish invaders. They had recently been subjected to vicious assaults by their enemies, the Aztecs. The Flower Wars were the result of a series of severe droughts in response to which the Aztecs sought new victims from neighbouring tribes to be sacrificed to their gods in a desperate bid to secure rain (see page 178).

In November 1519 Cortés and his army reached the glorious capital of the Aztec Empire itself (see plate 11).

Tenochtitlan, a city built in the middle of water and accessible by three separate causeways, was a fabulous artificial world of canals, walkways and bridges, the Venice of Central America. Canoes carried goods and people under bridges and across a vast network of five interconnected lakes. Two terracotta aqueducts, each six kilometres long, took bathing water from nearby springs to the city centre, since Tenochtitlan's 200,000 people were, like the Romans, devotees of spa baths.

At the time of Cortés's arrival the Aztec Empire was ruled by a King called Moctezuma, who was renowned for his hospitality. After welcoming Cortés and his army as guests – one theory is that Moctezuma thought the Spanish were gods fulfilling an Aztec prophecy – the ruler soon found himself a captive in his own palace. Cortés demanded an enormous ransom in gold as the price of his freedom. As the weeks passed and treasure flowed into the Spanish coffers, resentment built up inside the city at the continued presence of Cortés's warriors and their native allies, and at the huge ransom demand.

Stones and spears were hurled by the citizens at their puppet ruler, who Cortés paraded on a balcony in an effort to quell riots. A few days later Moctezuma lay dead. Accounts differ as to his death. Perhaps he was killed by the Spanish, who had come to regard him as a liability. Or maybe one of his humiliated subjects had scored a direct hit. Not long after, at the beginning of July 1520, hostile Aztec citizens caused the Spanish to flee the city, only for them to return the following year with an army significantly strengthened by a Spanish alliance with the Aztecs' neighbouring enemies.

## The impact of disease

Highly infectious diseases including smallpox, measles, typhoid and influenza originated in large mammals such as cows, pigs and sheep as long as 10,000 years ago. Following their domestication, the diseases jumped across the species barrier into human beings. The absence of these mammals in the Americas meant that, unlike Europeans, Native American people had built up no immunity against such infections. When Europeans arrived they unwittingly brought these diseases with them. Smallpox killed about 40 per cent of the Aztec population within a year.

Weakened by disease and besieged by Cortés's army, Tenochtitlan eventually fell into Spanish hands. More than 240,000 Aztecs are estimated to have died during a final eighty-day siege.

The way was now clear for Spanish colonization and conquest of the whole region. A viceroy of New Spain, as it was called, was appointed in 1524, and over the next sixty years a mixture of Spanish military superiority and smallpox devastated the Native Americans. In 1546 silver mines like those at Potosí were discovered at Zacatecas, in north-central Mexico, the target of another swathe of Spanish settlers eager to get rich quick. As they arrived they raided local villages to acquire slaves for use as labour.

Meanwhile, far to the south, Cortés's second cousin Francisco Pizarro had received imperial approval for a conquest of Peru in 1529 (see plate 11). With just 106 foot soldiers, sixty-two cavalry and three cannon, Pizarro defeated an Incan army estimated at 80,000. Faced with these apparently impossible odds, he borrowed tactics from his cousin Cortés, and on 16 November 1532 lured the Inca Emperor Atahualpa into a trap. Through an interpreter (another lucky find), arrangements were made for Spanish delegates to meet the Emperor in the central square of a hilltop town called Cajamarca, where gifts and tokens of friendship would be exchanged.

Atahualpa approached the town square accompanied by a small retinue of nobles and concubines. He had left his weapons behind as a mark of friendship and trust. Accounts of what happened next were written by the Spanish. They claim that the Emperor was handed a Bible and ordered to renounce his pagan religion and accept the word of Jesus Christ. When Atahualpa threw the Bible to the ground in confusion, Pizarro's men charged on horseback from all sides of the square to the accompaniment of cannon fire. The surprise attack provoked panic. Never before had the Emperor and his household seen horses or heard gunfire. Many of the unarmed Incas were slaughtered and the Emperor himself was captured and imprisoned in a small room.

With no one to lead them, the Inca army fled in panic. Over the next few months Atahualpa's 'ransom room' was piled high with treasure brought on the understanding of his eventual release. But when he was charged with twelve trumped-up crimes, including revolting against the Spanish, practising idolatry and murdering his brother Huascar, his fate was sealed.

Tribes once loyal to the leaderless Incas now switched sides and helped the Spanish forces conquer the Inca capital, Cuzco, where a new Spanish city was built. Pizarro later founded Lima as the capital of Spain's South American empire because it was within easy reach of the sea.

No one can be sure how many Native American people died during the holocausts of war, disease and slavery that accompanied the Spanish invasions of Mexico and Peru, but estimates range between two million and a hundred million. More than 90 per cent are thought to have been the victims of European diseases, dramatically changing the course of human history and clearing the way for colonization. By 1546, largely thanks to silver mines, vast quantities of new wealth were being shipped back to the growing power of Spain.

## Reformation, emigration and colonization

In 1527 Pope Clement VII refused a request from English monarch Henry VIII for a divorce from Holy Roman Emperor Charles V's aunt Catherine of Aragon.

It was a momentous decision. Hot-tempered Henry was outraged, and declared himself, and not the Pope, supreme head of the English Church. He then used this as an excuse to plunder ecclesiastical property. More than 800 abbeys and monasteries made rich by centuries of forest clearing (see page 216) were confiscated in the famous Dissolution of the Monasteries. And with the money Henry built himself a massive fleet. By his death in 1547 the British Royal Navy could boast fifty-seven well-armed ships.

Meanwhile, popular hysteria about the abuses of the Church of Rome had quickly turned into a full-scale European religious schism known as the Reformation. It was exacerbated by a combination of German monk Martin Luther's protests against corrupt practices such as the clergy's sale of pardons in exchange for absolving an individual's earthly sins and the mass printing of Lorenzo Valla's damning evidence that the Papacy's claim to its territories in Italy was based on a lie (see page 226). Faith in Jesus alone could save people from their sins, argued the eloquent Luther, not the payment of taxes or doing good works as decreed by the Catholic Church.

The rise of Protestantism reflected the growing independence and confidence of Europe's emerging powers. Thanks to early explorers, nations such as Britain and France could now see opportunities for enriching themselves from trade overseas. John Cabot had already impressed the merchants of Bristol with his voyage to North America, and Jacques Cartier, a French navigator, sailed to Canada in a series of expeditions for the French King Francis I in the 1530s, becoming the first European to see the St Lawrence River (see plate 11).

The Reformation made revolt against Spanish (Holy Roman) imperial rule much easier to justify. Christianity's single all-powerful God could now be deployed on all sides, each claiming for itself the one true Church. Emergent nations also pitched themselves headlong into the violent contest for access to global resources. Holland, Denmark and Sweden were the most fervently Protestant countries while France dithered, swinging in the wind between Catholic and reformed, sinking for a while into in its own desperate wars of religion (1562–98). Although England had been early to break ties with Rome, the question of which faith to follow continued to plague its politics well into the next century, provoking that country's own civil war between 1642 and 1651.

Such conflicts came at an incredible cost. Silver from Mexico and Peru, which poured into Spain from the 1560s onwards, didn't stay there long. It was quickly spent on firearms, armadas and mercenaries. The silver from the New World became the backbone of a new bullion-based economy across all Europe.

So quickly did Spain's wealth spread that by the time Philip II of Spain died in 1598 his country was bankrupt, its fortune scattered across the warring nations of Europe. So many loans to fund wars of religion had been taken out from banks in Genoa and Augsburg that 40 per cent of all Spanish income was being spent on interest payments alone. Philip's war legacy left Spain the sinking power of Europe.

Europe's strategic direction was now clear: a continent carved up into autonomous national fragments, each pursuing whatever policies suited its own individual interests in a global competition to secure wealth overseas.

In the autumn of 1620 a band of English pilgrims and their families set off on a traumatic voyage across the Atlantic on board their ship the *Mayflower*. England was plagued by religious disputes and they hoped to find a better life abroad, taking their reformed Protestant religion with them. Puritans swelled their numbers over the next twenty years as England fell into a period of bitter Civil War, inflamed by matters of religion so that by 1642 about 21,000 had emigrated to North America.

## Changing European appetites, tastes and attitudes

Sweet foods became commonplace in Europe with the arrival of cheap sugar from plantations overseas. Even poor people became addicted to tobacco and snuff, grown on plantations established on the east coast of North America, turning Europe into the soft-drugs centre of the world. Hot chocolate, a drink made from cacao beans, which grow naturally in Central America, was first sampled by Cortés while he was being entertained at the court of Moctezuma. By 1544 it was being drunk at the royal court in Spain, and within a hundred years people in France, England and other countries in western Europe had become addicted to its delicious flavour. French settlers established cacao plantations in the Caribbean, as did the Spanish in the Philippines. Demand led to more plantations and again the market grew.

With new European tastes came a renewed confidence in the belief that perhaps humans were, after all, set apart from and superior to all other forms of life on earth. It was an old idea, reinforced by the Christian Bible, now available in mass-produced editions printed in vernacular languages for all to read. Protestant preachers zealously confirmed from the opening Book of the Old Testament, Genesis, that God made man to have dominion over all the world, its creatures and nature's bounty.

Religious confirmation that the natural resources of the earth were indeed at man's disposal was ratified philosophically with the beginnings of empirical Western scientific thought. A radical book published in 1543 by Polish astronomer Nicholas Copernicus (1473–1543) demonstrated how the earth revolved around the sun. No longer was mankind at the end of a long, divine chain of being. Instead, the world was part of a much larger mechanical system of planets and stars, rotating according to physical laws, as first proposed by Greek philosophers like Thales (see page 149).

The greatest of all the philosophers who celebrated Europe's new-found confidence was René Descartes (1596–1650). This French philosopher, scientist and mathematician considered mankind could gain insights into the workings of nature by breaking it down into small parts that could be understood through observation and reason. Descartes believed that only humans have minds, reducing all other things, animate or inanimate, to mere machines that can be manipulated, dissected and exploited without feeling or scruple.

# European Conquest and Revolt

## Natural consequences

Although the destruction of natural woodland was a process that first began when human civilizations appeared 10,000 years ago, Europe's maritime strategy to develop colonies and trading posts all around the world accelerated the process into a violent new phase. Although cooking and heating were the most immediate human demands, requiring a constant supply of firewood, the chief reasons for such widespread deforestation were shipbuilding, iron smelting, salt extraction and agriculture. In the period 1650 to 1749, between 18.4 and 24.6 million hectares of forest disappeared in Europe. Compounding the problem was the lack of any coordinated replanting policy to ensure supplies for future generations.

Iron making, the manufacture of glass, bricks and ceramics, and salt extraction all placed huge demands on ancient forests, as wood was needed to fuel the furnaces these processes required. Europe's annual production of iron has been estimated at 40,000 tonnes a year in 1500, but by 1700 it had more than tripled. Following the Great Fire of London in 1666, it was decreed that to protect against future conflagrations all new buildings must be made of brick and stone, not wood. Ironically, this substantially *increased* the amount of timber required, because of the vast quantities of firewood needed to fuel the fires for baking so many bricks.

Deforestation in North America was driven by the first European settlers' need for pastureland for the fast-breeding domesticated animals they had brought with them as life-support systems. Columbus brought eight pigs to Hispaniola in 1492. They quickly spread to Mexico, taken there by conquistador expeditions, until their numbers in the wild became, in the words of the Spanish, *infinitos*.

On his second voyage, in 1493, Columbus brought with him some cows and horses. Within fifty years huge herds of cattle could be found as far apart as Florida, Mexico and Peru. The grassland pampas of South America provided perfect feeding grounds so that by 1700 these herds totalled an estimated fifty million animals. Domesticated sheep were first taken to America in the 1540s. They multiplied so fantastically that by 1614 there were 640,000 of them in the area around Santiago in Chile alone. Horses escaped and migrated from Mexico to the Great Plains, where they were re-domesticated by Native Americans, bringing a new way of life to the surviving tribes, most of which had fled to the interior of the continent to escape the encroaching European settlers.

From the prairies in the north to the pampas in the south, the Americas were swamped by new hoofed animals: goats, sheep, mules, horses, pigs and cattle brought from Europe and Asia. Within 250 years parts of America's landscape had been stripped bare, transformed beyond recognition by the never-ending grazing of these huge migrating herds.

## Potato famine, and the rise of monoculture

Growing commodities for worldwide export, such as tobacco (from the Caribbean), sugar cane (from the Americas and Asia), cotton (from North America), rubber (from South America), coffee (from Africa) and chocolate (from Mexico) provided the economic backbone of Europe's colonies. Crops like these not only meant more forest clearing, but many quickly exhausted the soil, leading to further expansion to find new areas of fertility. Usually only three or four tobacco crops could be sustained by a piece of land before it was abandoned, to be replanted in twenty or thirty years' time. In the meantime, more land was cleared.

While grazing animals and crops grown for export in the Americas caused a huge change in the natural landscape, domesticated plants taken across the world to be cultivated in Europe and Asia had consequences that were just as profound. Over thousands of years native Central American women had painstakingly domesticated wild *teosinte* into maize (see page 172) and as many as 300 varieties of potatoes were grown in Peru. Now, thanks to European globalization, Europe and much of Asia could reap the benefits of these nutritious crops too.

Maize was brought to Europe by the Spanish. It quickly became a valuable crop grown all around the Mediterranean, primarily as fodder for livestock. The cold climate of the Little Ice Age (*c.*1350–1850) meant that maize didn't take off in northern Europe until after 1850, when warmer conditions were re-established. However, it was successfully grown in southern China from about 1550 onwards. Between 1400 and 1770 the population of China exploded, from seventy to 270 million people – a rise of nearly 400 per cent, much of it accounted for by highly nutritious maize, which could be grown on higher, drier ground than rice.

The potato was introduced to Europe by a Spaniard returning from South America in about 1570. It eventually transformed European diets owing to its high nutritional value and the ease with which it could be grown and harvested, although at first European snobbery seems to have prevented its rapid uptake since it was a favourite food of the natives of the Andes, who were widely regarded by the Spanish as savages.

The South American potato's big European break came with its adoption by the peasants of Ireland, who frequently suffered food shortages. By the early 1800s Ireland was desperately addicted to a potato-based diet. When, in the 1830s, a fungal disease struck crops on the east coast of North America, its spores quickly spread on the winds as far as Peru, which is where the rot should have stopped. But such spores could now be spread by ships travelling across the Atlantic. By 1845 potato blight – probably carried on ships importing potatoes from Peru – had reached Germany, Belgium, England and then Ireland, where its progress caused complete collapse. During the great potato blight of 1846–9 more than one and a half million Irish people are thought to have died of starvation, disease and malnutrition after the total failure of three potato harvests in a row. More than a million more left Ireland, hoping for a better life in the American colonies or Australia.

Of the hundreds of different types of potatoes cultivated by the natives of South America, only as few as four varieties were ever brought across to Europe. This lack of biodiversity was one big reason why a single fungus could cause such widespread devastation.

## How animals were annihilated for their skins

As Europeans flocked to colonies established on the other side of the world, whether as adventurers, entrepreneurs or refugees, many animal species which had evolved over tens of millions of years became endangered or extinct. Flightless birds were especially vulnerable. The fearless dodo, a relative of the pigeon and native to the island of Mauritius, fell victim to Portuguese (and then Dutch) invaders who arrived from 1505.

Animals with furry skins were in particular peril. As a result of the cooling climate of the Little Ice Age, furs became an increasingly important commodity for trade in Europe from the fifteenth century onwards. European demand for furs drove Russian Cossacks to conquer the hugely hostile and previously unexplored environment of Inner Siberia. Novgorod, in western Russia, became a centre for the export of squirrel furs, exporting 500,000 skins a year by 1400. Urged on by rich merchant families such as the Stroganovs, Cossack peasants from south-eastern Europe moved through Siberia, trapping furs and selling them in European markets in exchange for guns. Their descendants eventually formed the backbone of imperial Russia's armies.

From as early as 1534 French settlers in North America had traded beaver furs with Native Americans. When hunters had exhausted one region they quickly moved on to another, travelling further inland until populations became exhausted. Fortified trading posts were established along the St Lawrence River by rival British and French trappers, who sided with native tribes in their efforts to out-hunt each other.

The same story applied to seals, walruses and whales, which all declined rapidly from about 1500 owing to the insatiable human appetite for skins, tusks and oil. In 1456 Atlantic walruses could still be found in the River Thames; now there are only 15,000 left worldwide. Today, artificial materials have replaced wild animal skins in many parts of the world. The practice of farming animals for their skins, rather than hunting wild stocks, has also been encouraged to prevent further extinctions.

## High time for a political rethink

Command of the high seas had now helped European rulers and merchants escape from medieval Muslim encirclement. Slave labour and the exchange of easy-to-produce arms and ammunition supplied Europe's traders with bullion, exotic foods, spices, silks, tea, coffee and chocolate from colonies in the New World and the Far East. Generally, these were not available to the population at large – how could they afford them? Instead, the masses continued to suffer as much as ever from famine, poverty and disease.

Growing inequality between Europe's rulers and their poverty-stricken subjects was exacerbated by the relentless warfare waged by European nations both within Europe and around the world. Unprecedented devastation was exported as far as the Americas and India in the Seven Years War starting in 1756. This conflict was described by British statesman and historian Winston Churchill as the first true world war, with more than one million lives lost.

How could a merciful, just, Christian God condone a world such as this? If Jesus Christ could perform miracles, why did he permit such inequality, wars and suffering? A fashionable new philosophy among European thinkers and politicians proposed that while a divine force had originally created the universe, it could not be responsible for intervening in its workings. Deism, as this concept came to be known, rejected supernatural events, miracles and any concept of divine revelation.

Such ideas fused with the scientific observations of Copernicus, Galileo and Isaac Newton, which showed that nature's laws were more rational and logical than divine or inspired. Perhaps a more scientific system of social order could unlock a better, more acceptable way of life for everyone – not just kings, clerics and merchants, who justified their luxurious lifestyles on the basis of either divine authority or the principle that might is right.

During his country's violent civil war from 1642 to 1651 English philosopher Thomas Hobbes (1588–1679) developed the idea that a ruler's political authority came not from God but from rational laws of nature. Hobbes argued that people voluntarily delegated their authority in the interests of their own self-preservation. Then in 1689 English philosopher John Locke (1632–1704) proposed a form of government based on a 'social contract' between rulers and the ruled. In Locke's view a ruler's authority not only came from the people, but could, if the contract were breached, also be legitimately taken away by the people.

Locke's *Two Treatises on Government* (1689) began a period now known as the Enlightenment, in which the concept of popular sovereignty became a powerful new force in the politics of Europe and its colonies. What gave people the right to own property was, said Locke, the fact that they worked to acquire it, extract wealth from it and defend it. Personal liberty was the inalienable natural right of all men for the protection of their private property. If governments breached that right, it followed through reason that people were justified in taking authority back into their own hands.

## *How freedom on one side of the pond ...*

Political ideas like these fell on fertile ground in the British colonies of North America. Taxes imposed to help recover the huge debts incurred by the gruelling Seven Years War were bitterly resented by American settlers, who were also fighting their own battles against dispossessed natives. Discontent grew greater when the British government refused to supply sufficient forces during major clashes such as Pontiac's Rebellion (1763–6), when Native American forces tried to drive European settlers out of Ottawa. By 1776, all thirteen American colonies felt sufficiently aggrieved to form a coalition and declare their independence from Britain.

The founding fathers of the United States succeeded in their aim of creating a separate state, independent of Britain, largely thanks to the gunpowder and battleships supplied by Britain's arch enemy, France. They justified their rebellion through the arguments of writers who took their lead from Locke. Fashionable deists Benjamin Franklin, John Adams and Thomas Jefferson were the chief architects of America's declaration of inalienable human rights, which, they said, had been so undermined by Great Britain that the creation of a new independent sovereign state was not only justified but an obligation under 'Nature's God'. The United States Bill of Rights (1791) enshrined the principle of personal liberty in a series of ten amendments to the new nation's constitution. Individual rights for the protection and exploitation of private property formed a cornerstone of American liberty and personal freedom.

However, some issues that should have been dealt with were brushed under the carpet. Women, slaves and Native Americans were not, in reality, equal in the eyes of America's founding fathers, despite the powerful opening statement of the Declaration of Independence that 'all men are created equal'. The tolerance of slavery later contributed to the outbreak of a bitter American civil war that cost nearly a million lives (see page 267).

*... was very different from freedom on the other*

Popular French disgust at the excesses of the King and his court, and the privileges enjoyed by the Catholic Church provoked revolutionary zeal just as impassioned as that in the United States. But ideas of freedom on this side of the world were very different from those incubating in America. Tying natural rights to parcels of land was far less important to the mob which liberated the prisoners from the Bastille in Paris on the night of 14 July 1789. After all, theirs wasn't a fight against a distant colonial power or fierce bands of dispossessed natives. Their struggle was to do with making sure everyone got fed and ridding their country of privilege. Liberty, equality and fraternity became their rallying cry. And anyone that stood in its way was brutally swept aside.

Following the storming of the Bastille, a new assembly abolished all special rights and privileges of the nobles, clergy, towns, provinces, companies and cities. In the 'Declaration of the Rights of Man and of the Citizen', published on 26 August, the basis of French liberty was firmly founded on abolishing inequality between classes of people and not, as in the United States of America's new constitution, on the inalienable rights of private landowners.

Popular freedom, in all its forms, was an infection that quickly spread across the world. On 20 July 1810 the citizens of Colombia (then called New Granada) declared their independence from Spain. More colonies in Central and South America followed: Venezuela in 1811, Argentina in 1816, Mexico, Guatemala, El Salvador, Honduras, Nicaragua and Costa Rica in 1821, and Brazil in 1822.

## Propaganda and national heroes

It didn't take long for Europe's other ruling classes to figure out how to make use of notions of liberty, equality and individual rights to boost their own grip on power.

For a start, it now became easier for rulers to recruit much larger armies. Since the 1530s firearms had made it possible to turn peasants into foot soldiers with only a few days' training. But armies stayed small, because the bigger they were, the more they cost to equip. Standing armies were a wasted expense when a country was not at war. However, once people became infected with the idea that ultimately *they* were sovereign, it became much easier for rulers to galvanize the masses into taking up arms and sacrificing themselves for the sake of an idea, or for the colours on a national flag or the melody of an anthem. In this way, ideas of national service were born.

In 1798 the French Republic passed a law declaring in its first article, 'Any Frenchman is a soldier and owes himself to the defence of the nation.' Napoleon Bonaparte, a general who seized political power in a military coup in 1799, was a genius at rallying France to the cause of defending its new libertarian principles. He was the first European statesman to introduce the idea of a conscript army. It quickly caught on. At the height of the Napoleonic Wars (1804–15), the French Emperor – as Napoleon became – managed to raise as many as 1.5 million troops, mostly from France. At the end of the wars, some 900,000 Napoleonic troops faced forces of about a million from a coalition of other European countries. No wars had ever been fought on such a scale before.

The birth of fighting for causes – good versus evil, freedom versus tyranny – ushered in a new age of propaganda and popular heroes. After Admiral Horatio Nelson defeated the French fleet at the Battle of Trafalgar in 1805, the British government built a statue and a square in the heart of London as a permanent reminder to its people of this hero who had led them in the defence of their country against tyranny. National champions like Nelson and Wellington, the British general who finally crushed Napoleon at the Battle of Waterloo in 1815, were given state funerals and buried in the nation's most sacred places.

# What on Earth Happened?

## *Towards a world of free trade and free people*

Another challenge for some of Europe's rulers was how to recover from the economic dislocation caused by the loss of the colonies on which much of their wealth was based.

France had lost Haiti and ceded most of its American colonies in a desperate bid for cash. The French colony of Louisiana was sold by Napoleon to the United States in 1803 for $15 million to help fund the wars against the British. Thanks to Latin America's independence movements Spain's overseas empire began to crumble from the start of the nineteenth century. And Britain could now no longer rely on exclusive supplies from the plantations of the newly independent United States of America.

One solution was to find new colonies elsewhere. Napoleon occupied Egypt in an attempt to protect French trade interests and block British routes to its colonies in India. Meanwhile, the British consolidated their position in India, extending the rule of the Honourable East India Company across most of the subcontinent by 1813. The conquest of Burma to an extent compensated Britain for its loss of North American timber supplies by gaining access to thousands of square kilometres of precious hardwoods.

Also, no longer able to send convicts to North America as indentured servants, Britain's gaze turned southwards to find an alternative place for the disposal of the large numbers of poor people locked up in the country's overcrowded jails. From 1788 to 1868 regular shipments of British convicts turned Australia, which had been home to an estimated one million previously undisturbed Aboriginals, into another satellite of Europe's global village.

But strategies like these didn't resolve the problem of what to do about trade with former colonies, such as the United States of America, which could no longer be exploited on an exclusive basis. What's more, with its millions of African slaves, the United States was at a huge economic advantage now that it was free to export its goods to the highest bidder anywhere in the world.

Thanks to tireless Quaker campaigners and evangelical Christians such as William Wilberforce (1759–1833), the British parliament voted in 1807 to outlaw slave trading throughout the British Empire. By 1833 Britain had declared not just the trade but slavery itself illegal throughout its empire. The British parliament now positioned itself as liberty's true champion, and in a determined effort to level the economic playing field British foreign policy was now directed at persuading its trading partners to follow suit.

The restoration of profitable trading relationships with former colonies was also assisted by the pen of a Scottish professor called Adam Smith. In *An Inquiry into the Nature and Causes of the Wealth of Nations* (1776) Smith proposed a new economic philosophy, arguing that some countries were naturally more efficient at making certain goods than others. If a country with a warm, dry climate suitable for growing raw materials like cotton was free to sell it to a hilly country that had plenty of rainfall to power watermills to manufacture finished clothes, then, said Smith, both countries would be better off.

Smith extended the idea of liberty to mean free trade between nations – the removal of monopolies, taxes and tariffs. Smith's economic liberty became the cornerstone of a new science called economics. Capitalism based on free trade between separate nations was a direct challenge to the protectionist concept underpinning the empires of Europe, in which wealth came exclusively from a nation's private colonies. In a world where some empires were beginning to break apart and new nations like the United States had no colonies of their own, this idea of free-market capitalism had considerable attractions.

A different kind of revolution was responsible for the success of the economic system called capitalism, which eventually became globally predominant. The Industrial Revolution was no less violent than the American or the French, but instead of trying to overthrow political authority, its sights were set on using scientific progress to unfetter humanity from the limitations of being part of the natural world.

# 13

# The Industrialized World

## (1800–1945 AD)

*How the human species finally freed itself from the shackles of nature, provoking a race to exploit the capital riches of the world*

ARE HUMANS FUNDAMENTALLY different from other animals? Today people seem divided on the issue. Some feel secure in their belief in man's separateness, even superiority, perhaps persuaded by the fact that no other animal has ever tried to send its own species to the moon and back, let alone succeeded in doing so.

Others think that Charles Darwin's discoveries, first published in 1859, proved beyond all reasonable doubt that humans evolved from animals and that the difference between man and monkey is only a matter of degree – or of brain size, to be precise. Humans, they say, may be good at inventing things that other animals cannot, but then was making an atomic bomb really such a smart idea? And what's all this recent anxiety about the climate and global warming? If humans are to blame for melting ice caps, rising sea levels, changing rainfall patterns and dreadful new droughts which may mean that soon hundreds of millions of human beings, not to mention other species, will perish, perhaps they're not so clever after all.

This dispute is at the core of the current debate about man's relationship with nature. Will the future of life on earth be best secured by man using his ingenuity to tackle and take responsibility for the great problems of climate change, energy supplies and shrinking biodiversity? Or should mankind revert to a simpler, less frenetic way of life, restoring to nature its traditional role of regulating and balancing the planet's life-support systems, regardless of the success or failure of any individual species?

The foundations of this mother of all debates date back about 200 years. Until then most civilized people were clear in their minds that in terms of living species mankind was a cut above the rest.

Followers of Judaism, Christianity and Islam believed that God had given man dominion over all other life and with the advent of guns and gunpowder he finally had the means to back this claim up. Once Europeans had connected the earth's previously separate continents, using their ships to transport artificially bred crops and animals from one part of the world to another, man's command over nature must have seemed almost complete.

Large human populations covered most of the globe. Even where they had been all but wiped out by disease, as in the Americas, stocks were rapidly replenished by fresh supplies of slaves or colonists from Africa and Europe. Numbers tell the story. Despite wars, plague and other natural disasters by 1802 the world's population had risen to a staggering one billion people – that's a rise of at least 500 per cent in less than 2,000 years.

But in 1798 an English economist called Thomas Malthus (1766–1834) published an essay that predicted imminent disaster. Within fifty years, he claimed, the human race would have increased to such an extent that there would not be sufficient food to sustain it. The problem, wrote Malthus in *An Essay on the Principle of Population*, was that the human population was growing far more quickly than the supply of food the earth could produce. If disasters resulting from human vices, such as war, didn't cut humanity's numbers sufficiently, then nature would take over, in the form of disease, famine and starvation, until the proportion of population to food supply regained its proper balance.

Malthus's essay came as a great shock to many people in Europe and America. They believed, mostly for religious reasons, that thanks to the gift of a superior intellect and a divine soul mankind was different from all other living things. But what if Malthus was right? It was almost as if his dire warnings were a direct challenge to the most creative minds of Europe and its American offshoots to make sure that his predictions couldn't come true.

## The advent of mass production

For centuries China led the world in technological and scientific innovation. Printing, gunpowder and the compass, three inventions which helped shape the modern world, all came from the East (see pages 202, 203, 205). But it wasn't from the East that man's newest inventions designed to overcome the limits of nature were to come. After all, who in China had ever heard of an Englishman named Malthus?

Since the mid-fifteenth century China had shunned approaches from the West. Its government's instincts were not directed towards the expansion of markets overseas. Following the rise of the Qing Dynasty in 1644, the strategy was simple: keep China's borders secure from invasions and other foreign influences, keep tribute payments from neighbours flowing in and, above all, prevent its prodigious numbers of peasants from clamouring for regime change. Without the pressure of external enemies, which had plagued the Song, the Qing's message to China's rural poor was as consistent as it was conservative: learn the works of Confucius, who teaches obedience to the family and the state, and if you're lucky you may win a well-paid job as a minor official in the enormous civil service. Otherwise, stick to growing rice.

The contrast with Britain in 1800 could not have been greater. This small island nation, naturally protected by the sea, was now at the centre of a worldwide system of fleets, markets and colonies. A knock here or there, such as the loss of its American colonies, was simply redressed by the acquisition of new imperial territories elsewhere (Burma, Malaysia, Singapore, Australia) or policies such as the abolition of slavery and the pursuit of capitalist free enterprise. When Britain was threatened by an energy crisis after its supplies of wood had been almost exhausted by the demands of shipbuilding, iron making, beer brewing, glass production, brick making and salt extraction, an alternative energy source was found underground in the form of coal. By 1800 most industries in Britain had converted from burning wood and charcoal to coke or coal.

Another incentive to be creative came from the ban on slave trading (see page 253), introduced in 1807, which stretched the nation's most ingenious minds to find ways of replacing slave labour with machines. This was considerably boosted by a system that gave individuals who came up with new ideas the chance to grow rich. Patents, which gave inventors a monopoly over sales of their ideas for a number of years, were first introduced in England by James I in 1623. By 1714 it was mandatory for inventors to publish their designs in exchange for their monopoly entitlement, encouraging creative minds to share their ideas as well as devise new and useful inventions.

It was within this innovative, entrepreneurial environment that Bolton barber Richard Arkwright (1732–92) came up with a revolutionary way of manufacturing cloth, inventing the world's first water-powered cotton mill. Arkwright's mill, opened in 1781 in the village of Cromford in Derbyshire, transformed the process of textile making by spinning thin, strong threads which were then fed into an automatic loom. In spite of a series of disputes over the rightful claim to the invention, by the time Arkwright died in 1792 he was a very wealthy man, with a fortune estimated at £500,000. From nothing, he had become one of the richest men in the world.

Despite the ingenuity of Arkwright's loom, his invention could work only next to suitably fast-flowing rivers or streams. Indeed, from the start of human history until about 1800 everything to do with man's relationship with the rest of the world had always been to some extent subject to nature's own operating systems. Energy came directly from the natural, solar-powered processes of the earth – either from life itself, animal or human, or from nature's life-sustaining cycles of wind and water.

Automation made possible by water power led to the advent of assembly lines with teams of labourers trained to do the same repetitive tasks day in and day out. Products could be made more quickly, more cheaply and in greater volumes than ever before. Whereas a craftsman had to be skilled in many disciplines to make a finished item, bustling around his workshop, taking time to find the right tools for different stages of the job in hand, the assembly-line worker simply waited for the arrival of the next half-made object as it passed down the line, ready to do his one simple task again and again and again. Little skill required. No time wasted.

It wasn't just in Britain that the idea of mass production had caught on. Eli Whitney (1765–1825) was a mechanical genius from Massachusetts, USA, who became familiar with the ideas of mass production after having worked in his father's nail-making workshop during the American Revolutionary War. By 1798 the newly independent United States, anxiously watching the rapidly escalating war between Britain and Napoleonic France, had recognized the need for armaments to secure its fledgling liberty. To the amazement of the American Congress, Whitney demonstrated how he could assemble ten separate guns from a single heap of interchangeable parts. They were so impressed that they awarded him a contract to produce 10,000 muskets.

But ships, windmills, waterwheels, canals and mass production in newfangled factories were all still products of man's ability to harness the forces of nature. Even the first steam engines, pioneered by Englishman James Watt in 1769, used the weight of atmospheric air to provide a limited source of power for pumping water out of mines. If mankind was to prevent Malthus's catastrophic predictions coming true it was essential to find ways of breaking free of nature's constraints and tapping into the resources that she herself used to create and sustain all life.

## Full steam ahead

When Cornish inventor Richard Trevithick (1771–1833) turned up the pressure on his Puffing Devil steam engine in 1801, the truly transformative effects of man's potential power over nature could at last be seen. This machine did not rely on the earth's natural forces at all. High-pressure steam meant that Trevithick's engine could be mounted sideways on a track and be made to pull a wagon without the help of gravity, atmosphere, wind or water. All it needed were the energy-rich raw materials of the earth itself, the leftovers of life once lived (coal, oil and natural gas are all such products). Simply by burning wood or coal in an oxygenated atmosphere, water could be heated in a high-pressure kettle to produce a fully independent source of portable power.

Railways transformed the landscapes of Britain, Europe and America. By 1890 they criss-crossed the whole of Britain, providing a convenient, fast, reliable transportation service that ran according to a timetable of human needs regardless of natural conditions. In the United States rail transport allowed the proper exploration and exploitation of the vast inner continental area, opening up new lands for plantations and mining. By 1890 the US railroad system stretched some 230,000 miles. Networks in Russia, Europe and in other Western colonies such as India and South Africa developed in parallel, providing mass overland transportation across the trading world.

Steam also powered the provision of electricity, pioneered by a clutch of American, French, Italian and German scientists. Having perfected the design for a cheap, mass-produced lightbulb, American inventor Thomas Edison went on to establish the world's first distribution system in 1882, linking fifty-nine customers in New York with mains electric power. In the same year, a steam power station came into operation in London, supplying energy to street lights and private houses nearby.

Today as much as 86 per cent of all electricity is still generated by steam-powered turbines heated by coal, oil, natural gas or nuclear fuels. Electricity gave rise to the first system for worldwide telegraphic communications, initially based on chemical battery power, trialled in France as early as 1810. In 1866 a transatlantic cable was laid on the seabed, linking Britain with the United States, thanks to the development of steam-powered ships, which had by then entered service in the British Royal Navy. By 1900 instant electronic communications networks linked every inhabited continent on the globe.

The power of steam was matched by the development of another artificial transportable power-production system, the internal combustion engine. In 1876 German scientists Nikolaus Otto and Gottlieb Daimler developed a four-stroke engine that used oil, in its refined state of petroleum, as an energy-rich explosive mixture from which they produced a lighter, faster system for motive power. Ransom Olds built the first American automobile factory in 1902 and Henry Ford applied mass-production techniques beginning in 1910. Road networks were upgraded by governments keen to promote trade and transport, urged on by people's desire to express their personal liberty by being able to travel independently where and when they chose.

Small, highly efficient engines that could power cars were soon mounted on wings, further defying nature's limits on man's mobile capabilities. In 1903 Orville and Wilbur Wright successfully piloted the first controlled, powered flight near Kitty Hawk, North Carolina. Aircraft became a vital component of military forces, providing reconnaissance and the possibility of delivering bombs from on high. War needs meant that the dynamics of mass production were quickly applied to aircraft manufacture. During the Second World War (1939–45) mass-production techniques allowed the United States to build almost 300,000 military planes in just five years.

Continents were now so close that it became possible to travel to the other side of the world in less than a day. In 1879 the US was producing nineteen million barrels of oil a year. By 2005 worldwide production was almost eighty-three million barrels a day.

The ultimate form of power, which does not occur naturally on earth, was pioneered by Albert Einstein (1879–1955). In 1905 this German-born genius spelled out a number of new theories that revised man's basic understanding of the laws governing the physical universe. Isaac Newton's theories of motion and gravity, although apparently correct for large objects, broke down at the atomic level, said Einstein. Most critically of all, he calculated that the enormous quantity of energy stored in an atom to hold its constituent parts together was a massive source of untapped power. The amount of energy inside a single atom was, Einstein worked out, equivalent to its mass multiplied by the speed of light (186,000 miles per second) squared, i.e. $E = mc^2$.

In August 1945 the residents of Hiroshima and Nagasaki in Japan were the first people to feel the power of this awesome, supra-natural force when atomic bombs were dropped on their cities by the American air force, each one killing as many as 70,000 people in an instant. Thousands more died in the deluge of invisible but lethal radioactive energy that lingered for years to come. In 1951 a means of harnessing this energy for peaceful purposes was demonstrated by a test reactor in the US state of Idaho. It showed that nuclear energy could provide another source of heat to evaporate water into steam for generating electricity.

## Molecular miracles

Man's ability to compete with nature was enhanced further by the discovery by German scientist Friedrich Wöhler (1800–82) that chemicals produced by life itself could be created artificially in a laboratory. While trying to concoct the compound ammonia cyanate in 1828, Wöhler, quite by accident, synthesized urea. The scientific world was astonished. Until then people had believed that a fundamental 'vital' force separated animate from inanimate matter. The artificial creation of a chemical of nature out of inanimate substances in a laboratory had been considered quite impossible.

The birth of organic chemistry, triggered by Wöhler's discovery, signalled the opening of a second front in man's knowledge of how to use the same materials as nature for his own ends. Life's 'modelling clay' is constructed from two main elements – carbon and hydrogen – which combine with traces of other elements and oxygen in an almost infinite variety of chains, curls and rings to produce the diverse stuff of living things. One of the richest sources of such ingredients is crude oil. Wöhler's discovery meant that it was now possible for mankind to learn how to model with this clay too – not yet for making life itself, but for synthesizing useful but unnatural materials.

In the 180 years since Wöhler's accidental synthesis of urea, mankind has modelled countless new substances and materials – from plastics to explosives – using oil or its aerated equivalent, natural gas, as ingredients. Two German scientists, Fritz Haber and Carl Bosch, developed a new artificial process for producing ammonia from nitrogen and hydrogen which could be used as an artificial fertilizer. Today, more than a hundred million tonnes of artificial fertilizers are produced each year for spreading on fields all over the world. The Haber–Bosch process is now reckoned to be responsible for sustaining up to 40 per cent of the world's population – that's as many as three billion people.

## Cracking the genetic code

Direct artificial intervention in the processes of life was the third frontier in man's push over the last 200 years to break free from the natural limits endured by his ancestors. Building on the pioneering work of Englishman Edward Jenner (1749–1823), Frenchman Louis Pasteur (1822–95) devised vaccinations that worked by injecting people with artificially weakened forms of diseases to provoke their bodies into building defences to ward off potential infection. By 1979 such vaccinations had eradicated smallpox from the world, possibly man's biggest triumph over one of nature's most persistent and devastating historical plagues.

Direct biological interventions were spurred on by Rosalind Franklin (1920–58), a British biophysicist whose X-ray images of DNA helped James Watson and Francis Crick to model nature's ultimate polymer, DNA, in 1953. Their work unlocked the control system inside every living cell that directs the process of evolution itself, thereby leading to the rise of the modern science of genetic engineering.

Since then scientists have replicated life in a test tube by cloning cells; genetically modified crops to make them grow fitter, faster and larger; and fought diseases with drugs and therapies that lengthen human lifespans. To cap it all, the Human Genome Project, launched in 1990, has codified the complex genes that make up humans themselves, giving modern scientists the keys with which to unlock the inner secrets of evolutionary mechanics.

Modern man's achievements would seem to suggest that he is indeed rather different from any other species that has ever lived. After all, what other living things have managed to interrupt, modify, compete with and even usurp nature's age-old operating systems? As for the dire warnings of Thomas Malthus: when he died in 1834 the world's population had just passed the one billion mark. By 1928 it had reached two billion; by 1961 three billion; by 1974 four billion; by 1987 five billion; and by 1999 six billion. The growth rate is such that for each extra billion humans added, it takes roughly half as long to add a billion more. Dramatically falling child death rates have been accompanied by substantially longer life expectancy. Artificial fertilizers, medicines, improved hygiene, fossil fuels, industrialized cities, mass production, organic chemistry and vaccinations are the cause. As of 2006 the world's net population grows by approximately 211,090 every day. Malthus was right. None of this would have happened if nature had had her way.

## The matter of race

Once mankind was unshackled from the limitations of the earth's natural forces, steamships could travel anywhere regardless of prevailing winds, railways could transport goods at high speeds without the need for human or animal power, and industrialists could manufacture limitless numbers of cheap finished goods using artificial as well as natural materials, unskilled labour and automatically powered machines.

Britain's industrial lead didn't last long. By 1870 France and the United States of America had caught up. Their factories were manufacturing everything from pots and pans to clothes, ships and weapons. New countries such as Italy (united in 1860) and Germany (formed in 1871) also joined the club of rapidly developing nations. Each followed a similar pattern: merchants grew rich off the profits of new enterprise while their workers stewed with discontent about low pay, poor working conditions and the lack of a real political voice. Liberty, equality and fraternity were still hollow words. Real power lay with cabals of aristocrats and hungry merchants who dominated parliamentary politics, or with imperialist tsars and autocratic kings.

It hadn't escaped the notice of some late-nineteenth- and early-twentieth-century commentators that the inventions that were changing the world all seemed to originate in the 'genius' of white Caucasian people – British, French, German, Italian or American. Samuel George Morton (1799–1851), professor of anatomy at the University of Pennsylvania, collected hundreds of human skulls from all over the world in an attempt to understand the source of Europe's apparent intellectual superiority. He claimed to be able to determine the respective mental abilities of different human races based on their average cranial capacity: the larger the brain, he said, the greater the intelligence.

Voyeuristic Europeans and Americans had ample opportunities to see the apparent inferiority of other races for themselves. During the 1870s human zoos displayed African Nubians and American Inuits alongside wild animals. They could be found at imperial exhibitions held in Hamburg, Antwerp, Barcelona, London, Milan, New York and Warsaw, which drew as many as 300,000 members of the public. The 1889 Exposition Universelle in Paris was visited by a remarkable twenty-eight million people. One of its main exhibits was a 'Negro Village' featuring 400 native Africans. Other exhibitions in Marseilles (1906 and 1922) and Paris (1907 and 1931) displayed natives in cages, often naked.

Deep racism was one of the factors at the heart of America's devastating Civil War (1861–5), which almost caused the Union to break up irrevocably. The status of African slaves had been under scrutiny ever since the Declaration of Independence statement in 1776 that 'all men are created equal' (see page 249). When Britain abolished slave trading in 1807 and then slavery throughout its Empire in 1833, pressure for change elsewhere grew greater. America's Northern states had little to lose from the abolition of slavery, having quickly industrialized with help from Britain. Not so the cotton-, tobacco- and sugar-plantation owners of the South, where slave labour underpinned the white way of life. Although the US Constitution was unequivocal about the equal rights of men, the legality of slavery was deemed a state matter, not a federal concern. Eleven Southern states refused to outlaw slavery using some ingenious mental gymnastics to justify their stance.

The questions as to whether new states should be admitted as 'slave' or 'free' further inflamed debate. When Abraham Lincoln, a Northerner, became President in 1861, eleven Southern states, led by South Carolina, formed their own confederation and declared themselves separate from the Union.

Between April 1861 and the spring of 1865 almost one million people died in a most bitterly fought civil war. The Northern states secured victory thanks to their superior industrial technology. Four million black African slaves were freed and three new amendments adopted into the US Constitution: outlawing slavery (the Thirteenth Amendment), granting black citizenship (the Fourteenth) and granting all men – but not women – the right to vote regardless of race, colour or creed (the Fifteenth). By 1877, after a painful period of 'reconstruction' in the South, all the former Confederate states had been sworn back into the Union.

But ideas of white supremacy endured. US Supreme Court Rulings in 1896 and 1908 allowed legal discrimination through the provision of public facilities that were 'separate but equal'. In reality this meant that until the Civil Rights movement of the 1960s many states in America ran a system of apartheid in which blacks were forbidden by law to attend the same schools as whites. They were also not allowed to share a taxi with whites or enter public buildings by the same doors. They had to drink from separate water fountains, use separate toilets, be buried in separate cemeteries and even swear in court on separate Bibles. They were excluded from public restaurants and libraries and barred from public parks with signs that read 'Negroes and dogs not allowed'.

## How Europeans claimed Australia and Africa

Between 1788 and 1900 Australia's Aboriginal population is estimated to have fallen by as much as 90 per cent owing to a combination of disease, land appropriation by overseas settlers and violence. The news of the discovery of gold in 1851 provoked a new wave of European colonization which increased Australia's population from 431,000 to 1.7 million two decades later. Roads, railways and telegraph lines quickly followed. Native people, as in America, found themselves in the middle of a confusing, unsympathetic world. European illnesses such as smallpox, influenza, measles and venereal diseases did most of the killing, although it is estimated that some 20,000 Aboriginals who got in the way were variously massacred by European whites.

Many white settlers hoped that over time Aboriginal culture would disappear altogether. Between 1869 and 1969 Christian missionaries, supported by the Australian government, systematically made Aboriginal children wards of the state, forcibly taking them to internment camps and orphanages where they were raised apart from their parents as agricultural labourers or domestic servants. In an effort to stamp out their culture, they were forbidden to speak except in English. According to a government inquiry published in 1997, more than 100,000 Aboriginal children were forcibly removed from their parents between 1910 and 1970. In a candid admission of what happened to these 'stolen generations', the report concluded: 'These violations continue to affect Indigenous people's daily lives. They were an act of genocide, aimed at wiping out Indigenous families, communities and cultures, vital to the precious and inalienable heritage of Australia.'

Europe's conquest of inland Africa was no less traumatic. At the beginning of the nineteenth century sub-Saharan Africa was still a patchwork of as many as 3,000 distinctive human groups speaking over 1,500 different languages. Most of the continent was dominated by Bantu farmers and herders, who over several centuries had spread from their ancient homeland in west Africa displacing hunter-gathering bands such as the bushmen (Khosians) and Pygmies.

France pioneered the first major European incursions in 1830, when its troops invaded Algeria, then a vassal state of the weakening Ottoman Empire. By 1834 French troops controlled a population of three million Muslims, and Thomas Bugeaud, the colony's first governor-general, began constructing roads for transporting goods and materials for export to Europe. By 1848 more than 100,000 French people had settled in the territory, cultivating the land and exporting cotton harvested by forced African labour.

Following the success of this first invasion, Europe's other capitalist nations found themselves in a race to grab as much land and labour, and as many commodities for as many markets, as possible. By the 1870s a renewed fervour for colonization – known as the Scramble for Africa – was fuelled by the demands of European industrialization (see plate 12).

The scramble was whipped up further by the arrival of a new power on the European stage – Germany. On 1 September 1870 France was humiliated at the Battle of Sedan by German-Prussian forces, which surrounded and captured the French Emperor Napoleon III and his army. Following this Franco-Prussian War (1870–1) Germany became unrivalled master of the River Rhine, around which lay prime land for industrialization with excellent transport links and power from natural fast-flowing rivers.

Flushed with victory, Chancellor Otto von Bismarck united twenty-five separate German states into a single mighty nation headed by the all-powerful Wilhelm I of Prussia. Africa's fate as the next theatre of European colonization was sealed by a conference in Berlin in 1884–5 orchestrated by Bismarck, at which the major powers of Europe agreed the terms under which the continent was to be sliced up between them like a melon. The stage was now set for the rapid and comprehensive creation by European powers of what has since become known as the Third World.

A condition of the Berlin Congress was that colonized land be put into 'economic use'. That meant either cultivating cash crops such as coffee, cacao, rubber, cotton and sugar to generate profits, or extracting minerals such as copper, diamonds and gold to pay for and feed Europe's appetite for industry. As Africa was occupied, its people, soil and society were pressed into producing goods mainly suitable for export to other countries. Africans were also denied the chance of investing in strategies to feed and sustain their own growing civilizations.

Nineteenth-century Europe's financial and material gains were made at the expense of the native populations of Asia, America, Africa and Australia. Grand buildings like the Royal Palace of Brussels still stand proud, lavishly refurbished by King Leopold II with his profits from Congolese ivory and rubber (see plate 12). By the time most African countries received their political independence in the second half of the twentieth century, their land had been exhausted, their raw materials removed, their economies sucked dry by loans, and trade agreements locked their populations in poverty. Worse still, their people had been ripped out of their traditional tribal and ethnic groupings, rearranged into new colonial territories and armed with Western guns.

European colonization extended the misery of Africa, which had begun with the demand for slaves in the Muslim world to the east and America to the west.

## Ideological misgivings

Karl Marx, a Jewish German social philosopher and economic theorist, wrote a famous diatribe against the capitalist nations in the heady climate of a Europe swept by revolutions. His *Communist Manifesto* directly challenged the ruling elites. Marx proposed a new type of society that would finally put an end to centuries of pernicious inequality between the rich and poor.

A series of disastrous crop failures, most importantly the potato blight that crippled Ireland, Belgium and Germany, led to popular rebellions in Italy, France, the German states and Poland in 1848. The cause of the unrest, according to Marx, was plain to see. Human history, he said, was a long series of struggles between rich and poor. As a result of industrialization that struggle was now being waged between capitalist businessmen (the bourgeoisie) and impoverished factory workers (the proletariat). The constant economic growth upon which Europe and America had based their strategies was now tottering. Capitalism's imminent collapse, said Marx, would lead to a new social order across the whole world in which equality and true freedom for the masses could be attained, if only the workers of the world would unite.

## Shenanigans in the Far East

Shortly after Marx wrote his prophetic manifesto, humanity's largest ever civil war broke out in China. Between 1850 and 1864 an estimated twenty million people perished in the Taiping Rebellion – that's twenty times more than in the American Civil War of around the same period.

# What on Earth Happened?

Chinese tea, silk and porcelain were highly sought-after commodities in Europe, but there was a problem: Chinese society was built on a philosophy of self-sufficiency. Since the mid-fifteenth century China had been a civilization independent of overseas fleets and trade with far-flung vassal colonies. Food and luxury goods were all manufactured in the home market. The Chinese Emperor himself explained as much in a letter he wrote to King George III of England in 1793, in response to a British request for trade: 'You, O King, live far away across the mighty seas ... The difference between our customs and moral laws and your own is so profound that our customs and traditions could never grow in your soil ... I have no use for your country's goods. Hence there is no need to bring in the wares of foreign barbarians to exchange for our own products ...'

Such self-satisfaction provoked the most extreme imperialist reaction. If the Chinese didn't want Western goods, then something had to be done to *make them* want them.

Officials in Britain's Honourable East India Company came up with the dishonourable solution of drug trafficking. An elaborate system was established whereby British traders would buy Chinese tea in Canton and issue credit notes to local traders, who could then redeem them against opium smuggled in by agents from Calcutta. Between 1750 and 1860 thousands of tonnes of opium grown in the poppy fields of Bengal were smuggled into China in exchange for silk, tea and porcelain. The trade was a masterstroke of ingenuity. Rather than the British paying for goods in valuable silver, locally grown opium could be used as currency instead. And the problem of China's self-sufficiency was solved by a freshly cultivated dependency on highly addictive drugs.

By the 1820s more than 900 tonnes of opium a year were flooding into China from Bengal. In 1838 the Chinese imperial government introduced the death penalty for anyone caught trading the drug. When the British refused to stop shipments, the Chinese government imposed a trading embargo. Two years later a British fleet arrived with the object of forcing the Chinese to revoke the ban. After the British seized the Emperor's tax barges, the Chinese government was forced to sue for peace in 1842. A treaty re-established trade links, ceded Hong Kong to Britain and allowed Christian missionaries to preach unhindered on Chinese soil.

These agents of God did more harm than all the poppy fields of India combined. In 1850 Hong Xiuquan, an unorthodox Christian convert, was so entranced by missionary teaching that he claimed to be the long-lost brother of Jesus Christ. Blessed with a charismatic personality, Xiuquan raised a giant peasant army to challenge the Qing government, which was, largely thanks to Britain, now impoverished and ineffective. Between 1853 and 1864 Xiuquan and his rapidly swelling band of followers established a rival state across southern China with its capital at Nanjing. The Heavenly Kingdom of Great Peace replaced the teachings of Confucius with the Christian Bible. Women were treated for the first time as equal to men. Opium, gambling, tobacco and alcohol were all banned.

But once installed in his new capital the movement's divine leader lost his zest for rule, instead choosing to spend more time with his extended family in his harem. In 1856 Britain used China's civil war as an opportunity to make more military mischief in a conflict known as the Second Opium War and attacked the port of Guangzhou. This conflict ended in 1860 with the occupation of Beijing by Western forces, who compelled the Chinese government, still battling Xiuquan's rebels in the south, to sign a new treaty which legalized the import of opium, authorized foreign warships to sail along the Yangtze River, established eleven new ports for trade with Britain, France, Russia and the United States, and paid a large indemnity in silver to compensate Britain for its recent loss of profits. How times had changed since the Chinese Emperor confidently penned his letter to George III in 1793!

Meanwhile, French and British forces supported the struggling Qing government and together finally put an end to the rebellion in 1864, but not before it had become one of the deadliest wars in human history in which an estimated twenty million people died.

By now China, exhausted by war and still reeling from the effects of opium, was easy prey for the vultures. By 1887 the French had their own Far Eastern empire, luring Vietnam and Cambodia (known as Indochina) away from China's sphere of influence. Ten years later German forces occupied the strategically important mainland coastal region of Jia Zhou. By this time the Japanese had established control over Korea.

All of which explains why another devastating Chinese rebellion broke out between 1899 and 1901. Traditionalist rural peasants, calling themselves the Boxers, wanted to rid their homeland of the pernicious influence of the West and its alien capitalist culture. Their forces invaded the imperial capital Beijing in June 1900, killing tens of thousands of Chinese Christians and taking thousands of Western foreigners living in the city hostage. An international force scrambled to the rescue. By August it had defeated the Boxer rebels, but then, in an echo of the disaster of the Fourth Crusade (see page 219), this cabal of mostly European nations went on to plunder Beijing itself, setting fire to its palaces and forcing the Emperor and Dowager Empress to flee.

The price of international 'rescue' was set at reparations of some £67.5 million, to be paid in precious silver by the imperial government of China and split amongst the members of the eight-nation alliance. Such a sum could be raised only by punishing new taxes on the rural population. Within ten years the imperial Chinese government had become so weak and was so loathed by its people that a popular revolution finally put an end to the 2,000-year-old institution, replacing it with a republic in January 1912. After decades of civil war and invasions, this fledgling republic itself succumbed to a communist takeover on 1 October 1949 led by party chairman Mao Zedong.

In the Far East Marx's predictions as to the course of capitalism and the rise of the suppressed proletariat had proved uncannily accurate. In Europe, similar revolutions turned out to be no less profound.

## Towards total war

Popular zeal for a return to a fairer way of life boiled over during the First World War. The Great War, as it became known, was fought mostly in Europe between 1914 and 1918. It was only slightly less devastating than China's Taiping Rebellion, with eighteen million people left dead, twenty-two million wounded and the slaughter of some eight million horses.

It began after the heir to the imperial Austrian throne, Archduke Franz Ferdinand, was murdered by a Serbian student in Sarajevo on 28 June 1914. What was intended as a brief incursion by Austria-Hungary into Serbia to seek revenge turned into a struggle between the nations of Europe.

Against the combined forces of imperial Germany, Austria and the Ottoman Empire was pitched an alliance of Britain, France and Russia, and from 1917 the United States, in a titanic struggle for control of Europe and its overseas colonies. In such a climate, popular revolutions took place. First to fall was Russia, after two separate revolts during 1917. Military humiliations inflicted by Japan in the east and Germany in the west had severely weakened the authority of Tsar Nicholas II. Inflation, food shortages and a battered economy ripened the conditions for revolt while rapid industrialization had increased urban populations but failed to provide them with a better quality of life.

When the women of Petrograd revolted over the shortage of bread in February 1917 they triggered a massive outpouring of popular discontent. In March Tsar Nicholas was forced to abdicate. The political radical Vladimir Lenin was smuggled back to Russia from Switzerland, where he was living in exile. By early November Lenin and his army of Bolshevik revolutionaries led by Leon Trotsky had seized formal power in Russia. In May 1918 the Tsar and his family were executed in cold blood – whether on local or central orders, no one knows. Now civil war broke out between the Marxist Bolsheviks' Red Army and the monarchist Whites backed by Britain, France, the USA and Japan. In June 1923 the Bolsheviks finally gained control of the country, leading to the world's first experiment with communism, in which new technology promised to provide the magic ingredient to make Marxist dreams of class equality at last come true.

Universal healthcare, equal rights for women and education for all formed the backbone of Lenin's socialist ideals. But Russia, being a predominantly peasant, rural society, did not have the industrial capacity to achieve such reforms. The New Economic Policy, introduced in 1921, allowed surplus agricultural yields to be sold by farmers as an incentive for them to produce more grain to help build Russia into a rich enough society to afford the technology it needed to make the dream of classlessness come true.

But Lenin died in 1924. His successor Joseph Stalin (1878–1953) purged the Communist Party and established a dictatorship as total as any in imperial times. Although his successive five-year plans, begun in 1928, transformed the Soviet Union from a backward, peasant society into a major industrial power, countless millions died of starvation owing to his confiscation of grain and food from farmers between 1932 and 1934. Stalin's Communist Party became a brutal ruling class, suppressing anything and everything that threatened its grip on power. Those who resisted were either executed or dispatched to labour camps in Siberia. By 1939 an estimated 1.3 million people had been interned in such camps, which were known as the Gulag.

## Hitler's attempt to restore German pride

Adolf Hitler (1889–1945) felt deeply let down by his country's leaders, who in the opinion of many in the German army had accepted a humiliating armistice agreement in 1918 which had burdened Germany with impossible war reparations. According to the terms of the Treaty of Versailles, signed on 28 June 1919, not only did Germany accept full responsibility for the Great War (article 231) but it had to pay reparations of a staggering 269 billion Reichsmarks in gold (£11.3 billion).

Waves of strikes had crippled the munitions factories of Germany, turning what Hitler had believed was almost certain victory into a humiliating surrender. Those responsible were, in his eyes, Jewish Marxists. What's more, Jewish bankers, he believed, were responsible for the rise of the capitalist powers themselves, with their moneylending and pursuit of profit. Thanks to them, Germany had been dragged into a war with an ignominious end, after which it was forced to admit guilt and pay enormous reparations that could be honoured only by borrowing more capital from Jewish bankers in the United States.

But what, exactly, was Hitler proposing instead?

Hitler outlined his belief in a system called eugenics, a philosophy that advocated selective human breeding, in a book he wrote in 1923 called *Mein Kampf* (My Struggle). 'Nature concentrates its greatest attention not to the maintenance of what already exists, but on the selective breeding of offspring in order to carry on the species. So in human life also it is less a matter of artificially improving the existing generation – which, owing to human characteristics is impossible in ninety-nine cases out of a hundred – and more a matter of securing from the very start a better road for future development.'

Hitler's grand plan was to force back the frontiers of Europe's globalized world and go back to the philosophy of ancient Sparta with its pure racial stock providing national security and social welfare (see page 151). But to wind the clock back now would require intervention on a massive scale. Hitler took it upon himself to bring this about.

Elections in July 1932 gave Hitler's Nazi Party an overall government majority and on 30 January 1933 Hitler was sworn in as Chancellor. Almost immediately the effects of his ideas when put into practice began to come clear. Germany's population, like many others', was rising fast. Hitler believed that his country needed more space since industrialization had led to overcrowding of the homeland. Eastward expansion became his top priority. Domestic economic revival and the provision of new land could both be accomplished through a massive programme of rearmament, designed to intimidate, and, if necessary, force Germany's neighbours into territorial concessions.

To put his plans into effect, Hitler introduced a totalitarian regime. He used emergency powers to suspend all democratic elections and then banned opposition parties. Next he introduced a secret police force to enforce conformity. Beginning in 1933, Hitler inaugurated a mass sterilization programme with the co-operation of the leaders of Germany's medical establishment. By 1945 more than 400,000 people had been sterilized against their will to eliminate them from the chain of heredity. Physically weak, homosexual, religious, ethnically mixed and criminal stock was being weeded out of the system.

In an extension of the programme, between 1939 and 1941 an estimated 75,000 to 250,000 people with 'intellectual or physical disabilities' were slaughtered through a system of forced euthanasia called Action T4. Later this was extended to what is now called the Holocaust during the Second World War, when between nine and eleven million people were executed in gas chambers, most of them Jews but also Christians, homosexuals and prisoners of war, as well as Polish and Romany people. Systematic genocide was at the apex of the Nazi regime's efforts to cleanse the racial stock of Germany and return to a mythological time when its people were genetically pure.

The implementation of theories of eugenics and racial hygiene, many of which were popular in pre-Second-World-War Europe and the United States of America, left deep and lasting scars in humanity's increasingly globalized civilizations. More than sixty-two million people are thought to have died in the Second World War, making it the most devastating human conflict in all history.

## Two wars, not one

But these deaths were really the result of two wars, both of which ultimately stemmed from the inexorable rise of industrialization. Hitler's European war was a struggle against what he saw as a Jewish plot to rape the world for profit, which must, he believed, be stopped from perverting the natural order of humankind for ever. The second war took place in the Far East, where Japan's brilliance at copying Western-style industrialization was equalled only by China's inability to protect its people from foreign interference.

Japan's aim was to colonize the Far East in much the same way that Europe had sliced up Africa. It wanted to secure permanent access to the raw materials it required for economic growth independent of the meddlesome powers of the West. That meant controlling the vast agricultural and mineral wealth of China, which, largely thanks to Soviet and Japanese intervention, had become embroiled in a drawn-out and bitter civil war starting in 1927.

In 1931 Japan invaded the north-eastern Chinese province of Manchuria and installed a puppet regime. In 1937 it launched an invasion of China with 350,000 soldiers and began a series of aerial bombing raids on cities all over the country. But Japanese advances had stalled by mid-1938, as Chinese resistance grew stronger under nationalist leader Chiang Kai-shek. By 1940 the war in mainland China was a stalemate and Japan was increasingly being strangled by economic sanctions from Western powers, which controlled its energy and oil supplies via their colonies in India, Burma, the Philippines, Malaysia, Indonesia and Singapore.

With Europe's major powers distracted by the struggle against Hitler, Japan waded into the Second World War with a surprise attack on the American Pacific fleet at Pearl Harbor, Hawaii on 7 December 1941. It hoped that, in their desperation to avoid the opening of a second front, Western nations would lift their sanctions, giving Japan free rein to complete its conquest of China. Despite initial successes, Japan never achieved a decisive victory and was ultimately forced to surrender after the United States dropped atom bombs on two cities in the summer of 1945.

By then Hitler's Reich was already finished. His attempts to reverse generations of interracial mixing solved nothing and just provoked yet more war, violence and slaughter. The scale of devastation was immense. Its effects dramatically altered the final fraction of our history – the last one thousandth of a second to midnight – still to come.

# 14

# What Now?

## (1945–present day)

*How the whole world was bound into a single system of global finance, trade and commerce. Can the earth and its living systems sustain humanity's ever-increasing demands?*

ON A WINDSWEPT, treeless, barren moor, three weird witches dance around a bubbling cauldron, casting spells that let them gaze into the future: 'When shall we three meet again? In thunder, lightning or in rain?'

Such is the setting for this opening scene of Shakespeare's *Macbeth*, about a man who would be king. It also works well as a backdrop for the final one thousandth of a second to midnight that represents the extraordinary sixty years that have followed the Second World War when seen on the scale of earth history as a twenty-four-hour clock. In that tiny fragment of time so much changed in both the human and the natural worlds that no number of books can hope to tell the whole story.

To help us see the job through, these witches will now conjure up the ghosts of three thinkers from the past whose prophetic insights bring into sharp focus dilemmas of today that may yet determine the future for all living things.

## Can capitalism survive?

The ghost of Karl Marx haunts anyone who believes in the supremacy and wisdom of the human system of economic organization called capitalism. Marx believed it to be merely a necessary historical phase which would one day be replaced by an altogether fairer society (see page 271).

In the first three weeks of July 1944 more than 700 bankers, representing the forty-four nations allied against Hitler's Germany, met in secret at Bretton Woods, deep in the forests of New Hampshire. Their goal was to devise a robust financial system that would not only repair the damage done by two devastating World Wars but would minimize the risk of such conflicts ever happening again.

The bankers agreed on the two wars' main causes. Industrialized nations had ignored the sacred mantra of free trade, as originally spelled out in the eighteenth century by Adam Smith (see page 253), and had instead engaged in a pernicious cycle of mercantile protectionism, exploiting their colonies as security for raw materials (for making goods) and consumer markets (for selling them). A series of economic blocs had competed for global supremacy, leading inevitably to conflict, especially when times got tough.

The stock market crash of 1929, which led to a period now known as the Great Depression of the 1930s, was one such time. Instead of a global system of central banks co-ordinating rescue, each colonial empire was confined to the limits of its own trading system – such as the Sterling Area in the British Empire. If Britain was struck by a slump, its colonies suffered appalling hardships as the one-way flow of produce to the mother nation stalled. Workers in the factories of the industrialized motherland suffered too, since few consumers in its overseas markets could now afford to buy finished goods. Spiralling unemployment led to social unrest which could be settled only by massive state intervention, often implemented through rearmament programmes, potentially leading, as in Nazi Germany, to global war.

The Bretton Woods system was designed to prove Marx wrong. Capitalism was not doomed, but required a single global system that allowed the free flow of capital and goods without exchange controls and government taxes. In the changed conditions following two World Wars, imperialist nations that had previously relied on their colonies for economic strength were now encouraged to relinquish them and establish an international collaborative financial framework instead. Free trade agreements would allow Smith's invisible hand of market forces to regulate the supply and demand of goods, taking away from individual nations the power of economic blackmail as well as the threat of being sunk without trace.

## Welfare states, democracy and universal suffrage

It was also thought that governments should create a 'safety net' for the welfare of their citizens, providing payments in the event of unemployment, healthcare for the poor and state pensions for the elderly and infirm. Welfare states were designed to alleviate economic hardship sufficiently to eliminate the likelihood of French-, Chinese-, Russian- or German-style popular revolts. Further reforms included universal adult suffrage, adopted between the wars by countries like Britain, which, after protracted lobbying by suffragettes, extended the right to vote to all women over the age of twenty-one in 1928. The huge nation of India followed in 1950 after gaining its political independence. The voting rights of blacks were at last enforced in the United States following the Civil Rights Act of 1964 and women finally got the vote in Switzerland in 1971. South African blacks were eventually enfranchised after the racist apartheid system collapsed in 1994, and on 20 January 2009 the United States inaugurated its first Afro-American President, Barack Obama.

# What on Earth Happened?

During the sixty years after the Second World War, free trade, welfare states and democratic governments underpinned by universal suffrage came to dominate the politics of much of the human world. The principles of capitalism and free trade were enshrined in a system of global exchange championed by the World Trade Organization, established in 1995. By 2007 it had 123 nations as members, with most of the world's remaining countries – including Russia, Libya, Iran, Iraq, Ethiopia, Algeria and Afghanistan – waiting to join.

The Soviet Union and China had not been party to the Bretton Woods Agreement. In October 1949 Mao Zedong's People's Republic of China declared itself a one-party state. The communists' defeated political rivals, Chiang Kai-shek's Kuomintang, fled to the small island of Taiwan, where they remain to this day, as capitalist converts firmly tied to the Western camp.

Between 1945 and 1991 China and the Soviet bloc confronted the capitalist West with closed, centrally managed systems backed up by massive armament programmes. Thanks to the doctrine of Mutually Assured Destruction (MAD), atomic weapons ultimately helped keep the peace between the ideologically divided communist East and the capitalist West during what was called the Cold War.

A number of flashpoints arose during this period that could have led to global war. They include the Cuban Missile Crisis of 1962, the Korean War (1950–3), the Vietnam War (1964–75) and the Soviet invasion of Afghanistan (1979). But then, starting in 1985, the Soviet Union (USSR) began to disintegrate through economic stagnation, and its satellite countries in Eastern Europe and around the Baltic Sea (Lithuania, Latvia and Estonia) snatched at the greater political and social freedoms offered to them by reforming Soviet leader Mikhail Gorbachev. Following a failed coup in 1991 the Soviet empire finally collapsed as former republics declared their independence – in December 1991 fourteen out of the fifteen Soviet states signed the Alma Ata Protocol effecting the dissolution of the Soviet Union. On Christmas Day President Gorbachev resigned as

# What Now?

President of the USSR, declaring the office extinct, and even Russia became a capitalist democracy of sorts. On 1 May 2004 seven former Soviet bloc countries (Estonia, Latvia, Lithuania, Poland, the Czech Republic, Slovakia, Hungary) formally joined the European Union. Romania and Bulgaria joined later, on 1 January 2007.

China remained a communist one-party state. Economic reforms introduced by party leader Deng Xiaoping in 1978 have brought it increasingly within the capitalist system of commerce and trade, culminating in its accession to the World Trade Organization in 2001. Communist China is modern capitalism's biggest growth area. The Asian economies of China and India have almost limitless supply of cheap manpower (see power of rice, pages 131–3). As a result, they are now on a path to take over from the United States as the kingpins of global capitalism.

Meanwhile, the imperial powers of Europe let their former colonies go. Sometimes the process happened peacefully, sometimes not. It took years for some of the new countries to find their feet – especially those, like French-controlled Algeria, whose populations included thousands of settlers from the colonial motherland.

## The discovery of oil, and the rise of extremism

Nations in the Middle East were transformed not only by political independence, but by the discovery beneath their deserts of huge reserves of crude oil.

In the 1930s disaffected British diplomat Jack Philby handed the United States a precious gift, through his close friendship with Arab ruler Ibn Saud. Following the collapse of Ottoman power at the end of the First World War, Ibn Saud conquered the Muslim holy cities of Mecca and Medina, and formed a new kingdom which he named after himself – Saudi Arabia, recognized internationally by the Treaty of Jeddah on 20 May 1927. Largely thanks to Philby's influence, US oil companies were granted exclusive rights to prospect the Saudi desert for oil.

By 1938 their searches had borne fruit. Aramco, formed by the American oil industry to exploit the reserves of Saudi Arabia, soon became the largest oil company in the world. By 1950 its profits were so huge that Ibn Saud demanded a 50 per cent share, threatening to nationalize the firm. In the end the US government compensated Aramco's shareholders by providing them with a tax break called the Golden Gimmick, equivalent to the amount siphoned off by the Saudi regime.

The oil money pouring into the Middle East transformed the influence of the region's rulers, whose grip on power was backed up by their sponsorship of a strict form of Sunni Islam. Wahhabism was an eighteenth-century reform movement, founded by Muhammad ibn Abd-al-Wahhab, that sought to purify Islam. It was subsequently adopted by the House of Saud, which had historically ruled the region of Najd in central Arabia, where Wahhabism first took hold.

Backed with money from the oil-hungry West and with tight control of Islam's holiest cities, this creed spread quickly through the region via religious schools, newspapers and outreach organizations. When Western powers created the State of Israel in 1947, carved out of Palestinian lands where the majority of the existing population were Muslims, a potent mix of Islamicism and anti-Western sentiment exacerbated the long-standing hostility between the Jewish and other Middle Eastern peoples that had its origins back in the pre-Christian world (see page 147–8). Racial war, bitter hatred and international terrorism still pour from this Middle Eastern conflict, which remains unresolved.

Between them, cheap Chinese labour and the rich oilfields of Arabia underpin today's global economy. They demonstrate that capitalism has no intrinsic requirement for democracy, despite some of its leading advocates declaring otherwise.

The desire for personal enrichment through the never-ending acquisition of material possessions – which Marx called 'commodity fetishism' – has, since the end of the Second World War, provided a common incentive for people to collaborate in business regardless of colour, politics, race or creed. Capitalism has proved remarkably robust. Despite a succession of crises such as the Middle Eastern oil shock of 1973, the Latin American debt crisis (1981–94), the great global stock market crash of 1987, the East Asian financial meltdown of 1997 and the hedge-fund crisis of 1998, the scheme of central bank interventions first proposed by the Bretton Woods bankers in 1944 has managed to recalibrate and rebalance the global economic system to keep underlying growth on track. Until 2008 the United States had avoided serious recession, with only two brief interruptions in 1987 and 2000, leading some politicians to claim that the traditional capitalist boom-and-bust cycle, one of Marx's main criticisms of the system, had finally been put to rest thanks to modern economic management.

However, the 'credit crunch' that began in the summer of 2007 has caused such optimists to reappraise their faith in free markets. Without massive central government intervention in many of the world's leading economies, including the US and Britain, the capitalist financial system would have completely collapsed during 2008. As a result, many of the world's biggest banks have either gone bankrupt or are now owned by taxpayers.

### The enemies of 'free trade' fight back

Unfortunately, the system of free trade, proudly trumpeted by advocates such as Ronald Reagan (US President 1981–9) and Margaret Thatcher (British Prime Minister 1979–90), has proved in reality to be far from free. Massive subsidies for farmers in Europe under the EU Common Agricultural Policy (CAP), introduced in 1958, meant that the playing field was uneven. Poor countries in

# What on Earth Happened?

Africa, whose economies had been shaped by their colonial past, depended on income from food exports to feed their people. But the rich countries artificially depressed prices through subsidies and import taxes, claiming that they had to do so to protect the livelihoods of their own farmers.

Mountains of European butter, lakes of wine and stocks of cheese and grain that far exceeded what Europe itself could consume were dumped at rock-bottom prices, putting Third World farmers out of business. Although many of these market abuses have since been addressed they have left a deep legacy of mistrust. Lacking an industrialized base, many poor countries have been forced to borrow funds from First World banks. Unable to pay back their loans, they have been caught in a vicious spiral of dependency. To add to their economic woes, many colonies won their political independence only for their governments to fall into the hands of corrupt, despotic rulers, who, with weapons sold to them by developed nations, greedily clung to power. Ethnic and tribal disputes have in many ex-colonies replaced the tyranny of arbitrary foreign rule.

These are some of the reasons why capitalism has failed to make amends for the colonialism of the past. Desperate people are resorting to desperate measures. While refugees flood from the barren wastes of places like the Democratic Republic of Congo and Somalia, terrorist groups recruit suicide bombers to their cause in the repressed oil-rich states of the Middle East. Fourteen of the nineteen terrorists who smashed three American airliners into the World Trade Center in New York and the Pentagon in Washington on 11 September 2001 came from the Kingdom of Saudi Arabia. Their actions were an extreme example of a devastatingly effective new way of making desperate voices heard. With such a dramatic increase in international terrorism, fuelled by the politics of envy, race and inequality, the spectre of Marx's warnings lives on in the twenty-first-century 'War on Terror'.

# What Now?

## *Can human populations keep on rising?*

Witch number two conjures up a ghost no less haunting. Thomas Malthus was so concerned about rising levels of human populations that he prophesied a time when nature would take revenge (see pages 256–7).

The massive increase in the population of the world during the twentieth century is directly linked to rising economic wealth. At 78.8 years, life expectancy in Britain is now thirty years higher than it was in 1900 – and more than thirty-two years higher than in sub-Saharan Africa today. By far the biggest recent increases in population have been in Asia. China and India between them contain nearly half the world's overall population of 6.7 billion – a number projected to rise to more than nine billion by 2050.

The fact that so many more people are now crowded on to the same-sized planet has dramatically changed life on earth in the last sixty years. Natural habitats have been devastated by rapid industrialization and the growth of towns and cities. Deforestation, mining, deep-sea trawling and intensive agriculture are some of the main causes of the massive decline in the number of species on earth.

## *A sixth mass extinction?*

A sixth extinction event may turn out to be no less profound than the five previous mass extinctions that are known to have occurred in prehistory (for an example, see Permian Mass Extinction, page 40). Human activities over the last few hundred years are now thought to be responsible for increasing natural rates of extinction by as much as 1,000 per cent, with some experts estimating that two million different species of plants and animals may already have fallen victim to habitat loss, increased farming, pollution and infrastructure projects such as the building of dams. The rate of extinctions today is reckoned to be between one hundred and one thousand times greater than the historic norm known as the background rate. According to the World Conservation Union Red List of Threatened Species, as many as 52 per cent of all major living species are in jeopardy; plant extinctions head the list, with 70 per cent of species reported to be at risk.

Deforestation accelerated dramatically during the twentieth century, especially in the tropics, as demand for hardwood products rose to new heights. Between 1920 and 1995 nearly 800 million hectares of tropical forests were cleared, an area approaching that of the United States of America. Between 1980 and 1990 roughly 15.4 million hectares of forest – an area almost double the size of the United Kingdom – were felled each year.

Such destruction has been driven by economics, usually regardless of the human or natural cost. Poor people in post-colonial countries desperately need a crop they can easily and cheaply trade for cash. Gang violence has become synonymous with illegal logging. There have been more than 800 land-related murders in the Amazon region over the past thirty years. Sometimes things got personal. Sister Dorothy Stang was an American nun who devoted her life to educating people living in the Amazon rainforest as to how they could extract natural forest products without resorting to cutting down trees. After reporting illegal loggers to the Brazilian authorities she began to receive death threats. On 12 February 2005, as she walked to a meeting in her village, she was shot by two gunmen at point-blank range. They then emptied another five bullets into her dead body.

Chopping down trees destroys more than just animals, insects and humans. It also sterilizes the earth itself. Soil quality is severely compromised in areas with no trees because the ground is exposed to erosion by the weather. Deforestation is also thought to have a significant effect on rainfall patterns, since it is through the natural process of transpiration that much of the world's water, locked up in the ground, ends up seeded in clouds (see page 29).

# What Now?

Hunting by humans is another major cause of extinctions. One extraordinary example, which occurred in the late nineteenth century, is the case of the North American passenger pigeon. These birds were once so numerous that their flocks regularly stretched more than a mile across the skies during springtime migrations from the south to their breeding areas in New England. Human hunting began in earnest in the 1860s and 1870s to provide a source of cheap meat for the growing cities on the east coast of the United States. In 1869 Van Buren county in Michigan sent more than seven million of the birds to markets in the east. Such extreme levels of hunting meant that by 1914 the passenger pigeon, a species which once numbered more than five billion individuals, was added to the list of the extinct.

The same story may soon be repeated for thousands of other species, some as common as the cod. A study released in 2006 concluded that one third of all fishing stocks worldwide have now collapsed to less than 10 per cent of their previous levels and that if current fishing trends continue the seas will be virtually empty of edible fish by the year 2050. Bottom-trawling, the practice of dragging long trawl nets along the sea floor, churns up seabeds so severely that the damage to deep-sea ecosystems is far greater than any amount of man-made pollution that leaches into the oceans.

Pollution caused by the huge rise in human population is another reason for the rapid decline in the diversity of living things. Air pollution comes from the burning of fossil fuels, causing rainwater to become acidic. Metal foundries and petrochemical plants are sources of poisonous contaminants that destroy delicate ecosystems. Landfill sites release methane and harmful chemicals like cadmium, found in discarded electronic products, which poison the surrounding soil. In 2007 Britain had the worst record for landfill use in Europe, discarding some twenty-seven million tonnes of waste into dumps that now extend across 227 square kilometres.

Today the number of households in China is increasing at twice the rate of its population growth due to increasing divorce rates and more families living apart as young people seek employment in cities. If everyone in China led a lifestyle similar to that of people in Europe and America, it would require roughly double the amount of raw materials currently used by the world's entire population. Just to keep up with China's huge demand for power its government is currently commissioning two new coal-fired power stations every week.

## The perils of global warming

The need for resources to power the economic growth driven by the capitalist system led to an increase in global oil production to almost eighty-three million barrels a day in 2005.

The consequences of burning fossil fuels are now well understood. Atmospheric carbon dioxide levels have increased dramatically since the 1800s, when fossil fuel deposits ignited man's first wholly independent source of power, in the form of high-pressure steam (see page 260). Between 1832 and 2007 levels of $CO_2$ have risen from 284 parts per million to 383. Carbon dioxide, like methane, is a gas which has a major impact on the earth's temperatures by absorbing infrared radiation. Its increasing levels in the atmosphere are reckoned to be the most likely cause of a recent rise in global temperatures that has already led to the shrinking of many of the world's major glaciers, melting of the ice caps, changes in sea levels and shifting patterns of rainfall.

The geopolitical effects of global warming are already starting to unfold. A war in Darfur, a region of western Sudan the size of France, began in February 2003. It was triggered by decades of drought and soil erosion, probably caused by changing rainfall patterns as a result of global warming. In an echo of what provoked Mongolian tribes to unite under Genghis Khan (see page 206), camel-he ding

# What Now?

Arab Baggara tribes moved from their traditional grazing grounds to farming districts further south in search of pasture and water. As a result of their attacks on the non-Arab population more than 2.5 million people are thought to have been displaced by October 2006, of whom approximately 400,000 have died of disease, malnutrition or starvation.

Further south in Africa, the HIV virus is destroying the human immune system, causing the death of millions of people left defenceless against common infections. First diagnosed in 1981, the virus somehow jumped the species barrier from monkeys to humans. Since then it has killed more than twenty-five million people, mostly Africans, and infected as many as forty-six million more. There are currently more than a million orphaned South African children, most of them infected themselves, since their parents died from the disease, which is easily passed through body fluids such as breast milk.

Is this what Malthus predicted when he said that one day the human population would be levelled by nature's intervention through 'sickly seasons, epidemics, pestilence, and plague', and 'gigantic inevitable famine'?

## Can science find a solution?

The most agonizing question of all is that of the third and last witch. Her visions belong to the ghost of the man who many regard as the most influential scientist, naturalist and thinker of all time.

The reason Charles Darwin was so reluctant to publish the theories described in *On the Origin of Species* and *The Descent of Man* was simply that their conclusions led to the question of whether humans are fundamentally different from other animals. Many people today find Darwin's prophetic warning that 'Man still bears in his bodily frame the indelible stamp of his lowly origin' hard to accept, either for religious reasons or simply because evidence from all around suggests that humans are not susceptible to the same rules of survival and extinction.

Mankind's ability to sidestep nature's systems shows no sign of abating. Since the Second World War his cunning has developed systems that have radically changed the way we relate to each other and to the world around us. Televisions, computers, video games, mobile phones, text messaging and the Internet have taken ordinary people into unnatural worlds where no wildlife can possibly get in their way. Seasons have been abolished as obstacles in the way of consumer choice, with the emergence of air-conditioned supermarkets which can source and deliver tens of thousands of different lines of refrigerated foodstuffs from around the world, twenty-four hours a day, 365 days a year.

Broadcast media, which emerged in a truly mass-consumer form only in the 1950s, transformed the ability of manufacturers to sell their products through advertising. Modern economic growth can now rely on marketing agencies developing elaborate strategies for convincing millions of consumers to buy products not found in nature that no one really needs. Fashions and fads are essential ingredients in modern man's 'virtual world', which further increases the distance between the human world, nature and other living things.

Western science is the self-appointed protector of man's artificial world. Synthesized drugs have engineered longer lifespans; couples who can't have children naturally now have the chance through IVF; and slim-hipped women who in the past would probably have died during childbirth can now elect to have Caesareans that minimize the risks to their own health.

Such innovations tamper with the fundamental fabric of nature herself – the path of natural evolution through which species survive or fail based on each generation's natural adaptations to its surroundings. Artificial selection has been applied by humans to animals and plants since the advent of selective breeding and agriculture more than 10,000 years ago, but modern science, with its recent understanding of life's genetic code, DNA, aspires to giddy new heights. In the short term its aims are to help genetically engineer out life-threatening diseases or to develop drought-resistant crops. In the long term such 'solutions' compound the problems of ever-increasing human populations making demands on the same resource-depleted, environmentally wrecked planet.

How far distant is this approach from Hitler's attempt to interrupt nature's flow to produce his master race, weeding out the weak from society, allowing the strong and wealthy who can afford expensive treatments to prosper and thrive?

## Dilemmas, ancient and modern

Despite modern appearances, are humans really so different, so apart from nature? What will happen when the earth's oil runs out? The global addiction to fossil fuels is likely to prove even harder to kick in the twenty-first century than imperial China's addiction to imported opium in the nineteenth (see page 272). Unless dramatic new levels of investment are made in nuclear energy and renewable energy sources, man's fossil-fuel-dependent virtual reality could be unplugged by global conflicts over increasingly scarce energy supplies. Financial markets may buckle under the weight of inflation as demand for food and energy soars.

The mantra of ever-increasing economic expansion assumes a world with limitless resources. As discovered by the Roman Empire (see page 163), territorial and economic growth cannot be assured ad infinitum. Plundering the wealth of other continents – a Roman habit inherited first by European explorers and later by Western governments and business corporations – has already been stretched to its limits by the takeover of North America by European settlers and the Scramble for Africa. For how much longer can cheap Asian labour subsidize living standards in the democracies of the West?

What about developing alternative lifestyles that are more sustainable in the long term? Darwin concluded that man has evolved, inescapably, as part of the natural world. Perhaps now is the time to relearn how to live within nature's means, as some, like Mahatma Gandhi and his followers, have tried to demonstrate. Switch off the electricity, turn out the lights, sell the car, grow vegetables, walk to work, bring back the small local school, learn a craft, buy only what you need, make your neighbours your friends and have fun in simple, traditional ways such as playing cards, storytelling, drama, dancing and building dens outdoors.

But Darwin's conclusion that humans evolved in the same way as all other life forms suggests that people aren't naturally well adapted to long-term, rational planning. It has always been the blind watchmaker – nature – that determines, however randomly, the long-term state of life on earth, while individual species either collaborate or battle in the here and now. Evolution depends on the strongest survivors passing on useful traits to their successors, while the weakest fall into obscurity and eventually extinction.

Humans today appear to follow their natural instincts every bit as much as their ancestors did. Modern democracies, like hedge-fund managers, plan around the here and the soon-to-be. Their concern is not with making sacrifices in the present for the sake of alleviating possible risks in an uncertain future. As one twenty-first-century President of the United States famously declared, modern Western lifestyles are 'blessed'. The pursuit of life, liberty and happiness in the present is what most often seems to count.

Those who hold this view believe humans should continue to live as they do now, except perhaps for a few tweaks here and there. These are the sceptics who believe that all the fuss about finite raw materials and overpopulation is some elaborate hoax propagated by fanatics and societies' envious have-nots.

Others believe humans, unlike other animals, do have within themselves the capacity for a rational escape from their evolutionary origins. Huge investment in a search for new sources of raw materials, for example by colonizing the moon, could be a stepping stone for exploration elsewhere. Techniques to capture and store carbon dioxide emissions before they leak out into the atmosphere could be perfected and made mandatory throughout the world. Proposals to limit $CO_2$ emissions could be driven by a comprehensive trading system in which governments, companies and individuals bid to purchase a fixed number of credits that cap the total amount produced. Consumers could make a start by making short-haul aeroplane flights morally unacceptable – a modern-day taboo, to take a leaf out of the Australian Aboriginals' book (see page 166).

Such efforts would have to be applied globally, in a rational, consistent and universal manner. Governments would have to agree to caps on $CO_2$ emissions for their military operations too. Thousands of years of tribal conflict, more recently manifested in nationalistic pride and sporting contests, would have to be set aside for the sake of the greater global good, and for generations to come. It could happen. The European Union and the United Nations are examples of attempts to end centuries of tribal rivalries that have got in the way of collective, thoughtful, long-term policy.

## Three final questions as the clock strikes midnight

What if the depletion of the earth's finite natural resources does bring about the fall of global capitalism? What if climate change really is the beginning of nature's check on the exponential rise of human populations? What if humanity's evolutionary instincts prevent it from collectively reaching beyond the short-term satisfaction of its immediate material desires? If the warnings of Marx, Malthus and Darwin do indeed come to pass, their prophecies will take centre stage in the next act in the drama that is life on earth.

## What on Earth Happened?

Now, at last, the clock finally strikes midnight on our twenty-four-hour history. What on earth happens next promises to be a lively beginning to the first one thousandth of a second in a brand new day.

*For full notes, references and a forum for feedback and debate,*
*please visit www.whatonearthhappened.com*

# Time's Tables

WHO AND WHAT have had the biggest impacts on shaping the destiny of the planet, life and people? Is it the earth itself, other life or people who are most in control of events historically, today and in the future?

Peak events puncture history's horizon, each one making its own unique but interconnected contribution to the unfolding story of planet, life and people. The following tables feature only the most significant events as discovered on my own personal journey through the saga of *What on Earth Happened?*

# What on Earth Happened?

## Top Ten **Natural Events that Shaped the World**

|  | Page | Event | Date (years ago) | Why? |
|---|---|---|---|---|
| 1 | 6 | Collision of the earth and Theia that created our moon | 4.49 billion | The ultimate collision between two early planets that resulted in the formation of our moon, and the earth's magnetic shield that protects life against solar radiation. |
| 2 | 40 | Creation of Pangaea | 300 million | This single super-continent challenged plants and animals to find ways of living inland — leading to the evolution of seed-bearing trees and hard-shelled eggs. |
| 3 | 41 | Volcano that erupted for over a million years creating the Siberian Traps | 252 million | The Siberian Traps were formed by this huge volcanic event that also contributed to the Permian Mass Extinction — the largest ever in pre-history. |
| 4 | 50 | Indian volcano that created the Deccan Traps | 65.5 million | Huge quantities of carbon dioxide from this eruption, possibly triggered by part of the meteorite impact that also struck Mexico at this time, caused climate temperatures to see-saw out of control, contributing to a devastating mass extinction. |
| 5 | 50 | Asteroid that smashed into Mexico 65.5 million years ago | 65.5 million | A six-mile-wide asteroid smashed into the Yucatán Peninsula (Mexico) with a force 10,000 times greater than all nuclear warheads in existence today, triggering a mass extinction of species, including the dinosaurs. |

# Time's Tables

| | Page | Event | Date (years ago) | Why? |
|---|---|---|---|---|
| 6 | 62 | Crashing of Indian plate into Asia that created the Himalayas | 40 million | This mountain range is thought largely responsible for a dramatic cooling of the earth over the last forty million years, as water vapour cooled by the peaks created monsoon rains that dissolved large volumes of carbon dioxide from the air. |
| 7 | 64 | Great American Interchange connecting North and South America | 3 million | As a result of this land-merger, animals from two continents were able to mingle, and a new ocean current, the Gulf Stream, spluttered into life, warming Europe and the Middle East, eventually helping the establishment of human civilizations. |
| 8 | 79 | Toba eruption in Indonesia | 75,000 | This volcano may have nearly wiped out the species Homo sapiens, but in the end reduced populations to between 1,000 and 10,000 individuals, creating unusual genetic similarity within our species. |
| 9 | 95 | Younger Dryas | 12,700 | Sudden cooling of the climate followed by a rapid warming led to the first human experiments with agriculture and animal domestication – the advent of farming. |
| 10 | 112, 118 | Eruption of Thera | 3,635 | Tsunamis triggered by this volcanic eruption devastated several advanced early Mediterranean civilizations such as the Minoans in Crete and the Egyptians, giving violent horse and chariot invaders such as Hyksos and Mycenaeans a chance to establish themselves. |

# What on Earth Happened?

## Top Ten **People that Changed Human History**

| | Page | Person | Date | Why? |
|---|---|---|---|---|
| 1 | 92 | Hammurabi | 1810–1750 BC | A King of Babylon who wrote one of the earliest comprehensive legal codes, establishing the principle that an accused is innocent until proven guilty. |
| 2 | 139 | Ashoka | 304–232 BC | An Indian king who spread the ideals of Buddhism throughout Asia. He was the first ruler to put animal and human rights on an equal footing. |
| 3 | 160 | Jesus Christ | 2 BC–36 AD | The pacifist son of a Jewish carpenter whose miraculous powers helped his followers believe he was the son of God. Jesus's death on a cross ultimately led to the establishment of what is now the world's biggest religion, Christianity, adopted as a state creed by the Roman Empire in 391 AD. |
| 4 | 187 | Mohammed | 570–632 AD | An Arabic trader who revealed a series of divine messages that led to the establishment of Islam, now the world's second largest religion. The rise and spread of Islamic political and trading empires helped to connect Eastern and Western cultures. |
| 5 | 235 | Hernán Cortés | 1485–1547 | A Spanish mercenary and conquistador who masterminded the destruction of the Aztec empire of Mexico through a mixture of luck and cunning. Amongst his company was an African slave who brought deadly smallpox to the Americas. |
| 6 | 260 | Richard Trevithick | 1771–1833 | A Cornish inventor who, with the assistance of a neighbour (William Murdoch), was the first successfully to build a high-pressure steam engine that could provide power without the assistance of atmospheric pressure. This invention gave humanity its first mobile power source and ushered in a new age of industrialization. |

# Time's Tables

| | Page | Person | Date | Why? |
|---|---|---|---|---|
| 7 | 263 | Friedrich Wöhler | 1800–82 | A German chemist who artificially manufactured the first organic chemical, urea. Before this time people believed all chemicals produced by living things could not be made by man. His discoveries led to the birth of organic chemistry from which derive everything from plastics and synthesized drugs to explosives and artificial fertilizer. |
| 8 | 16, 255, 296–7 | Charles Darwin | 1809–82 | An English naturalist who developed a new theory on the origins of life, published in 1859. Darwin's theory of evolution by natural selection suggested that species can become extinct. It provided powerful evidence to support the view that the earth was billions of years old and that all living creatures are ultimately related to a common ancestor, including humans, who, he claimed, were descended from apes. |
| 9 | 271, 282 | Karl Marx | 1818–83 | A Jewish German political philosopher who predicted the eventual demise of Capitalism. His Communist Manifesto inspired a number of revolutionaries, leading to an epic ideological struggle between modern civilizations. |
| 10 | 277 | Adolf Hitler | 1889–1945 | An Austrian veteran of the First World War who so despised Western powers for their part in Germany's humiliating surrender in 1918 that he became obsessed with restoring all life on earth to a 'natural order'. Hitler attempted to re-create a master human race that could eventually breed 'impure' stock out of existence. Hitler's ideas led to a second global war that stimulated the invention of atomic energy and rocket technology. |

# What on Earth Happened?

## Top Ten **Fruits and Seeds of Human History**

|   | Page | Item | Date | Why? |
|---|------|------|------|------|
| 1 | 122 | Rice | 7000 BC in China and Korea | Today's massive human population owes as much to the cultivation of rice as it does to artificial fertilizers. This plant can feed more humans per hectare than any other crop. |
| 2 | 92 | Wheat | 7000 BC in Middle East | Today's artificially cultivated varieties only began to be farmed by humans following the cold Younger Dryas period c.12,700 years ago. Their labours produced a domesticated crop with large seeds that held firmly to the stalk (this made grinding and harvesting easier). |
| 3 | 172 | Maize | 5000 BC onwards in Central America | Painstakingly bred from wild teosinte by early Central American farmers, maize eventually became the staple crop for all indigenous American peoples. By the sixteenth century European explorers had spread maize around the world. |
| 4 | 272 | Poppies | 4000 BC onwards in Asia, the Middle East and Europe | The medicinal use of opium goes back to the first early Neolithic farmers but by the nineteenth century opium extracted from poppy seeds had become a major international commodity. Morphine, another derivative, is still one of the world's most popular painkillers. |
| 5 | 245 | Potatoes | 3000 BC in South America but 1600 onwards in Europe | Hundreds of varieties of this highly nutritious vegetable were selectively cultivated by South American natives, although only four were exported by sixteenth-century European settlers to Europe. A lack of diversity led to devastating blights in nineteenth-century Europe and mass emigrations to the Americas and Australia. |

# Time's Tables

| | Page | Item | Date | Why? |
|---|---|---|---|---|
| 6 | 193 | Sugarcane | 3000 BC in South-East Asia | Deforestation to clear ground for sugar plantations in the New World led to dramatic changes in the landscape and ushered in a new era of slavery, which eventually spilled out into armed conflict in the American Civil War. |
| 7 | 124, 199 | Mulberry trees | 2500 BC in China | Leizu, a Chinese queen, is said to have discovered how threads from the cocoon of a moth larva could be woven into silk. Later a new paper-making process was discovered that used the bark of mulberry trees. Paper is a major contributor to economic growth and global deforestation. |
| 8 | 272 | Tea | Cultivated in China from before c.1000 BC | This camellia leaf was used medicinally by Chinese rulers and by Buddhist monks to keep them awake for prayers. The British became addicted to tea by the nineteenth century – so much so that its supply from China was secured by the illegal exchange of opium, grown in Bengal, which provoked international conflict. |
| 9 | 148 | Olives | 700 BC in Mediterranean | An energy-rich crop that grows in craggy soil and requires no hard labour to cultivate. Wealth from olives provided ancient Greek cities with enough time and leisure to pursue scientific investigations and new experimental societies including democracy and republicanism. |
| 10 | 269 | Quinine | c.1600 in South America | This extract from the bark of the cinchona tree provided European settlers with their first effective protection against the deadly disease malaria, spread by mosquitoes. It therefore became a passport to the successful European colonization of Africa, eventually cultivating the conditions for creating what is now known as the Third World. |

## Top Ten **Living Creatures that Shaped Life on Earth**

|   | Page | Creature | Date (years ago) | Why? |
|---|------|----------|------------------|------|
| 1 | 18 | Corals | 540 million | These tiny sea creatures have built some of the sea's most vibrant habitats. Coral islands are the skeletal remains of countless numbers of these marine organisms which have substantially reduced atmospheric $CO_2$ levels with their reef-building antics. |
| 2 | 19 | Jellyfish | 530 million | These were the first sea creatures to develop cell tissues with specialized functions that later evolved in other species into separate organs. The deadly sting of some jellyfish provoked other creatures to defend themselves by making large protective shells. |
| 3 | 20 | Sea squirts | 500 million | These animals are rooted to the sea bed and feed off microsopic food by filtering water through their bodies. Baby sea squirt larvae swim using a primitive chord that beats the water. In their descendants these chords evolved into backbones, from which the family of vertebrates (called chordate) and eventually humans emerged. |
| 4 | 22 | Lungfish | 420 million | The first vertebrate fish whose ancestors experimented with escaping the terror of the high seas by using a primitive air-breathing lung adapted from one of their gills. It also learned to walk across muddy river estuaries using its fins, precursors to the tetrapods, the world's first four-legged animals. |
| 5 | 32 | Velvet worms | 420 million | Ancestors of today's velvet worms developed stubby legs that helped them move faster across the sea floor to seek food, making them ideally suited to experiment with life on land where they re-nourish the soil. Eventually the velvet worm's many legs and segmented bodies evolved into insects. |

# Time's Tables

| | Page | Creature | Date (years ago) | Why? |
|---|---|---|---|---|
| 6 | 32 | Dragonflies | 350 million | These creatures adapted slits once used for breathing underwater into flaps that helped them fly from place to place. Dragonflies were also the first creatures to gain a view of life on land through an ingenious system of compound eyes. Increased levels of oxygen in the air meant they once grew as large as seagulls are today. |
| 7 | 35 | Honeybees | 150 million | Descended from wasps, these flying insects developed a taste for nectar and pollen, a fancy that stimulated plants and trees all over the world to cover the land in blossom. Social behaviour that evolved in bees' nests signalled nature's ability to construct complex civilizations out of large communities of living creatures. |
| 8 | 47 | Termites | 200 million | These insects evolved from cockroaches and beetles and were part of nature's proving ground for creatures whose lives depended on social behaviour (like humans). Their collective intelligence, exhibited through language, rulers, teamwork, agriculture, education and sacrifice, later became hallmarks of civilized human society. |
| 9 | 57 | Gorillas | 7 million | Ancestors of today's gorillas were the first members of the great ape family to experiment with living on the ground instead of up in the trees. As the climate dried out during the Ice Ages and grasslands replaced much of the world's forests, it was from the mild-mannered, vegetarian gorilla that humanity's most direct ancestor evolved. |
| 10 | 96 | Grey wolves | 300,000 | Today's domestic dogs are directly descended (as a sub-species) from the grey wolf that evolved during the Ice Ages. Without the help of dogs, early farmers would have struggled to keep control of their flocks of animals on which their sustenance depended. |

# What on Earth Happened?

## Top Ten Extinct Creatures that Shaped Life on Earth

| | Page | Creature | Date (years ago) | Why? |
|---|---|---|---|---|
| 1 | 16 | Trilobite | 530 million | These were the first living creatures thought to have been able to see using compound eyes (sight later re-evolved on land in dragonflies). |
| 2 | 38 | Tiktaalik | 375 million | This four-legged animal adapted to living on land by being the first creature to use a neck to lift and swivel its head from side to side, helping it to hunt for food and better detect danger. |
| 3 | 39 | Ichthyostega | 350 million | Young offspring of these sea creatures colonized the land to protect themselves from predators in the sea. Their descendants evolved into the world's first dedicated land animals, the amphibians. |
| 4 | 39 | Hylonomus | 315 million | This was the first creature known to have developed a hard-shelled egg, allowing it to breed inland, beginning the domination of life on land by reptiles, the family to which all dinosaurs belonged. |
| 5 | 39 | Dimetrodon | 260 million | A mammal-like reptile whose ingenious back-mounted sail allowed it to warm up its blood to hunt early in the day when other reptiles were still too cold. Warm-bloodedness later allowed mammals to hunt at night when they were safer from dinosaur attack. |
| 6 | 41 | Lystrosaurus | 230 million | A warm-blooded mammal-like reptile that somehow survived the Permian Mass Extinction (252 million years ago) and therefore preserved a vital evolutionary link between mammal-like reptiles and their descendants, the mammals. |

# Time's Tables

| | Page | Creature | Date (years ago) | Why? |
|---|---|---|---|---|
| 7 | 47 | Sinosaurop-teryx | 140 million | A dinosaur that developed the use of feathers as a means of insulation. These were later adapted by birds for flight, showing that birds are living descendants of the dinosaurs. |
| 8 | 55 | Hyracotherium | 35 million | A dog-like creature that roamed the forests of North America which evolved into the horse. Horses then migrated across the Alaskan land-bridge into Asia where they were eventually domesticated by man 7,000 years ago, dramatically altering the course of human history by providing a new source of transportation as well as military and agricultural power. |
| 9 | 68 | Australo-pithecus | 3 million | The earliest known ape that walked on two feet, freeing its hands to be able to carry food and make tools. Motor skills to control intricate hand-movements stimulated the growth of brain size, which required more food, which required better tools for hunting – provoking an evolutionary spiral that led to the development of human brains which are four times larger than those of our closest genetic relatives, bonobos and chimpanzees. |
| 10 | 237 | Variola Major | Declared extinct in 1979 | A deadly virus that spread to humans following the domestication of animals after the last Ice Age melt 12,000 years ago. In the twentieth century alone the virus was responsible for as many as 500 million human deaths. Before then, it accounted for the decimation of indigenous American and Australian populations when European settlers spread the disease. The virus was the first to have been completely eradicated from nature by man. |

## Top Ten **Threats to Life on Earth**

| | Page | Threat | Why? |
|---|---|---|---|
| 1 | 51 | Meteorite strike | That's what finished off the dinosaurs 65.5 million years ago and at some point experts say another boulder of a similar size or bigger is bound to collide into the fragile earth, causing another mass extinction of species. So dark are many of these objects in space that there may not be too much warning, either. |
| 2 | 289 | Man-made pollution | The entire manufacturing output of all plastics made since the early 1900s will exist for thousands of years to come because none of it biodegrades. CFCs from fridges and aerosols continue to wreak havoc with the ozone layer. Nuclear waste from the world's 441 nuclear power plants will stay highly toxic for tens of thousands of years. |
| 3 | 62, 256 | Climate change | Melting ice-caps, shifting rainfall patterns, floods, droughts and extreme weather events that destroy harvests are some of the predicted consequences of the continuing increase in atmospheric $CO_2$ from 284 ppm (parts per million) in 1832 to 383 ppm today. The rise is down to modern humans pumping out fossil fuel pollution into the atmosphere, like a massive global volcano. |
| 4 | 256, 265 | Over-population | For tens of thousands of years human populations stayed at a roughly stable level of around five million. Then, with the birth of agriculture after the last Ice Age melt, settled civilizations piled on the population pressure. By the time of Jesus Christ numbers had soared to c.200 million. By 1804 the total rocketed past the one billion mark to become nearly seven billion today, tipping the world's living systems into ecological imbalance. |
| 5 | 179, 216, 290 | Deforestation | The itch to settle led humans to abandon living in forests because farming required felling trees for fields, turning lands once lush with vegetation into desert and scrub. Deforestation is a big cause of the current mass extinction of species and is also damaging the earth's natural capacity to soak up climate-changing carbon dioxide. |

| | Page | Threat | Why? |
|---|---|---|---|
| 6 | 244, 256 | Shrinking biodiversity | As living things get transported by humans from one habitat to another in the modern globalized world, species become exposed to new predators, and without time to adapt to survive, many become extinct. Loss of trees, sterilization of the soil through over-farming and the use of pesticides and over-fishing are giving rise to concerns that humans are increasingly vulnerable in a world that has lost its ecological balance. |
| 7 | 293 | Inequality | Farming gave rise to permanent human settlements in which some people controlled supplies of stored food while others became dependent. Domesticated horses gave others military superiority, reinforced by bronze weapons and chariots. Roughly a third of the modern human population is overfed whilst another third is malnourished, giving rise to social grievances and international terrorism. |
| 8 | 237 | Disease | Living in close proximity to farm animals spawned diseases that have plagued humans ever since they began to live in towns and cities. Smallpox, a virus which originated c.12,000 years ago and jumped to humans from cows, is human history's biggest killer. Today viruses such as HIV Aids (originated in monkeys), avian influenza (from birds) and ebola (from fruit bats) could be just as lethal. |
| 9 | 293 | Famine | Genetically modified foods that are disease and drought resistant offer the hope of salvation from death by famine for some people. However, the deliberate manipulation of nature's operating systems is fiercely opposed by those who believe humans are not adequately equipped to take over from nature as custodians of the earth's living systems. |
| 10 | 284 | Global war | The potential for humans to wipe out most living things as well as themselves has only existed since the dawn of the bio-engineering and nuclear ages in the mid-twentieth century. Proliferation has recently increased the risk that such an outcome could take place through a state-sponsored global war over natural resources (e.g. oil) or by maverick groups of disaffected individuals. |

# What on Earth Happened?

## Top Ten How We Know What Happened Happened

| | Page | Item | Date | Why? |
|---|---|---|---|---|
| 1 | 4 | The Big Bang | 13.7 billion years ago | Echoes from this monumental, universe shattering event were unexpectedly detected in 1964 by American scientists Arno Penzias and Robert Wilson using a home-made space radio-telescope |
| 2 | 41 | Lystrosaurus fossils | 250 million years ago | This mammal-like reptile, looking like a cross between a hippopotamus and a pig, somehow survived the biggest mass extinction of species on earth 252 million years ago. Its fossils, found on every continent, help prove that Alfred Wegener's theory of plate tectonics is correct. |
| 3 | 51 | Iridium layer | 65.5 million years ago | High concentrations of a rare type of the metal iridium, not naturally occurring on the earth, were found in a layer of clay just at the moment when dinosaur relics disappear from the fossil record. First discovered in the early 1970s, the same tell-tale sign of a massive meteorite impact has since been found in rocks all over the world. |
| 4 | 81 | Altamira caves | 20,000 years ago | Eight-year-old Spanish child Maria Sautuola couldn't believe her eyes when she noticed paintings of huge bison on the ceiling of a cave in Spain. They turned out to be among the oldest expressions of human art ever known, painted by hunter-gathering people more than 20,000 years ago. |
| 5 | 127 | Oracle bones | c.1600 BC | Ancient writing that resembles Chinese today was etched on oracle bones and turtle shells discovered near the Royal Tombs of Yin where Shang rulers buried their dead. More than 20,000 have been discovered, revealing questions put by kings to the gods in their capacity as intermediaries between earth and heaven. |

# Time's Tables

| | Page | Item | Date | Why? |
|---|---|---|---|---|
| 6 | 104 | Nineveh tablets | c.600 BC | A staggering 20,000 tablets of cuneiform writing, unearthed in the 1840s, have transformed our historical understanding of ancient Sumerian, Assyrian and Babylonian civilizations. The Royal Library of King Ashurbanipal contained everything from king lists and epic histories (Gilgamesh) to complex mathematical treatises. |
| 7 | 145 | Cyrus cylinder | 539 BC | Discovered in 1879 under the walls of Babylon, this inscribed cylinder details what is hailed as the first charter of human rights. Tolerant Persian King Cyrus abolished slavery and even paid for the reconstruction of the Jewish Temple in Jerusalem after it was destroyed by Babylonian King Nebuchadnezzar. |
| 8 | 140 | Ashoka pillars | c.264 BC | Indian King Ashoka was so dismayed at the horrific casualties of the Battle of Kalinga that he converted to Buddhism and vowed to dedicate his reign to restoring peace on earth for all living things. His achievements were recorded on a series of pillars, one of which still stands outside the city of Sarnath, near Varanasi, in India. |
| 9 | 177 | Sacred Cenote of Chichen Itza | 300 BC–800 AD | In 1897 American archaeologist Edward Thompson dredged a small lake that contained sacrificial knives, plates and other artefacts revealing the grim business of Central and South American human sacrifice. Desperate rulers believed these practices would encourage the gods to bring them good fortune and rain to water their crops. |
| 10 | 201 | Caves of the Thousand Buddhas | 900 AD | Early twentieth-century Hungarian archaeologist Aurel Stein discovered a trove of more than 40,000 perfectly preserved Buddhist texts, many hand-written by monks, which included the oldest dated printed document ever found, the Diamond Sutra (868 AD). |

# What on Earth Happened?

Top Ten **Unsolved Mysteries about What on Earth Happened**

| | Page | Item | Why? |
|---|---|---|---|
| 1 | 4 | What happened before the Big Bang? | Is our universe just the next in a long line of bangs and crunches? Is it one of many parallel universes, each one spurred into existence by other big bangs with their own different laws of fundamental physics, creating a kind of multiverse? Or, is there some form of superior intelligence that created our universe and life on earth? |
| 2 | 6 | What triggered life on Earth? | Amino acids delivered on meteorites from outer space? A chemical soup concocted at the mouth of sea-floor volcanic vents? A chance spark of life accidentally triggered by a primordial lightning storm? An alien or divine architect? |
| 3 | 34 | What caused the first flowers to bloom? | Charles Darwin called it an 'abominable mystery', and even today experts have no clear idea. Was it the presence of pollinators such as bees, or did bees emerge only after flowers were there to provide a diet of pollen and nectar? |
| 4 | 58 | Who was the missing common ancestor of humans and chimpanzees? | Modern genetics show that the split between chimps and humans occurred no more than about four to seven million years ago. But what was this creature like? |
| 5 | 66 | What caused Australopithecus to swivel on to two feet? | Walking on two feet has as many advantages as disadvantages to apes who came down from trees to live in grassland savannahs. With brains no larger than those of a chimpanzee it wasn't simply intelligence that provoked human ancestors to rise up on two feet. So what was it? |
| 6 | 72 | When did humans learn to talk? | Guesstimates range from between 50,000 and 110,000 years ago, but no one can be sure. Language gave humans a big advantage in being able to organize themselves to hunt more efficiently. |

# Time's Tables

| | Page | Item | Why? |
|---|---|---|---|
| 7 | 89 | What caused the Pleistocene extinctions in the Americas and Australia? | Large animals (megafauna) rapidly disappeared once Homo sapiens populated Australia 40,000 years ago and then the Americas 12,000 years ago. Was it overhunting, climate change, a mixture of the two, or something else, such as disease, that caused such devastation? |
| 8 | 155 | What happened to the tomb of Alexander the Great? | Once the most popular tourist attraction of the Roman world, all records of the location of Alexander's golden tomb have since disappeared from history, not yet recovered by archaeologists. |
| 9 | 180 | How did the ancient Nazca people construct their giant geoglyphs? | Fashioned sometime between 300 BC and 800 AD, these people made more than 70 geometric and natural shapes, some as long as 270 metres, by brushing arid desert grit to one side into a pattern of paths. But how could they have made such intricate shapes when the only way of seeing what they had done was from hundreds of feet up in the air? |
| 10 | 134, 160 | Is there such a thing as life after death? | From the animistic beliefs of hunter-gathering man to the monotheistic religions of Judaism, Christianity and Islam and from Hindu reincarnation to the Buddhist nirvana, human history is one long record of the belief in a force beyond earthly existence. But is it just a delusion as some modern scientists claim? |

# Acknowledgements

**THE TWO YEARS** I have spent researching, writing and now editing this incredible story would have been entirely impossible were it not for the unwavering support of my wonderful wife and two daughters. A big thank you also to our dog, Flossie. It would have been quite impossible to work out where on earth to begin and end each chapter without our many countryside walks.

I have also greatly benefited from the generosity, enthusiasm and support of my parents, family and friends, for which I am eternally grateful. The publishing team at Bloomsbury has been a complete delight to work with at every stage of the project for both the illustrated hardback and now this abridged paperback. Their professionalism and expert guidance is second to none. In particular I would like to thank Richard Atkinson for his constant support, enthusiasm and determination at every stage of the conception, birth and ongoing delivery of the What on Earth? series of books. My sincere thanks also to Trâm-Anh Doan for so skilfully navigating this paperback edition from first edit to final print.

Other thanks go to all those unknown trees that have been sacrificed in the course of telling this extraordinary tale. There's a good 300 million years of evolutionary wizardry just in the paper between these covers.

Finally, I dedicate this book to the memories of two special people. Dodo, my grandmother, would have taken such a keen interest in this whole project. Also to Christo, my late great-uncle and namesake, whose enormous generosity and passionate interest in other people knew no bounds and still inspires me every day. May the spirit of Great Dixter live on!

# Further Reading

## General histories

*A World History* by William McNeill (Oxford University Press, 1967)
*A New Green History of the World* by Clive Ponting (Penguin, 2007)
*Civilizations* by Felipe Fernandez-Armesto (Macmillan, 2000)
*The Universe Story* by Thomas Berry and Brian Swimme (HarperCollins, 1994)
*The Ancestor's Tale* by Richard Dawkins (Houghton Mifflin, 2004)
*Maps of Time* by David Christian (University of California Press, 2004)
*Collapse* by Jared Diamond (Viking Penguin, 2005)
*A Little History of the World* by E. H. Gombrich (Yale University Press, 2005)

## Other helpful books

*Wonderful Life* by Stephen Jay Gould (Hutchinson Radius, 1990)
*The Secret Life of Trees* by Colin Tudge (Penguin, 2006)
*Life* by Richard Fortey (Vintage, 1999)
*Oxygen* by Nick Lane (Oxford University Press, 2002)
*In the Beginning* by John Gribbin (Viking Penguin, 1993)
*The Civilisation of the Goddess* by Marija Gimbutas (Harper San Francisco, 1991)
*Gunpowder* by Jack Kelly (Atlantic Books, 2004)
*Deforesting the Earth* by Michael Williams (University of Chicago Press, 2003)
*Science and Civilization in China* by Joseph Needham (Cambridge University Press, 1986)
*Plows, Plagues and Petroleum* by William Ruddiman (Princeton University Press, 2005)
*Climate History and the Modern World* by H.H. Lamb (Methuen, 1982)
*The Ages of Gaia* by James Lovelock (Oxford University Press, 1988)
*On the Origin of Species* by Charles Darwin (Harvard University Press, 1964 – facsimile of original edition of 1859)
*The First Eden* by David Attenborough (William Collins, 1987)
*Guns, Germs and Steel* by Jared Diamond (Norton, 1997)

# Index

11 September 2001, 288

Abbasid dynasty, 190, 192–3
Abu Hureyra, 96
Adams, John, 249
Afghanistan, 138, 155, 284
Africa, 55–7, 95, 157, 288, 293
    exploration and
        colonization, 228–9,
        231–3, 235, 256,
        269–70, 279
    and human evolution,
        70–2
    and human migrations,
        73–4, 78–81, 165
    independence, 270–1
    indigenous peoples, 168,
        266, 269–70
    sub-Saharan, 229, 269,
        289
    Scramble for Africa,
        269–70, 295
agriculture, 90–7, 115–17,
        125, 243, 287–9,
        294–5
    in Americas, 171–2
    medieval, 215–16, 219,
        223
Ahuitzotl, King, 179

Akkad, 106
Akrotiri, 120
Alaska, 55, 63, 82
alcohol, 27, 273
Alexander the Great, 154–6,
    158
Alexander VI, Pope, 227
Alexandria, 140, 154
al-Fazari, Mohammed, 196
Algeciras, siege of, 209, 222
Algeria, 269, 284–5
Algiers, 194
al-Khwarizmi, 194–5
al-Kindi, 194
Alma Ata Protocol, 284
al-Ma'mun, 192
al-Maqqari, 193
Alps, 12, 156, 219
al-Zarqali, 197
Amazonia, 166–7, 290
Ambrose, Bishop of Milan, 162
amphibians, 13, 20, 39
Anatolia, 120, 142
Andes mountains, 180–1, 245
Angkor Wat, 140–1
animals
    breeding and
        domestication, 90–1,
        96–8, 103, 237, 294

    endangered, 246, 289–90
    evolution of, 10–11,
        38–58
    furs and skins, 83, 246–7
animism, 167–70
apes, 16–17, 53, 56–8, 63, 74
aqueducts, 175, 193, 237
Arabia, 56, 183, 187, 190,
    285–6
Arabic, 192, 194–5, 218, 224
Aral Sea, 190
archaeopteryx, 47
Arctic, 64, 168–9
Argentina, 64, 250
Aristotle, 153–4, 161, 193,
    224
Arkwright, Richard, 258–9
Armenia, 157
Arnarson, Ingólfur, 217
artificial selection, 90–2, 117,
    294
Ashoka the Great, 139–41
Asia, 55–7, 62–3, 88, 120,
    143, 175–6, 206, 289
    exploration and
        colonization, 233,
        244–5, 270
    and human migrations,
        72–5, 81–2

# Index

indigenous peoples, 168,
  270
Asia Minor, 142, 144, 157,
  223
Assyria, 102, 104, 106, 113,
  145
asteroids, 50–1
astronomy, 105, 149, 192,
  196–7, 218
Atahualpa, Emperor, 238–9
Athens, 147–51
Atlantic Ocean, 64, 158,
  233–4
atmosphere
  carbon dioxide levels, 62,
    292
  composition of, 9, 13
  oxygen levels, 29–31, 34
atomic bombs, 255, 262–3,
  280, 284
Attila the Hun, 210–11
Augustus, Emperor, 157
Australia, 53–4, 165–6, 246,
  252, 258, 270
  Aboriginals, 165–6, 168,
    252, 268–70, 297
  and human migrations, 81,
    83, 165
  mammalian extinction,
    87–90, 165
Australopithecus, 68, 84
Austria, 63, 81, 117, 275
Avars, 214
Avebury, 116
Avicenna, 195
Awash River, 66
*Azatan* knights, 158
Aztecs, 173, 177–80, 183,
  235–8

Babylon, 102, 104, 145, 149,
  155, 171, 173
Bacon, Roger, 222
bacteria, 8–11, 13, 41
Baghdad, 192–4, 196, 215,
  224
Bai Qi, 129
Balsas River, 172
Baltic tribes, 212, 214
Bangladesh, 138
banks, 224, 241
Banquet of Chestnuts, 227
Barbastro, Siege of, 197

barley, 92, 95, 102, 106, 108,
  171–2
Bastille, storming of, 250
Bay of Arguin, 229
Beijing, 207, 273–4
Belgium, 245, 271
Bell Beaker Culture, 144
Bengal, 273
Bering Strait, 82
Berlin Congress, 270
Bethlehem, 160
Bhagavad Gita, 133–4
Bhutan, 141
Bible, 144–6, 160, 238, 242,
  268, 273
Big Bang, 4
Bismarck, Otto von, 270
Black Death, 56, 220–1, 223
Black Sea, 189, 210, 215, 222
Bolivia, 231
*Book of Lord Shang*, 130
*Book of the Dead*, 111
Borgia, Cesare, 227
Borneo, 56, 169
Borobudur, 140
Bosnia, 225
Bosporus, 147, 149
Boudicca, 157
bows and arrows, 83, 88,
  132–3, 211
Boxgrove Man, 74
Brazil, 56, 232, 235, 250
Bretton Woods agreement,
  282–4, 287
Britain, 74–5, 82, 93, 143,
  213, 283, 287, 289,
  291
  abolition of slavery, 253,
    258, 267
  colonies and empire, 167,
    240, 249, 252–3, 258,
    282
  industrialization, 258–60,
    265
  and opium wars, 272–4
  Roman conquest, 157–8
  and world wars, 275–6
Brittany, 116
bronze, 84, 91, 115, 118, 124,
  126, 134, 142–4
Buddha, 136–7, 139, 150,
  160, 203
Buddhism, 136–41, 200

Bugeaud, Thomas, 269
Bukhara, 195
Bulgaria, 285
bull-vaulting, 119
Burgess Shale, 15–16
burials, 96, 126
  megalithic, 115–16
Burma, 252, 258, 280
Byzantine Empire, 192, 217

Cabot, John, 235, 240
Cabral, Pedro, 235
Cai Lun, 199
Cairo, 194, 224
Cajamarca, 238
Calakmul, 174
Calcutta, 272
calendars, 173
Calicut, 235
Caliphs, 190–4, 198, 234
Cambodia, 140, 274
Cambrian Period, 15, 17–19,
  30
camels, 53–5, 63, 86–7, 89
  camel herders, 169, 292
Canada, 14, 38, 46, 64, 240
Cannae, Battle of, 156
cannon, 204, 222–3, 238
Canton, 272
Cape Bojador, 229
Cape of Good Hope, 232
Cape Verde Islands, 234
capitalism, 253, 258, 271, 275,
  282–3, 285–8, 297
carbon dioxide, 9, 11, 23, 27,
  62, 292, 297
Carboniferous Period, 25,
  33, 38
Caribbean, 235, 242, 244
Carter, Howard, 112
Carthage, 156–8, 211
Cartier, Jacques, 240
Caspian Sea, 207–8
Catherine of Aragon, 239
Catherwood, Frederick, 174
cattle, 53, 55, 108, 135, 171,
  237, 243–4
Caucasus mountains, 142
cave paintings, 81
Caves of the Thousand
  Buddhas, 201, 203
Celtic peoples, 168–9
Central America, 171–80,

# Index

183, 233, 235–7, 242, 244, 250
Central Asia, 64, 80, 132, 190, 201, 208, 214
Cerro Rico, 231
Ceuta, 228
Ceylon, 103
Chaac, 173
Chandragupta Maurya, 138
Changping, Battle of, 129
Charlemagne, 213–14, 216, 219, 226
Charles V, Emperor, 239
Chiang Kai-shek, 280, 284
Chichen Itza, 177
Chile, 181, 244
chimpanzees, 57–8, 67–70, 79
China, 15, 56, 121–32, 198–209, 213, 257–8, 272–5, 279–80, 284–5
  and Buddhism, 140
  communist revolution, 275, 283–4
  Cultural Revolution, 130–1
  Great Burning of Books, 130–1, 198
  and human migrations, 71, 73, 81
  imperial bureaucracy and examinations, 121, 199–200, 202, 219
  and medieval Europe, 210, 220–2
  and opium wars, 272–4, 295
  population growth, 164, 202, 245, 289, 292
  and rice cultivation, 122–3, 285
  and Second World War, 279–80
  and spread of Islam, 191–2, 197–8, 214
  terracotta army, 131–2, 199
  unification, 127–32, 138, 199
chocolate, 172, 242, 244, 247
Cholas, 204
Christianity, 144, 160–3, 167, 169, 215, 240, 256
  and China, 273–4

and Islam, 187, 189, 191, 197
and medieval Europe, 216, 219
Chu, 129
Churchill, Winston, 247
Clarke, Ronald, 68
Clement VII, Pope, 239
climate change, human-induced, 85, 255–6, 292, 297
clothes, 83, 91, 172, 221, 253
Clovis I, 212
coal, 26, 258, 260, 292
Cold War, 284
Colombia, 250
Columbus, Christopher, 183, 197, 217, 232–5, 243
*Communist Manifesto*, 271
compass, 121, 196, 205, 208, 257
computers, 48, 294
Confucius (Kongzi), 128–9, 199, 257, 273
Congo, 270, 288
Constantine, Emperor, 162, 226
Constantine XI, Emperor, 222
Constantinople, 162, 192, 211–12, 214, 217, 219
  fall of, 222–3, 225
continents, 61–4
Copán, 174
Cope, Edward, 43
Copernicus, Nicholas, 242, 248
copper, 84, 91, 115, 118, 125, 142, 176, 223
corals, 18–19
Cordoba, 193–4, 234
Cornwall, 142
Corsica, 211
Cortés, Hernán, 235–8, 242
Cossacks, 246
Costa Rica, 250
cotton, 36, 114, 172, 244, 253, 267
Council of Chalcedon, 213
Council of Nicaea, 162
Crécy, Battle of, 222
'credit crunch', 287
Cretaceous Period, 36–7, 49
Crete, 118–20
Crick, Francis, 264

Crimea, 207, 220
crocodiles, 39, 109, 159
crusades, 217–19, 223, 225, 274
Cuba, 235
Cuban Missile Crisis, 284
Cuzco, 181, 239
cycads, 29, 33, 37
Cyrus the Great, 145–6, 162
Czech Republic, 285

da Gama, Vasco, 235
Daimler, Gottlieb, 261
Damascus, 192, 212
Dante, 223–4
Danube, River, 116, 147, 158, 212, 215
Darfur, 292–3
Darius I, 146–7, 149
Darius III, 154–5
Darwin, Charles, 16–17, 34, 80, 88, 255, 293, 296–7
Dayak peoples, 169
de Aguilar, Gerónimo, 236
de Landa, Friar Diego, 174
deforestation, 216, 219, 240, 243, 289–90
deism, 248
democracy, 148, 153, 284, 286, 296
Den Xiaoping, 285
Denmark, 240
Derby, Earl of, 222
Descartes, René, 242
Devonian Period, 19, 21, 39
*Diamond Sutra*, 201
Diaz, Bartholomew, 232
*Dimetrodon*, 39–40, 43
dingoes, 165–6
dinosaurs, 38, 42–7, 49–52, 55, 61–2
Dio Cassius, 159
diptorodonts, 87
diseases, 96, 237–8, 264, 268
Dissolution of the Monasteries, 239
Domesday Book, 215
*Donation of Constantine*, 226–7
dreamtime, 165
druids, 168
duckbilled platypus, 53

# Index

Eanes, Gil, 229
earth
    and asteroid strikes, 51
    axial spin, 85
    collision with Theia, 5–6, 9
    iron core, 6
    origins of life on, 6–8
    tectonic cycle, 12–13
East Asian financial meltdown, 287
East China Sea, 122, 204
East India Company, 252, 272
Ebola virus, 57
Ecuador, 181
Edison, Thomas, 261
Edward II, King, 220
Egypt, 94, 144–5, 149, 154–5, 192, 252
    ancient, 107–14, 119, 123, 173, 183
    and Buddhism, 140
    Hyksos invasion, 112, 176
    and Islam, 189
    Roman conquest, 157–8
Einstein, Albert, 262
El Salvador, 250
electricity, 261
Ellesmere Island, 38
England, 65, 116, 222, 242, 245
    medieval, 215–16, 219–21, 225
    Norman Conquest, 215–16
    religion and civil war, 240–1
English Channel, 65, 74, 82, 93
Enlightenment, 248
Eocene Period, 52
Eratosthenes, 196
Eretria, 147
Estonia, 284–5
Ethiopia, 66, 68, 79, 284
Euphrates, River, 94, 103–4, 106
Europe, 64–5, 88, 93, 163, 175–6
    Bronze Age, 143–4
    and colonies, 244–7, 256, 269–71, 279, 285
    farming and settlement, 95, 98

and human evolution
    and migrations, 70, 74–5, 80
    industrialization, 260–1
    Iron Age, 125
    and Islam, 190, 198, 208–9
    medieval, 209–30
    megalithic culture, 115–20
    and plague, 212, 220–1
    politics and economics, 247–9, 253, 257, 271
    population levels, 212, 216, 219–20, 223
    Roman, 159
    and twentieth-century wars, 275–80
European Union, 285, 287–8, 297
Evans, Sir Arthur, 118

Ferdinand, King, and Queen Isabella, 233
Fertile Crescent, 94–6, 121, 171
fertilizers, artificial, 264–5
feudalism, 214–15, 221–2
Fibonacci, Leonardo, 194–5, 224
Finland, 168
fire, 72, 74, 83
firearms, 203–4, 208–9, 222, 241, 251, 260
First World War, 275
fish, 10, 13, 16, 18–19, 20–2, 39, 291
*fitna* (Muslim civil wars), 190
flight, 262, 297
Flower Wars, 179, 236
flowers, 26, 34–5, 47–8
Ford, Henry, 261
fortune-telling, 126–7
fossil record, 14–17
    and flowering plants, 34–5, 37
Foulke, William, 43
France, 63, 65, 76, 81–2, 157, 240, 249, 270–1
    and colonies, 240, 242, 252, 269, 274, 285
    French revolution, 250, 283
    industrialization, 261, 265

and Islam, 189–90, 194, 197, 212, 214
    medieval, 211–16, 219, 221, 225
    and Napoleonic Wars, 251, 259
    and world wars, 275–6
Francis I, King, 240
Franco-Prussian War, 270
Franklin, Benjamin, 249
Franklin, Rosalind, 264
Franks, 212–15
Franz Ferdinand, Archduke, 275
Frazer, Sir James, 167–8
Frederick Barbarossa, Emperor, 218
fruit, 36, 138
fungi, 27–9, 33–4, 41
    and potato blight, 245–6

Galapagos Islands, 88
Galen, Claudius, 195
Galerius, Emperor, 161
Galilee, 161
Galileo, 248
Gandhi, Mahatma, 296
Ganges, River, 132–3, 137, 155
gas, 260, 263
Gaugamela, Battle of, 155
Gaul, 157
genetics, 264–5, 295
Genghis Khan, 206–8, 292
George III, King, 272, 274
Georgia, 207
Gerard of Cremona, 195, 197
Germany, 47, 169, 211–12, 216, 245, 266, 270–1
    and world wars, 275, 277–80, 282–3
Gibbon, Edward, 190
Gibraltar, 80
Gilgamesh, King, 104, 107
Giza, Great Pyramid of, 107–8, 110–11
Gold Coast, 233
gold, 176, 180, 183, 193, 233, 237, 268
Golden Horde, 220
Gondwana, 53
Gorbachev, Mikhail, 284
Gorham's Cave, 80
gorillas, 57–8, 70

# Index

Goths, 158
Granada, 233, 235
grapes, 102, 108, 213
grasses, 37, 94–6, 171–2
Gray, Tom, 66
Great Barrier Reef, 18
Great Depression, 282
Great Fire of London, 243
Great Lakes, 64–5, 86
Great Plains, 244
Great Wall of China, 131, 204, 207
Greece, 140, 147, 225
    ancient, 72, 113, 138, 147–55, 175, 195–6
Greek gods, 150, 161
Greenland, 64, 206, 225–6
Gregory VIII, Pope, 218
Guangzhou, 273
Guatemala, 250
Gulf Stream, 64
gunpowder, 121, 140, 203–5, 208, 222–3, 225, 249, 257

Haber–Bosch process, 264
Haddonfield, New Jersey, 43
Hagar Qim, 116
Haiti, 252
Hàn Dynasty, 125, 199, 210
Hannibal, 156–7
Hào, 127
Harappa, 113–14, 116
Harun al-Rashid, 192
Hastings, Battle of, 215
He, Emperor, 199
Hell Creek Formation, 45
Henan Province, 126, 128
Hendrickson, Sue, 45
Henry IV, Emperor, 218
Henry V, King, 221
Henry VII, King, 235
Henry VIII, King, 239–40
Henry the Navigator, Prince, 228–9, 232, 234
Herodotus, 146
Himalayas, 12, 62, 132, 141
Hinduism, 132–5, 137–8, 140
Hipparchus, 196
Hispaniola, 235, 243
history, 101, 106–7
Hitler, Adolf, 152, 277–80, 282, 295

Hittites, 124
HIV, 293
Hobbes, Thomas, 248
Holland, 240
Holocaust, 279
Holy Roman Empire, 213, 225, 240
Homer, 118, 144
*Homo erectus*, 71–5, 78–9, 82
*Homo ergaster*, 74
*Homo habilis*, 68–71, 84
*Homo heidelbergensis*, 74–5
*Homo rhodesiensis*, 75
*Homo sapiens idaltu*, 79
Honduras, 250
Hong Kong, 273
Hong Xiuquan, 273
Hooker, Joseph, 34
hoplites, 151–2
Horner, Jack, 46
horses, 53, 55, 63, 86–7, 89, 96, 129, 133, 156, 176, 219
    in Americas, 243–4
    and cavalry, 197–8
    domestication of, 143–4
    and Spanish conquests, 235, 239
    and stirrups, 197, 214–15
House of Wisdom, 193–4, 224
Huaorani, 166
Huascar, 239
Hubei Province, 220
Huitzilopochtli, 179
human rights, 249
humans
    adaptations to climate change, 85–6
    brain size, 67–70, 75, 255, 266
    ethnic groups, 80
    evolution of, 11, 13–14, 16–17, 40, 57–8, 66–83
    farming and settlement, 90–8
    and genetic variation, 79
    and hunter-gatherer lifestyle, 83–4
    and mammalian extinctions, 88–90
    migrations, 73–4, 78–83
    population levels, 79–80,

84, 171, 256–7, 265, 289, 293
    and selective breeding, 150–2, 277–9
    uniqueness of, 242, 255–7, 293–6
    walking upright, 66–70, 75
Hundred Schools of Thought, 128, 131, 140
Hundred Years War, 221
Hungary, 208, 225, 285
Huns, 162, 211
hunting, 72, 83, 88, 94–5, 139, 291
Hyksos, 112, 176

ibn al-Haytham, 196
Ibn Saud, 285–6
Iceland, 83, 206, 217, 226
Incas, 181–3, 219, 235, 238–9
incest taboo, 166
India, 56, 62, 132–42, 193–4, 232, 247, 252, 261, 280
    and Alexander the Great, 154–5
    caste system, 134–5
    centralization, 138–9
    and human migrations, 73, 81, 165
    independence, 283
    modern, 114, 122, 285
    and opium wars, 272–3
    population growth, 164, 289
    religions, 134–41, 200
Indian Ocean, 18, 62–3, 205
Indonesia, 56, 79, 235, 280
Indus, River, 114, 155
Indus Valley Civilization, 113–15, 117–20
Indus Valley dancing girl, 142
Industrial Revolution, 26, 253
inheritance, 13–14
insects, 31–3, 35, 41, 122
    social, 47–50
internal combustion engine, 261–2
Inuits, 266
investment schemes, 204–5, 208
Ionians, 147

# Index

Iran, 94, 106, 146, 284
Iraq, 94, 102, 104, 284
Ireland, 116, 143, 245–6, 271
iron, 6, 84, 91, 176, 183, 243, 258
   China and, 121, 124–7, 132
   iron oxides, 9, 125
irrigation, 103, 106, 123, 193
Islam, 140, 167, 187–91, 256, 286
   and African colonization, 228–9, 271
   and ancient texts, 192–3, 218, 224
   and Constantinople, 212, 222–3, 225
   and spread of learning, 192–7, 208–9
   and trade system, 223–6
Isle of Wight, 44, 46
Israel, 76, 94, 144–5, 286
Issus, Battle of, 154
Italy, 63, 158, 266, 271
   and *Donation of Constantine*, 226–7, 240
   Italian Renaissance, 223–4, 227
   medieval, 211–13, 216, 223–5

Jacquerie, 221
Jainism, 137–8
James I, King, 258
Jani Beg, 220–1
Japan, 128, 140, 165, 235, 274–6, 279–80
Java, 56, 71, 140
Jeddah, 286
Jefferson, Thomas, 249
Jenner, Edward, 264
Jericho, 97–8, 171
Jerusalem, 145–6, 160, 171, 196–7
   and crusades, 217–19
Jesus Christ, 160–2, 167, 188–9, 191, 238, 240, 247, 273
jewellery, 81, 91, 114, 176, 194
Jews, 144–6, 148, 159, 191, 196, 218, 277, 279, 286

Jia Zhou, 274
Jigme Singye Wanngchuk, 141
*jihad*, 198
Jin Dynasty, 203–4, 207
Johanson, Donald, 66
John I, King, 228
John II, King, 232
Jordan, 144
Judaea, 157, 160, 256
Judaism, 167, 189
Julius II, Pope, 234
Julius Caesar, 157
Jupiter, 105
Jurassic Period, 49
Jurchens, 203
Justinian I, Emperor, 211–12

Kaaba, 187–8
Kaffa, 220–1
Kalinga, Battle of, 139
Karnak, 112
Kents Cavern, 75
Kenya, 71
Keraits, 206
Khosians, 269
Khufu (Cheops), Pharaoh, 107, 110
Khwarazm, 207
Kiev, 207, 215
knights, 197, 213–14, 219
Knossos, 118–20
Koran, 187, 191–2, 198
Korea, 128, 140, 274
Korean War, 284

La Venta, 173
Laetoli, 66
Lagos, 228–9
Lake District, 65
Lake Turkana, 71
Laozi, 140
Lascaux, 81
Latin, 195–7, 218
Latin American debt crisis, 287
Latvia, 284–5
Lauralia, 53
laws, 92, 130
   natural, 153–4, 248
Layard, Austen, 103–5
Le Moustier, 76
Leakey, Richard, 71
Lebanon, 94, 117, 140, 157
Leizu, 123–4

Lenin, Vladimir, 276
Leo I, Pope, 213
Leo III, Pope, 213
Leonardo da Vinci, 223–4
Leopold II, King, 270
Leopold V, Duke of Austria, 218
Li Si, 130
Liao, 203
liberty, 248–50, 253, 262, 266
Libya, 284
Lima, 239
Lin'an, 203
Lincoln, Abraham, 267
lions, 54–5, 71, 86–7, 89–90, 159
Lisbon, 197, 232
Lithuania, 214, 284–5
Little Foot, 68
Little Ice Age, 206, 225, 245–6
llamas, 53, 181
Lloyd-Stephens, John, 174
Locke, John, 248–9
Lombards, 211–13
longbows, 219, 221
Lothal, 115
Louisiana, 251
Lu, 128
Lucy, 66–70, 76, 84
Lumbini, 136
Luoyang, 128
Luther, Martin, 240
Lycurgus, 151

Macedonia, 147, 154
Mackie, Willia, 25
Madeira, 234
Mahabharata, 133
Mahajnapadas, 138
Mahavira, 137
Mahindra, 140
Mainz, 211
maize, 172, 175–6, 245
Malaysia, 56, 258, 280
Maldives, 18
Mali, 169
Malintzin, 236
Malta, 116, 211
Malthus, Thomas, 256–7, 260, 265, 289, 293, 297
mammals, 175
   evolution of, 13, 20, 40, 52–8

323

# Index

extinctions, 86–7
  and genetic variation, 79
  and infectious diseases, 237
Manchuria, 203, 279
Mantell, Gideon, 42–3, 45
Manzikert, Battle of, 217
Mao Zedong, 131, 275, 284
Marathon, Battle of, 147
Marcus Crassus, 158
Mars, 6, 33, 105
Marsh, Othniel, 43
Martel, Charles, 190, 197, 212–13
Martin, Paul, 88
Marx, Karl, 271–2, 275, 282–3, 287–8, 297
Massagetae, 146
Masson, Charles, 113
mathematics, 105, 149, 173, 192, 194–5, 198, 208, 218
Mauritania, 229
Mauritius, 246
Maya, Queen, 136
Mayans, 173–9, 183, 236
*Mayflower*, 241
Mecca, 187–8, 196, 285
Media, 155
medicine, 192, 195–6, 264–5, 294
Medieval Warm Period, 213
Medina, 196, 285
megafauna, 86–7
Mehmed II, Sultan, 222–3
Mehrgarh, 114
Memphis, 111
Mendel, Gregor, 13–14
Menes, King, 110
Mercury, 105
Merkits, 206
Mesopotamia, 94, 102–4, 108, 118, 132, 142–3, 173
Mexico, 51, 171–3, 238–9, 241, 243–4, 250
Mezquita mosque, 194
Michelangelo, 223
Michigan, 27, 291
Middle East, 55, 62, 120–1, 132, 155, 158, 163, 168, 175
  Bronze Age, 142–4
  farming and settlement, 95, 97–8

and human migrations, 73, 78, 81
Iron Age, 125
  and Islam, 189, 193, 198
  and oil, 285–8
  and writing, 101–2
  *see also* Fertile Crescent
Miletus, 149
Milky Way, 3–5
Miller, Stanley, 7–8
Minoan civilization, 118–20
*Missal of Silos*, 192
Mnajdra, 116
Moche, 180–1
Moctezuma, King, 179, 237, 242
Mohacs, Battle of, 225
Mohammed, 187–91, 193, 196, 198
Mohi, Battle of, 208
monastic orders, 216
Mongolia, 55, 162, 292
Mongols, 206–8, 220
monkeys, 53, 56, 62, 67, 167, 255, 293
moon, 6, 33, 117, 120, 255, 297
Morocco, 192, 229
Morton, Samuel George, 266
Moses, 106, 145, 160, 188
Mosul, 103
Mount Hira, 188
Mount St Helens, 79
Mount Taishan, 131
Mount Taygetos, 151
Mount Toba, 79–80
mulberries, 124, 193, 199
Mungo Man, 165
musical instruments, 76–7
Muye, Battle of, 127

Nahuatl language, 236
Najd, 286
Nanjing, 273
Napoleon III, Emperor, 270
Napoleonic Wars, 251, 259
national heroes, 251
Native Americans, 171–83, 266, 270
  and European settlement, 246, 249
  and horses, 244
  and Spanish conquest, 174, 176, 183, 235–9

Natufians, 94–7, 109, 117, 171
natural selection, 16–17, 90
Nazca, 180–1
Neanderthals, 74–81, 85
Near East, 115–16, 157, 159
Nebuchadnezzar II, 155
Nelson, Horatio, 251
Nepal, 136–7
Netherlands, 169
New Guinea, 165
New South Wales, 165
New Zealand, 83
Newton, Isaac, 196, 248, 262
Nicaragua, 250
Nicholas II, Tsar, 275–6
Nile, River, 94, 108–10, 113, 123, 157
Nineveh, 104
Nordic people, 169–70
Normans, 215
North Africa, 88, 107–8, 118, 159, 194, 198, 211, 228
North America, 55, 63–5, 233, 243, 249, 295
  European colonization, 240–5
  and human migrations, 82, 165
  indigenous peoples, 171, 246
  mammalian extinction, 86–90
  and Viking exploration, 217
North Atlantic, 206, 213
North Pole, 81
Norway, 65, 168, 217, 226
Novgorod, 246
Nubians, 266
nuclear energy, 263, 295

Obama, Barack, 283
obsidian, 97–8
Odoacer, 163
Ögedei Khan, 208
oil, 260, 262–3, 280, 285–7, 292, 295
Old Stone Age, 69
Olds, Ransom, 261
olives, 148–9
Olmecs, 173, 176, 183

# Index

Olympic Games, 152, 162
Omo River skulls, 79
opium wars, 272–4, 295
organic chemistry, 263, 265
Orkney, 116, 120
Orléans, 211
Ostrogoths, 211
Ottawa, 249
Otto, Nikolaus, 261
Ottoman Empire, 225, 269,
    275, 285
Owen, Richard, 42
oxygen, 9–10, 13, 125, 263
    atmospheric levels, 29–31,
    34

Pachacuti, 181
Pacific islands, 82, 231
Pacific Ocean, 63–4, 166
Padmasambhava, 141
Pakistan, 113–14, 139
Palenque, 174
Palestine, 189, 286
Panama, 64, 82
pandas, 53, 56, 121
Pangea, 40–1, 44, 53
Papal States, 225–6
paper, 121, 191–2, 194–5,
    198–200, 205, 208
Paso de la Amada, 177
passenger pigeon, 291
Pasteur, Louis, 264
patents, 258
Patterson, Penny, 57
Pearl Harbor, 280
peasants' revolts, 221
Penan tribe, 169
Pereira, Duarte Pacheco, 232
Permian Mass Extinction, 21,
    38, 40–1, 43
Persepolis, 146, 155
Persia, 103, 154–6, 162, 189,
    197, 213
Persian Empire, 145–8, 158
Persian Gulf, 94, 102, 205,
    235
Persians, 113, 138, 211
Peru, 181, 231, 238–9, 241,
    243, 245
Petrarch, 223
Petrograd, 276
Phaistos, 118–19
Pharaohs, 107–8, 110–12, 183

Philby, Jack, 285–6
Philip II, King, 218, 241
Philippines, 242, 280
Phoenicians, 156, 233
photosynthesis, 9, 26
Picts, 158
pigs, 53, 55, 171, 237, 243–4
Pippin, King, 226–7
pirates, 228
Pizarro, Francisco, 235, 238–9
placentals, 54–6
plants
    endangered, 289–90
    evolution of, 10–11, 13,
        23–37
    flowering, 34–5
    and oxygen levels, 30
    primitive, 23–4
    and seed dispersal, 35–7
    selection and
        domestication, 244–5,
        294
plate tectonics, 12, 33
Plato, 150, 152–3, 161, 224
Pleistocene Overkill, 89
Poitiers, 189
Poland, 271, 285
Polynesia, 165, 168–9
Pompey, 157
Pontiac's Rebellion, 249
Pontic Steppe, 143
Pontius Pilate, 160
Popes, 198, 212–13, 217, 219
    and *Donation of Constantine*,
        226–7, 240
*Popol Vuh*, 175
Portugal, 44, 116, 216
    and voyages of exploration,
        228–30, 232–5
potatoes, 172, 245–6
Potosí, 231–2, 238
pottery, 81, 91, 114, 143–4
Prakrit, 139
printing, 121, 200–1, 205,
    208, 227, 257
Prometheus, 72
Protestantism, 227, 240–2
Ptolemy's *Almagest*, 192
Puritans, 241
Pygmies, 269
pyramids, 107–8, 110–11
    Native American, 179–81
Pyrenees, 189, 219

Qi, 130
Qin Kingdom, 129–30
Qin Shi Huang (Ying Zheng),
    130–2, 199
Qin Xiaogong, 130
Qing Dynasty, 257, 273–4
Quakers, 253
Quetzalcoatl, 173

railways, 260–1, 265
rain, 11, 23, 290
    and human sacrifice,
        178–80, 236
Ramadan, 193
Ravenna, 211
Reagan, Ronald, 287
Red Sea, 146
Reformation, 240
reincarnation, 134–5
religion, 76, 84, 91–2
    Egyptian, 107, 110–11
    Indian, 132–41
    and mother goddess,
        117–18
    Native American, 173,
        177, 180
    and Roman Empire, 160–3
    Sumerian, 104–5
    *see also* animism;
        Buddhism;
        Christianity;
        Hinduism; Islam;
        Jainism; Taoism
reptiles, 13, 16, 20, 38–42
    *see also* dinosaurs
Rhine, River, 116, 158, 211,
    270
Rhynie, 24–6
rice, 122–3, 126–7, 131–3,
    171–2, 193, 202, 258,
    285
Richard I, King, 218
roads, 159, 176, 181, 261
Roman Catholic Church, 212,
    240, 250
Roman Empire, 124, 156–63,
    224
    decline and fall, 162–3,
        165, 210–12, 218, 295
    entertainments, 159–60,
        163
    and religion, 160–3
    and slavery, 156–9, 163

# Index

Romania, 285
Romans, 105, 113, 155–63, 175
Rome, 158–60, 195, 198, 211, 213, 224, 227
Romulus Augustus, Emperor, 163
Rouen, 215
Royal Navy, 240, 261
Rus, 215
Russia, 40, 64, 143, 208, 261, 274, 284–5
    and human migrations, 82, 165
    revolution and civil war, 275–6, 283

sabre-toothed cats, 86, 90
Sacred Cenote, 178
sacrifices, 168, 170
    human, 126, 170, 177–80, 183, 236
Saga of Erik the Red, 217
Sahara Desert, 109, 169, 193, 228–9
St Lawrence River, 240, 247
Sajó River, 208
Saladin, 218
Salamis, Battle of, 148
Salem, 68
Samaria, 145
Samarkand, 192
Sami, 168–9
San Lorenzo, 173
Sanghamitra, 140
Sanskrit, 132, 134
Santiago, 244
Santo Domingo de Silos, 192
Santorini, 120
Sardinia, 211
Sargon the Great, King, 106
Sassanid Empire, 162, 189
Saudi Arabia, 285–6, 288
science, 149, 153, 192, 195–6, 208, 218, 294
Scipio, 157
Scotland, 21, 30, 116, 120, 158, 225
Scythia, 155
Scythians, 146–7
sea
    prehistoric inhabitants, 17–22

salt levels, 12–13
sea levels, 65, 93–5, 102, 255
sea temperatures, 63
Second World War, 262, 281, 284, 287, 294
Sedan, Battle of, 270
seeds, 24, 29, 35–6, 92–3, 95–8
Selim I, Sultan, 225
Serbia, 225, 275
Seven Years War, 247, 249
seven-day week, 105
Seychelles, 18
Shandong, 131
Shang Dynasty, 126–7
Shang Yang, 130
sheep, 53, 55, 96, 103, 108, 171, 237, 244
Shen Kuo, 205
Shia Muslims, 190
shipbuilding, 243, 258
ships, 91, 249, 256, 265
    caravels, 228
    Chinese, 204–5
    Greek, 148
    Roman, 156–7
    triremes, 146, 148
Shrewsbury, Earl of, 222
Siberia, 40–1, 208, 246, 277
Sibi, 114
Sicily, 197, 211
silk, 123–4, 126–7, 132, 247, 272
Silk Road, 124, 204, 220
silver, 176, 180, 183, 225, 231–3, 238, 241, 272, 274
Singapore, 258, 280
slavery, abolition of, 253, 258, 267
Slavic peoples, 215
Slovakia, 285
Slovenia, 76
Smith, Adam, 253, 282–3
snakes, 117, 120, 122, 173
social contract, 248
Socrates, 150, 161
solar wind, 5–6, 8
Solnhofen, 47
Solomon, King, 188
Solon, 148
Somalia, 288

Song Dynasty, 202–6, 213, 257
South Africa, 261, 283, 293
South America, 53, 56, 63–4, 82, 166, 244–6
    European conquest, 233, 235–9
    liberation movements, 250, 252
    native civilizations, 171–2, 176, 180–3
South Pacific, 168
South Pole, 63
Southern Ocean, 63
Soviet Union, 276–7, 279, 284
Spain, 116, 118, 143, 158, 192
    American colonies, 235–9, 241, 242, 250, 252
    and Carthaginians, 156–7
    and Islam, 189, 193–7, 208–9, 212, 214, 217, 224, 233
    medieval, 211–12, 214, 216, 225
    *Reconquista*, 197
    and voyages of exploration, 233–4
Sparta, 151–2, 278
Spartacus, 158
spears, 71, 76, 81, 83, 88, 132
sponges, 17–19
sports, 119, 152, 177
Sri Lanka, 140, 204
Stalin, Joseph, 276
Standard of Ur, 143
Stang, Sister Dorothy, 290
Stein, Aurel, 201
stirrups, 197, 214–15
Stonehenge, 116–17
Straits of Gibraltar, 70
Sturn, 105
Sudan, 292
Suez Canal, 146
Sufis, 192, 198
sugar, 193, 234–5, 241, 244, 267
Suleiman the Magnificent, Sultan, 225
Sumatra, 79
Sumeria, 102–7, 113–14, 119
sun, 5, 9, 117, 149

326

# Index

Sunni Muslims, 190, 286
supercontinents, 12, 40
Susa, 155
Sweden, 168, 240
Switzerland, 63, 65, 276, 283
Sylvester I, Pope, 226
Syria, 94, 96, 157, 189

taboos, 166, 168, 170, 297
Taiping Rebellion, 272, 275
Taiwan, 284
Taizu, Emperor, 202
Taj Mahal, 113
Taklamakan Desert, 201
Talas, Battle of, 190–1
Tang Dynasty, 200–1, 203
Tanzania, 66
Taoism, 140
Tao-te-Ching, 140
tarpans, 143
Tasmanian Tiger, 54
Tatars, 206
Tattvartha Sutra, 137
taxes, 92, 110, 182, 221, 227, 249, 253, 274
Tehtys Sea, 62–3
Tenochtitlan, 179, 236–8
teosinte, 172, 245
termites, 47, 49–50
Texcoco, 179
Thailand, 140
Thales, 149, 153, 242
Thames, River, 247
Thatcher, Margaret, 287
Thebes, 111–12, 171
Theia, 5–6, 8
Theodosius I, Emperor, 162
Thera, 119
Thompson, Edward, 177–8
Thrace, 147
Tibet, 62, 122, 141
Tigris, River, 103, 106, 146
Tikal, 174
Tiktaalik, 38–9
Timbuktu, 169
Timor, 168
tin, 115, 118, 142, 223
Titus, Emperor, 159
Tlacopan, 179
Tlaloc, 178–9
Tlaxcalans, 236
Tlaxcalteca, Kingdom of, 179
tobacco, 241, 244, 267, 273

Toledo, 195, 217, 224
Tollund Man, 170
Toltecs, 178
Tomyris, Queen, 146
tools, 69, 72–3, 76–7, 81, 124, 133, 166
Totonacs, 236
Tours, Battle of, 190, 197
trade, 91, 102, 115, 118, 194
    and China, 204–5, 272–4, 285
    free trade, 252–3, 282–4, 287
    and Islamic, 223–6
    and Vikings, 214
Trafalgar, Battle of, 251
Treaty of Tordesillas, 234
Treaty of Versailles, 277
trees
    and agriculture, 116
    evolution of, 10, 13, 23–37
    and oxygen levels, 30
    and reproduction, 29, 33
    see also deforestation
Trevithick, Richard, 260
Triassic Period, 41
Trojan Wars, 144
Trotsky, Leon, 276
troubadours, 197
Tunis, 224
Tupac, 181
Turk, Ivan, 76
Turkana Boy, 71, 73, 79
Turkey, 94, 98, 120, 124, 142, 147, 149
Turks, 222–3
Tutankhamun, 112
Tyler, Wat, 221
Tyre, 154

Umaswati, 137
Umayyad dynasty, 193
United Nations, 297
United States of America, 249–50, 257–61, 265, 271–2, 274, 291, 296
    and credit crunch, 287
    Declaration of Independence, 249, 267
    dinosaur fossils, 43, 45–6
    and oil, 285–6
    slavery and black people, 252–3, 267–8, 283

    and twentieth-century wars, 275–7, 279–80
Upanishads, 135
Ur, 106, 145
Urban II, Pope, 217–18
Urban the Hungarian, 222
Urey, Harold, 6–8
Uruk, 104, 106
Uyghurs, 206
Uzbekistan, 192, 195

vaccinations, 264–5
Valencia, 192
Valla, Lorenzo, 227, 240
Vandals, 158, 211
Vedas, 132–3, 135
vegetarianism, 135, 138–9
Venezuela, 25
Venice, 223–5
Venus, 6, 33, 105, 173
Venus of Willendorf, 81, 117
Vespasian, Emperor, 159
Vestal Virgins, 162
Vienna, 225
Vietnam, 128, 140, 274
Vietnam War, 284
Vikings, 214–15, 225–6
Vila do Infante, 228
villages, 83, 91, 94, 108
Visigoths, 211
volcanoes, 5, 12, 40–1, 79–80, 120
von Meyer, Hermann, 47

Wahhabism, 286
Walcott, Charles Doolittle, 14–15
Wales, 116, 142
Wang Tao-shih, 201
'War on Terror', 288
water buffalo, 123, 211
Waterloo, Battle of, 251
Watling Street, Battle of, 157
Watson, James, 264
Watt, James, 260
weapons, 84, 88, 116, 124, 142–4
    see also bows and arrows;
    firearms; cannon;
    longbows; spears
welfare states, 283–4
Wellington, Duke of, 251
wheat, 92–3, 95, 102, 106, 108, 171–2

# Index

wheels, 91, 105–6, 133, 143–4
    Native Americans and,
        175–6, 181
White, Lynn, 214
Whitney, Eli, 258–9
Wilberforce, William, 253
Wilhelm I, Kaiser, 270
William the Conqueror, 215
William VIII of Aquitaine, 197
Williams, Maurice, 45
Wöhler, Friedrich, 263
women, 95, 117–20, 244, 249,
    267, 283, 294
    Spartan, 151–2
Wood, Stan, 30–1
Woolley, Leonard, 143
woolly mammoths, 85–6

World Conservation Union,
    290
World Trade Organization,
    284–5
Wright, Orville and Wilbur,
    262
writing, 101–2, 106–7
    Chinese, 127, 131
    Native American, 173–4
Wu, Emperor, 199–200
Wu region, 125
*Wujing Zongyao*, 205
Wyrd, 169–70

Xerxes, 147
Xiongnu, 210

Yangshao people, 123
Yangtze River, 122, 125, 129,
    203–4, 274
Yanjing, 207
Yellow Emperor, 123–4
Yellow River, 122–3, 127
Yin, 126–7
Younger Dryas, 95–6
Yucatán Peninsula, 51, 174,
    178, 236

Zacatecas, 238
Zacuto, Abraham, 197
Zama, Battle of, 157
zero, 173, 194
Zheng Guo, 131
Zhou Dynasty, 127–9